D1823349

Pictures Every Child
Should Know

A SELECTION OF THE WORLD'S ART
MASTERPIECES FOR YOUNG PEOPLE

[ILLUSTRATED]

By

DOLORES BACON

Illustrated by Murat Ukray

ILLUSTRATED &

PUBLISHED BY

e-KİTAP PROJESİ & CHEAPEST BOOKS

www.cheapestboooks.com

Copyright, 2015 by e-Kitap Projesi

Istanbul

ISBN:

978-150-5-99219-9

Copyright© Printing and publication rights belong to the author's & Publisher's own restriction, using and working. According to the law of intellectual and artistic works, without permission in part or in whole not re-produced or re-published. Welding can be done by showing short excerpts..

Table of Contents

ILLUSTRATED FROM GREAT PAINTINGS

ACKNOWLEDGMENTS

Besides making acknowledgments to the many authoritative writers upon artists and pictures, here quoted, thanks are due to such excellent compilers of books on art subjects as Sadakichi Hartmann, Muther, C. H. Caffin, Ida Prentice Whitcomb, Russell Sturgis and others.

INTRODUCTION

Man's inclination to decorate his belongings has always been one of the earliest signs of civilisation. Art had its beginning in the lines indented in clay, perhaps, or hollowed in the wood of family utensils; after that came crude colouring and drawing.

Among the first serious efforts to draw were the Egyptian square and pointed things, animals and men. The most that artists of that day succeeded in doing was to preserve the fashions of the time. Their drawings tell us that men wore their beards in bags. They show us, also, many peculiar head-dresses and strange agricultural implements. Artists of that day put down what they saw, and they saw with an untrained eye and made the record with an untrained hand; but they did not put in false details for the sake of glorifying the subject. One can distinguish a man from a mountain in their work, but the arms and legs embroidered upon Mathilde's tapestry, or the figures representing family history on an Oriental rug, are quite as correct in drawing and as little of a puzzle. As men became more intelligent, hence spiritualised, they began to express themselves in ideal ways; to glorify the commonplace; and thus they passed from Egyptian geometry to gracious lines and beautiful colouring.

Indian pottery was the first development of art in America and it led to the working of metals, followed by drawing and portraiture. Among the Americans, as soon as that term ceased to mean Indians, art took a most distracting turn. Europe was old in pictures, great and beautiful, when America was worshipping at the shrine of the chromo; but the chromo served a good turn, bad as it was. It was a link between the black and white of the admirable wood-cut and the true colour picture.

Some of the Colonists brought over here the portraits of their ancestors, but those paintings could not be considered "American" art, nor were those early settlers Americans; but the generation that followed gave to the world Benjamin West. He left his Mother Country for England, where he found a knighthood and honours of every kind awaiting him.

The earliest artists of America had to go away to do their work, because there was no place here for any men but those engaged in clearing land, planting corn, and fighting Indians. Sir Benjamin West was President of the Royal Academy while America was still revelling in chromos. The artists who remained chose such objects as Davy Crockett in the trackless forest, or made pictures of the Continental Congress. After the chromo in America came the picture known as the "buckeye," painted by relays of artists. Great canvases were stretched and blocked off into lengths. The scene was drawn in by one man, who was followed by "artists," each in turn painting sky, water, foliage, figures, according to his specialty. Thus whole yards of canvas could be painted in a day, with more artists to the square inch than are now employed to paint advertisements on a barn.

The Centennial Exhibition of 1876 came as a glorious flashlight. For the first time real art was seen by a large part of our nation. Every farmer took home with him a new idea of the possibilities of drawing and colour. The change that instantly followed could have occurred in no other country than the United States, because no other people would have travelled from the four points of the compass to see such an exhibition. Thus it was the American's *penchant* for travel which first opened to him the art world, for he was conscious even then of the educational advantages to be found somewhere, although there seemed to be few of them in the United States.

After the Centennial arose a taste for the painting of "plaques," upon which were the heads of ladies with strange-coloured hair; of leather-covered flatirons bearing flowers of unnatural colour, or of shovels decorated with "snow scenes." The whole nation began to revel in "art." It was a low variety, yet it started toward a goal which left the chromo at the rear end of the course, and it was a better effort than the mottoes worked in worsted, which had till then been the chief decoration in most homes. If the "buckeye" was hand-painting, this was "single-hand" painting, and it did not take a generation to bring the change about, only a season. After the Philadelphia exhibition the daughter of the household "painted a little" just as she played the piano "a little." To-day, much less than a man's lifetime since then, there is in America a universal love for refined art and a fair technical appreciation of pictures, while already the nation has worthily contributed to the world of artists. Sir Benjamin West, Sully, and Sargent are ours: Inness, Inman, and Trumbull.

The curator of the Metropolitan Museum in New York has declared that portrait-painting must be the means which shall save the modern artists from their sins. To quote him: "An artist may paint a bright green cow, if he is so minded: the cow has no redress, the cow must suffer and be silent; but human beings who sit for portraits seem to lean toward portraits in which they can recognise their own features when they have commissioned an artist to paint them. A man *will* insist upon even the most brilliant artist painting him in trousers, for instance, instead of in petticoats, however the artist-whim may direct otherwise; and a woman is likely to insist that the artist who paints her portrait shall maintain some recognised shade of brown or blue or gray when he paints her eye, instead of indulging in a burnt orange or maybe pink! These personal preferences certainly put a limit to an artist's genius and keep him from writing himself down a madman. Thus, in portrait-painting, with the exactions of truth upon it, lies the hope of art-lovers!" It is the same authority who calls attention to the danger that lies in extremes; either in finding no value in art outside the "old masters," or in admiring pictures so impressionistic that the objects in them need to be labelled before they can be recognised.

The true art-lover has a catholic taste, is interested in all forms of art; but he finds beauty where it truly exists and does not allow the nightmare of imagination to mislead him. That which is not beautiful from one point of view or another is not art, but decadence. That which is technical to the exclusion of other elements remains technique pure and simple, workmanship--the bare bones of art. A thing is not art simply because it is fantastic. It may be interesting as showing to what degree some imaginations can become diseased, but it is not pleasing nor is it art. There are fully a thousand pictures that every child should know, since he can hardly know too much of a good thing; but there is room in this volume only to acquaint him with forty-eight and possibly inspire him with the wish to look up the neglected nine hundred and fifty-two.

ILLUSTRATIONS:

FRONTISPIECE

The Avenue, Middleharnis, Holland—*Hobbema*

The Avenue, Middleharnis, Holland--*Hobbema*

MADONNA OF THE SACK--*Andrea del Sarto*
A fresco that still remains on the wall of the cloister in Florence, where it was painted

Madonna of the Sack--*Andrea del Sarto*

DANIEL—*Michelangelo*

One of the frescoes on the ceiling of the Sistine
Chapel at Rome that illustrate the whole Bible

Daniel--*Michael Angelo (Buonarroti)*

THE ISLE OF THE DEAD—*Böcklin*
A sombre scene, befitting a sombre subject. The straight lines are specially noticeable.

The Isle of the Dead--*Arnold Böcklin*

THE HORSE FAIR—*Rosa Bonheur*
A famous canvas that can be seen in the Metropolitan Art Gallery, New York City

The Horse Fair--*Rosa Bonheur*

SPRING—*Botticelli*

All the lightness and grace of the season are in this allegory. A
noted critic considers this the most beautiful picture in the world

Spring--*Alessandro Botticelli*

THE HAY-WAIN—*Constable*
The hay-cart is not the most conspicuous thing in this picture
which has been called by other names—"Landscape," "Noon," etc.

The Hay Wain--*John Constable*

A Family Picture—*Copley*

The prim little lady in front seems more dressed up than her mother

A Family Picture--*John Singleton Copley*

THE HOLY NIGHT—*Correggio*
Another name for the picture is "The Adoration of
the Shepherds," which seems to explain it better

The Holy Night--*Correggio (Antonio Allegri)*

DANCE OF THE NYMPHS—*Corot*
One of the earliest, but also one of the best works of
this master of light and shade, trees and atmosphere

Dance of the Nymphs--*Jean Baptiste Camille Corot*

THE VIRGIN AS CONSOLER—*Bouguereau*

The mother of the dead child seems to need all the
help from heaven the Virgin Mary can bring down

The Virgin as Consoler--*Wm. Adolphe Bouguereau*

THE LOVE SONG—*Burne-Jones*
A song without words it seems to be, and directed
by the lady player to the youth at her right

The Love Song--*Sir Edward Burne-Jones*

MYSTIC MARRIAGE OF ST. CATHERINE—*Correggio*
The Saint of Alexandria considered herself the bride
of Christ, having been married to him in a vision

The Mystic Marriage of St. Catherine--*Correggio*

MOSES BREAKING THE TABLETS OF THE LAW—*Doré*
This is one of the illustrations of
the Doré Bible, published in 1865

Moses Breaking the Tablets of the Law--*Paul Gustave Doré*

THE NATIVITY—*Dürer*

Compare this with the Italian pictures of sacred subjects. The feeling is quite different

The Nativity--*Albrecht Dürer*

THE SPANISH MARRIAGE—*Fortuny*
The signing of the register, elsewhere a solemn occasion,
this artist has turned into a scene of gay frivolity

The Spanish Marriage--*Mariana Fortuny*

MRS. RICHARD BRINSLEY SHERIDAN—*Gainsborough*

Notice the sweetly pensive expression of the face, the lovely
hand and arm, and the transparency of the draperies

Mrs. Richard Brinsley Sheridan--*Thomas Gainsborough*

THE SWORD DANCE—*Gérome*

Compare with Scottish Sword Dance, where Highlander
tiptoes back and forth over sword to music of bagpipes

The Sword Dance--*Jean Léon Gérôme*

GIOVANNA DEGLI ALBIZI—*Ghirlandajo*

The tablet states that if art could have painted her mind and manner, no picture on earth would have been more beautiful

Portrait of Giovanna degli Albizi--*Ghirlandajo (Domenico Bigordi)*

THE NURSE AND THE CHILD—*Franz Hals*

Probably the artist kept these two amused with some
of his drolleries while he painted their picture

The Nurse and the Child--*Franz Hals*

MEETING OF ST. JOHN AND ST. ANNA—*Giotto*
A fourteenth century fresco, showing great
advance on the few paintings that preceded it

The Meeting of St. John and St. Anna at Jerusalem--*Giotto (Di Bordone)*

THE AVENUE, MIDDLEHARNIS, HOLLAND—*Hobbema*
The trees may typify a land denuded of former greatness, but to the right is
a thrifty Dutch homestead and garden, to the left a suggestive church spire

The Avenue--*Meyndert Hobbema*

THE MARRIAGE CONTRACT—*Hogarth*

The first act in a great moral drama of five acts called "Marriage
à la Mode." The series hangs in the National Gallery, London

The Marriage Contract--*Wm. Hogarth*

THE LIGHT OF THE WORLD—*Holman Hunt*

Perhaps the most popular picture of a sacred subject ever painted. It is in Keble College, Oxford

The Light of the World--*William Holman Hunt*

ROBERT CHESEMAN OF DORMANSWELL—*Holbein*
Notice the delicacy of the falconer's hand, the hood and
bell on the bird

Robert Cheseman with his Falcon--*Hans Holbein, the Younger*

THE BERKSHIRE HILLS—*Inness*

Observe the fine perspective of the distant highlands, and the little cottage nestling under the trees

The Berkshire Hills--*George Inness*

THE OLD SHEPHERD'S CHIEF MOURNER—*Landseer*
The dog in joy and the dog in sorrow, with his own
kind, with human kind—Sir Edwin painted them all

The Old Shepherd's Chief Mourner--*Sir Edwin Henry Landseer*

ARTIST'S PORTRAIT—*Masaccio*
The most original artist between Giotto and
Raphael. He died before he was thirty

The Artist's Portrait--*Tommaso Masaccio*

ACIS AND GALATEA—*Lorrain*

Polyphemus on the cliff seems too large for his sheep, but
he is a giant who will soon hurl a mountain on the lovers

Acis and Galatea--*Claude Lorrain*

RETREAT FROM MOSCOW—*Meissonier*
Horses and men alike have a dejected air, but notice the set face of Napoleon

Retreat from Moscow--*Jean Louis Ernest Meissonier*

THE ANGELUS—*Millet*
The sound of the bell travels far on the still air of
evening, from the church spire on the horizon

The Angelus--*Jean François Millet*

IMMACULATE CONCEPTION—*Murillo*
The artist has seized an opportunity to
paint the happy little children he loved

The Immaculate Conception--*Murillo (Bartolomé Estéban)*

HAYSTACK IN SUNSHINE—*Monet*

An example of the work of the impressionistic school

Haystack in Sunshine--*Claude Monet*

THE SISTINE MADONNA—*Raphael*
By many critics considered to be
the greatest painting in the world

The Sistine Madonna--*Raphael (Sanzio)*

THE NIGHT WATCH—*Rembrandt*

The faces did not come out strongly enough from the artist's glorious shadows to please his patrons, who had bespoken portraits

The Night Watch--*Rembrandt (Van Rijn)*

THE DUCHESS OF DEVONSHIRE AND HER DAUGHTER—*Reynolds*
Notice the baby's chubby feet, and the lovely arm of the mother

The Duchess of Devonshire and Her Daughter--*Sir Joshua Reynolds*

The Last Supper--*Leonardo da Vinci*

I ANDREA DEL SARTO

(Pronounced Ahn'dray-ah del Sar'to)

Florentine School

1486-1531

Pupil of Piero di Cosimo

Italian painters received their names in peculiar ways. This man's father was a tailor; and the artist was named after his father's profession. He was in fact "the Tailor's Andrea," and his father's name was Angelo.

One story of this brilliant painter which reads from first to last like a romance has been told by the poet, Browning, who dresses up fact so as to smother it a little, but there is truth at the bottom.

Andrea married a wife whom he loved tenderly. She had a beautiful face that seemed full of spirituality and feeling, and Andrea painted it over and over again. The artist loved his work and dreamed always of the great things that he should do; but he was so much in love with his wife that he was dependent on her smile for all that he did which was well done, and her frown plunged him into despair.

Andrea's wife cared nothing for his genius, painting did not interest her, and she had no worthy ambition for her husband, but she loved fine clothes and good living, and so encouraged him enough to keep him earning these things for her. As soon as some money was made she would persuade him to work no more till it was spent; and even when he had made agreements to paint certain pictures for which he was paid in advance she would torment him till he gave all of his time to her whims, neglected his duty and spent the money for which he had rendered no service. Thus in time he became actually dishonest, as we shall see. It is a sad sort of story to tell of so brilliant a young man.

Andrea was born in the Gualfonda quarter of Florence, and there is some record of his ancestors for a hundred years before that, although their lives were quite unimportant. Andrea was one of four children, and as usual with Italians of artistic temperament, he was set to work under the eye of a goldsmith. This craftsmanship of a fine order was as near to art as a man could get with any certainty of making his living. It was a time when the Italian world bedecked itself with rare golden trinkets, wreaths for women's hair, girdles, brooches, and the like, and the finest skill was needed to satisfy the taste. Thus it required talent of no mean order for a man to become a successful goldsmith.

Andrea did not like the work, and instead of fashioning ornaments from his master's models he made original drawings which did not do at all in a shop where an apprentice was expected to earn his salt. Certain fashions had to be followed and people did not welcome fantastic or new designs. Because of this, Andrea was early put out of his master's shop and set to learn the only business that he could be got to learn, painting. This meant for him a very different teacher from the goldsmith.

The artist may be said to have been his own master, because, even when he was apprenticed to a painter he was taught less than he already knew.

That first teacher was Barile, a coarse and unpleasing man, as well as an incapable one; but he was fair minded, after a fashion, and put Andrea into the way of finding better help. After a few years under the direction of Piero di Cosimo, Andrea and a friend, Francia Bigio, decided to set up shop for themselves.

The two devoted friends pitched their tent in the Piazza del Grano, and made a meagre beginning out of which great things were to grow. They began a series of pictures which was to lead at least one of them to fame. It was in the little Piazza, del Grano studio that the "Baptism of Christ" was painted, a partnership work that had been planned in the Campagnia dello Scalzo.

"The Baptism" was not much of a picture as great pictures go, but it was a beginning and it was looked at and talked about, which was something at a time when Titian and Leonardo had set the standard of great work. In the Piazza del Grano, Andrea and his friend lived in the stables of the Tuscan Grand Dukes, with a host of other fine artists, and they had gay times together.

Andrea was a shy youth, a little timid, and by no means vain of his own work, but he painted with surprising swiftness and sureness, and had a very brilliant imagination. Its was his main trouble that he had more imagination than true manhood; he sacrificed everything good to his imagination.

After the partnership with his friend, he undertook to paint some frescoes independently, and that work earned for him the name of "Andrea senza Errori"-- Andrea the Unerring. Then, as now, each artist had his own way of working, and Andrea's was perhaps the most difficult of all, yet the most genius-like. There were those, Michael Angelo for example, who laid in backgrounds for their paintings; but Andrea painted his subject upon the wet plaster, precisely as he meant it to be when finished.

He was unlike the moody Michael Angelo; unlike the gentle Raphael; unlike the fastidious Van Dyck who came long afterward; he was hail-fellow-well-met among his associates, though often given over to dreaminess. He belonged to a jolly club named the "Kettle Club," literally, the Company of the Kettle; and to another called "The Trowel," both suggesting an all around good time and much good fellowship The members of these clubs were expected to contribute to their wonderful suppers, and Andrea on one occasion made a great temple, in imitation of the Baptistry, of jelly with columns of sausages, white birds and pigeons represented the choir and priests. Besides being "Andrew the Unerring," and a "Merry Andrew," he was also the "Tailor's Andrew," a man in short upon whom a nickname sat comfortably. He helped to make the history of the "Company of the Kettle," for he recited and probably composed a touching ballad called "The Battle of the Mice and the Frogs," which doubtless had its origin in a poem of Homer's. But all at once, in the midst of his gay careless life came his tragedy; he fell in love with a hatter's wife. This was quite bad enough, but worse was to come, for the hatter shortly died, and the widow was free to marry Andrea.

After his marriage Andrea began painting a series of Madonnas, seemingly for no better purpose than to exhibit his wife's beauty over and over again. He lost his ambition and forgot everything but his love for this unworthy woman. She was entirely commonplace, incapable of inspiring true genius or honesty of purpose.

A great art critic, Vasari, who was Andrea's pupil during this time, has written that the wife, Lucretia, was abominable in every way. A vixen, she tormented Andrea from morning till night with her bitter tongue. She did not love him in the least, but only what his money could buy for her, for she was extravagant, and drove the sensitive artist to his grave while she outlived him forty years.

About the time of the artist's marriage he painted one fresco, "The Procession of the Magi," in which he placed a very splendid substitute for his wife, namely himself. Afterward he painted the Dead Christ which found its way to France and it laid the foundation for Andrea's wrongdoing. This picture was greatly admired by the King of France who above all else was a lover of art. Francis I. asked Andrea to go to his court, as he had commissions for him. He made Andrea a money offer and to court he went.

He took a pupil with him, but he left his wife at home. At the court of Francis I. he was received with great honours, and amid those new and gracious surroundings, away from the tantalising charms of his wife and her shrewish tongue, he began to have an honest ambition to do great things. His work for France was undertaken with enthusiasm, but no sooner was he settled and at peace, than the irrepressible wife began to torment him with letters to return. Each letter distracted him more and more, till he told the King in his despair, that he must return home, but that he would come back to France and continue his work, almost at once. Francis I., little suspecting the cause of Andrea's uneasiness, gave him permission to go, and also a large sum of money to spend upon certain fine works of art which he was to bring back to France.

We can well believe that Andrea started back to his home with every good intention; that he meant to appease his wife and also his own longing to see her; to buy the King his pictures with the money entrusted to him, and to return to France and finish his work; but, alas, he no sooner got back to his wife than his virtuous purpose fled. She wanted this; she wanted that--and especially she wanted a fine house which could just about be built for the sum of money which the King of France had entrusted to Andrea.

Andrea is a pitiable figure, but he was also a vagabond, if we are to believe Vasari. He took the King's money, built his wretched wife a mansion, and never again dared return to France, where his dishonesty made him forever despised.

Afterward he was overwhelmed with despair for what he had done, and he tried to make his peace with Francis; but while that monarch did not punish him directly for his knavery; he would have no more to do with him, and this was the worst punishment the artist could have had. However, his genius was so great that other than French people forgot his dishonesty and he began life anew in his native place.

Almost all his pictures were on sacred subjects; and finally, when driven from Florence to Luco by the plague, taking with him his wife and stepdaughter, he began a picture called the "Madonna del Sacco" (the Madonna of the Sack).

This fresco was to adorn the convent of the Servi, and the sketches for it were probably made in Luco. When the plague passed and the artist was able to return to Florence, he began to paint it upon the cloister walls.

Andrea, like Leonardo, painted a famous "Last Supper," although the two pictures cannot be compared. In Andrea's picture it is said that all the faces are portraits.

Just before the plague sent him and his family from Florence a most remarkable incident took place. Raphael had painted a celebrated portrait of Pope Leo X. in a group, and the picture belonged to Ottaviano de Medici. Duke Frederick II., of Mantua, longed to own this picture, and at last requested the Medici to give it to him. The Duke could not well be refused, but Ottaviano wanted to keep so great a work for himself. What was to be done? He was in great trouble over the affair. The situation seemed hopeless. It seemed certain that he must part with his beloved picture to the Duke of Mantua; but one day Andrea del Sarto declared that he could make a copy of it that even Raphael himself could not tell from his original. Ottaviano could scarcely believe this, but he begged Andrea to set about it, hoping that it might be true.

Going at the work in good earnest, Andrea painted a copy so exact that the pupil of Raphael, who had more or less to do with the original picture, could not tell which was which when he was asked to choose. This pupil, Giulio Romano, was so familiar with every stroke of Raphael's that if he were deceived surely any one might be; so the replica was given to the Duke of Mantua, who never found out the difference.

Years afterward Giulio Romano showed the picture to Vasari, believing it to be the original Raphael, neither Andrea nor the Medici having told Romano the truth. But Vasari, who knew the whole story, declared to Romano that what he showed him was but a copy. Romano would not believe it, but Vasari told him that he would find upon the canvas a certain mark, known to be Andrea's. Romano looked, and behold, the original Raphael became a del Sarto! The original picture hangs in the Pitti Palace, while the copy made by Andrea is in the Naples Gallery.

The introduction of Andrea to Vasari was one of the few gracious things, that Michael Angelo ever did. About Andrea he said to Raphael at the time: "There is a little fellow in Florence who will bring sweat to your brows if ever he is engaged in great works." Raphael, would certainly have agreed, with him had he known what was to happen in regard to the Leo X. picture.

Notwithstanding Andrea's unfortunate temperament, which caused him to be guided mostly by circumstances instead of guiding them, he was said to be improving all the time in his art. He had a great many pupils, but none of them could tolerate his wife for long, so they were always changing.

Throughout his life the artist longed for tenderness and encouragement from his wife, and finally, without ever receiving it, he died in a desolate way, untended even by her. After the siege of Florence there came a pestilence, and Andrea was overtaken by it. His wife, afraid that she too would become ill, would have nothing to do with him. She kept away and he died quite alone, few caring that he was dead and no one taking the trouble to follow him to his grave. Thus one of the greatest of Florentine painters lived and died. Years after his death, the artist Jacopo da Empoli, was copying Andrea's "Birth of the Virgin" when an old woman of about eighty years on her way to mass stopped to speak with him. She pointed to the beautiful Virgin's face in the picture and said: "I am that woman." And so she was--the widow of the great Andrea. Though she had treated him so cruelly, she was glad to have it known that she was the widow of the dead genius.

PLATE--THE MADONNA DEL SACCO

(Madonna of the Sack)

This picture is a fresco in the cloister of the Annunziata at Florence, and it is called "of the sack" because Joseph is posed leaning against a sack, a book open upon his knees.

Doubtless the model for this Madonna is Andrea del Sarto's abominable wife, but she looks very sweet and simple in the picture. The folds of Mary's garments are beautifully painted, so is the poise of her head, and all the details of the picture except the figure of the child. There is a line of stiffness there and it lacks the softness of many other pictures of the Infant Jesus.

PLATE--THE HOLY FAMILY

In this picture in the Pitti Palace, Florence, Andrea del Sarto represents all the characters in a serious mood. There are St. John and Elizabeth, Mary and the Infant Jesus, and there is no touch of playfulness such as may be found in similar groups by other artists of the time. Attention is concentrated uponJesus who seems to be learning from his young cousin. The left hand, resting upon Mary's arm is badly drawn and in character does not seem to belong to the figure of the child. A full, overhanging upper lip is a dominant feature in each face.

Other works of Andrea del Sarto are "Charity," which is in the Louvre; "Madonna dell' Arpie," "A Head of Christ," "The Dead Christ," "Four Saints," "Joseph in Egypt," his own portrait, and "Joseph's Dream."

II MICHAEL ANGELO (BUONARROTI)

(Pronounced Meek-el-ahn-jel-o (Bwone-ar-ro'tee))

Florentine School

1475-1564
Pupil of Ghirlandajo

This wonderful man did more kinds of things, at a time when almost all artists were versatile, than any other but one. Probably Leonardo da Vinci was gifted in as many different ways as Michael Angelo, and in his own lines was as powerful. This Florentine's life was as tragic as it was restless.

There is a tablet in a room of a castle which stands high upon a rocky mount, near the village of Caprese, which tells that Michael Angelo was born in that place. The great castle is now in ruins, and more than four hundred years of fame have passed since the little child was born therein.

The unhappy existence of the artist seems to have been foreshadowed by an accident which happened to his mother before he was born. She was on horseback, riding with her husband to his official post at Chiusi, for he was governor of Chiusi and Caprese. Her horse stumbled, fell, and badly hurt her. This was two months before Michael Angelo was born, and misfortune ever pursued him.

The father of Angelo was descended from an aristocratic house--the Counts of Canossa were his ancestors--and in that day the profession of an artist was not thought to be dignified. Hence the father had quite different plans for the boy; but the son persisted and at last had his way. When he was still a little child his father finished his work as an official at Caprese and returned to Florence; but he left the little Angelo behind with his nurse. That nurse was the wife of a stonemason, and almost as soon as the boy could toddle he used to wander about the quarries where the stonecutters worked, and doubtless the baby joy of Angelo was to play at chiseling as it is the pleasure of modern babies to play at peg-top. After a time he was sent for to go to Florence to begin his education.

In Florence he fell in with a young chap who, like himself, loved art, but who was fortunate enough already to be apprenticed to the great painter of his time--

Ghirlandajo. One happy day this young Granacci volunteered to take Michael Angelo to his master's studio, and there Angelo made such an impression on Ghirlandajo that he was urged by the artist to become his pupil.

All the world began to seem rose coloured to the ambitious boy, and he started his life-work with enthusiasm. At that time he was thirteen years old, full of hope and of love for his kind; but his good fortune did not last long. He had hardly settled to work in Ghirlandajo's studio than his genius, which should have made him beloved, made him hated by his master. Angelo drew superior designs, created new art-ideas, was more clever in all his undertakings than any other pupil--even ahead of his master; and almost at once Ghirlandajo became furiously jealous. This enmity between pupil and master was the beginning of Angelo's many misfortunes.

One day he got into a dispute with a fellow student, Torregiano, who broke his nose. This deformity alone was a tragedy to one like Michael Angelo who loved everything beautiful, yet must go through life knowing himself to be ill-favoured.

In height he was a little man, topped by an abnormally large head which was part of the penalty he had to pay for his talents. He had a great, broad forehead, and an eye that did not gleam nor express the beauty of his creative mind, but was dull, and lustreless, matching his broken, flattened nose. Indeed he was a tragedy to himself. In the "History of Painting" Muther describes his unhappy disposition:

"In his youthful years he never learned what love meant. 'If thou wishest to conquer me,' in old age he addresses love, 'give me back my features, from which nature has removed all beauty.' Whenever in his sonnets he speaks of passion, it is always of pain and tears, of sadness and unrequited longing, never of the fulfilment of his wishes."

Then, too, Michael Angelo had a quarrelsome disposition, and he was harsh in his criticism of others. He hated Leonardo da Vinci more for his great physical beauty than for his genius. He quarreled with most of his contemporaries, never joined the assemblies of his brother artists, but dwelt altogether apart. His was a gloomy and melancholy disposition and he never found relief outside his work.

He was all kinds of an artist--poet, sculptor, architect, painter--and although he worked with the irregularity of true genius, he worked indefatigably when once he began. It is said that when he was making his "David" he never removed his clothing the whole time he was employed upon the work, but dropped down when too exhausted to work more, and slept wherever he fell.

His first flight from the workshop of Ghirlandajo was to the gardens of the great Florentine prince, Lorenzo de' Medici, who had sent to Ghirlandajo for two of his best pupils. He wished them to come to his gardens and study the beautiful Greek statues which ornamented them. The choice fell to Angelo and Granacci. Probably those statues in Lorenzo's garden were the first glimpses of really great art that Michael Angelo ever had. Certain it is that he was overwhelmed with happiness when he was given permission to copy what he would, and at once he fell to work with his chisel. His first work in that garden was upon the head of an old faun; and Lorenzo, walking by, curious to know to what use the lad was putting his opportunity, made a criticism:

"You have made your faun old," he said, "yet you have left all the teeth; at such an age, generally the teeth are wanting."

Angelo had nothing to say and the prince walked on, but when next he came that way, he found that Angelo had broken off two of the faun's teeth; and this recognition of his criticism pleased Lorenzo so much that he invited Angelo to live with him. At first his father objected. He felt himself to be an aristocrat, and sculpture and painting were indeed low occupations for his son, who he had resolved should be nothing less than a silk merchant. Nevertheless, the prince's command, united with the son's pleading, compelled the father to give up his cherished dream of making a merchant of him, and Angelo went to live in the palace.

Then indeed what seemed a beautiful life opened out. He was dressed in fine clothing, dined with princes, and possibly he was grateful to his patron. Some historians say so, and add that when Lorenzo died Angelo wept, and returned sadly to his father's house to mourn, but this tale seems at odds with what else we know of Angelo's unangelic, envious and bitter disposition. It is quite certain, however, that with the death of Lorenzo, Angelo's, fortunes became greatly changed. Another prince followed in line--Pietro de' Medici--but he was a poor thing, who brought little good to anybody. He had small use for Michael Angelo's genius, but it is said that he did give him one commission. After a great storm one day, he asked him to make a snow-man for him, and Angelo obligingly complied. It was doubtless a very beautiful snow-man, but although it was Angelo's it melted in the night, even as if it had been Johnny's or Tommy's snow-man, and left no trace behind.

In Rome there was a high and haughty pope on the throne--Julius II.--who had probably not his match for obstinacy and haughtiness, excepting in the great painter and sculptor. When Angelo went to Rome, he was bound to come in conflict with Julius for it was popes and princes who gave art any reason for being in those days, and the Church prescribed what kind of art should be cultivated. Michael was to come directly under the command of the pope and such a combination promised trouble. Kings themselves had to remove their crowns and hats to Julius, and why not Michael Angelo? Yet there he stood, covered, before the pope, opposing his greatness to that of the pope. Soderini says that Angelo treated the pope as the king of France never would have dared treat him; but Angelo may have known that kings of France might be born and die, times without number, while there would never be born another Michael Angelo. There could be nothing but antagonism between Angelo and Julius, and soon after the artist returned to Florence; but the necessity for following his profession enabled Julius to tame him after all, and it is said that the pope led him back to Rome, later, "with a halter about his neck." This must have been agony to Angelo.

Back in Rome, he was commissioned to make a tomb for the pope. He had no sooner set about the preliminaries--the getting of suitable marble for his work--than he began to quarrel with the men who were to hew it. When that difficulty was settled, and the marble was got out, he had a set-to with the shipowners who were to transport the stone, and that row became so serious that the sculptor was besieged in his own house.

At another and later time, when he was engaged upon the frescoes of the Sistine Chapel, he was made to work by force. He accused the man who had built the scaffolding upon which he must stand, or lie, to paint, of planning his destruction. He suspected the very assistants whom he, himself, had chosen to go from Florence, of having designs upon his life. He locked the chapel against them, and they had to turn away when they went to begin work. Because of his insane suspicion he did alone the enormous work of the frescoes. Doubtless he was half mad, just as he was wholly a genius.

By the time he had finished those frescoes he was so exhausted and overworked that he wrote piteously to his people at home, "I have not a friend in Rome, neither do I wish nor have use for any." This of course was not true; or he would not have made the statement. "I hardly find time to take nourishment. Not an ounce more can I bear than already rests upon my shoulders." Even when the work was done he felt no happiness because of it, but complained about everything and everybody.

If Angelo thought this an unhappy day, worse was in store for him. Julius II. died and in his place there came to reign upon the papal throne, Leo X. If Michael Angelo had been restricted in his work before, he was almost jailed under Leo X. Julius had been a virile, forceful man, and Michael Angelo was the same. Since he must be restrained and dictated to, it was possible for the artist to listen to a man who was in certain respects strong like himself, but to be under the thumb of a weak, effeminate person like Leo, was the tragedy of tragedies to Angelo. That was a marvellous time in Rome. All its citizens had become so pleasure-loving that the world, stood still to wonder. When the pope banqueted, he had the golden plates from which fair women had eaten hurled into the Tiber, that they might never be profaned by a less noble use than they had known. From all this riot and madness of pleasure, Michael Angelo stood aside with frowning brow and scornful mien. He approved of nothing and of nobody--despising even Raphael, the gentle and loving man whom the pleasure-crazed people of Rome paused to smile upon and love. The pope said that Angelo was "terrible," and that he filled everybody with fear.

Finally, Rome so resented his frowning looks and his surly ways that work was provided for him at a distance. He was sent to Florence again to build a facade. While there, the city was conquered, and Angelo was one who fought for its freedom, but even so, he fled just at the crisis. Thus he ever did the wrong thing--excepting when he worked. In Florence he had planned to do mighty things, but he never accomplished any one of them. He planned to make a wonderful colossal statue on a cliff near Carrara, and also he resolved to make the tomb of Julius the nucleus of a "forest of statues."

Michael Angelo never married, but he was burdened with a family and all its cares. He supported his brothers and even his nephews, and took care of his father. All of those people came to him with their difficulties and with their demands for money. He chided, quarreled, repelled, yet met every obligation. He would sit beside the sick-bed of a servant the night through, but growl at the demands of his near relatives--and it is not unlikely that he had good reason.

At last he withdrew himself from all human society but that of little children, whom he cared to speak with and to please. He would have naught to do with men of genius like himself; and when he fell from a scaffolding and injured himself, the physician had to force his way through a barred window, in order to get into the sick man's presence to serve him.

An illustration of his determined solitude is given in the "Young People's Story of Art:"

"There had long been lying idle in Florence an immense block of marble. One hundred years before a sculptor had tried to carve something from it, but had failed. This was now given to Michael Angelo. He was to be paid twelve dollars a month, and to be allowed two years in which to carve a statue. He made his design in wax; and then built a tower around the block, so that he might work inside without being seen."

Everything Angelo undertook bore the marks of gigantic enterprise. Although he never succeeded in making the tomb of Julius II. the central piece in his forest of statues, the undertaking was marvellous enough. His original plan was to make the tomb three stories high and to ornament it with forty statues, and if St. Peter's Church was large enough to hold it, the work was to be placed therein; but if not, a church was to be built specially to hold the tomb. When at last, in spite of his difficulties with workmen and shipowners, the marbles were deposited in the great square before St. Peter's, they filled the whole place; and the pope, wishing to watch the progress of the work and not himself to be observed, had a covered way built from the Vatican to the workshop of Angelo in the square, by which he might come and go as he chose, while an order was issued that the sculptor was to be admitted at all times to the Vatican. No sooner was this arrangement completed than Angelo's enemies frightened the pope by telling him there was danger in making his tomb before his death; and with these superstitions haunting him Julius II. stopped the work, leaving Angelo without the means to pay for his marbles. With the doors of the Vatican closed to him, Angelo withdrew, post haste to Florence--and who can blame him? Nevertheless, the work was resumed after infinite trouble on the pope's part. He had to send again and again for Angelo and after forty years, the work was finished. There the sequel of the sculptor's forty-years war with self and the world stands to-day in "Moses," the wonderful, commanding central figure which seems to reflect all the fierce power which Angelo had to keep in check during a life-time.

The command of Julius that he should paint the ceiling of the Sistine Chapel aroused all his fierce resistance. He did it under protest, all the while accusing those about him of having designs upon his life.

"I am not a painter, but a sculptor," he said.

"Such a man as thou is everything that he wishes to be," the pope replied.

"But this is an affair of Raphael. Give him this room to paint and let me carve a mountain!" But no, he must paint the ceiling; but to render it easier for him the pope told him he might fill in the spaces with saints, and charge a certain amount for each. This Angelo, who was first of all an artist, refused to do. He would do the work rightly or not at all. So he made his own plans and cut himself a cardboard helmet, into the front of which he thrust a candle, as if it were a Davy lamp, and he lay upon his back to work day and night at the hated task. During those months he was compelled to look up so continually, that never afterward was he able to look down without difficulty. When he had finished the work Julius had some criticisms to make.

"Those dresses on your saints are such poor things," he said. "Not rich enough-- such very poor things!"

"Well, they were poor things," was Angelo's answer. "The saints did not wear golden ornaments, nor gold on their garments."

After Julius II. and Leo X. came Pope Paul III., and he, like the other two, determined to have Angelo for his workman. Indeed all his life, Michael Angelo's gifts were commanded by the Church of Rome. It was for Paul III. he painted the "Last Judgment." His former work upon the Sistine Chapel had been the story of the creation. All his work was of a mighty and allegorical nature; tremendous shoulders, mighty limbs, herculean muscles that seemed fit to support the universe. These allegories are made of hundreds of figures. To-day they are still there, though dimmed by the smoke of centuries of incense, and dismembered by the cracking of plaster and disintegration of materials.

Angelo's methods of work, as well as their results, were oppressive. In his youth, while trying to perfect himself in his study of the human form, he drew or modelled, from nude corpses. He had these conveyed by stealth from the hospital into the convent of Santo Spirito, where he had a cell and there he worked, alone.

He was concentrated, mentally and emotionally, upon himself. The only remark he made after the blow from Torregiano was, "You will be remembered only as the man who broke my nose!" This proved nearly true, since Torregiano was banished, and murdered by the Spanish Inquisition.

All sorts of anecdotes have floated through the centuries concerning this man and his work. For example, he made a statue of a sleeping cupid, which was buried in the ground for a time that it might assume the appearance of age, and pass for an antique. Afterward it was sold to the Cardinal San Giorgio for two hundred ducats, though Michael Angelo received only thirty. Nevertheless, he died a rich man, after having cared for a numerous family, while he himself lived like a man without means. All the tranquillity he ever knew he enjoyed in his old age.

It was characteristic of his perversity that he left his name upon nothing that he made, with one exception. Vasari relates the story of that exception:

"The love and care which Michael Angelo had given to this group, 'In Paradise,' were such that he there left his name--a thing he never did again for any work--on the cincture which girdles the robe of Our Lady; for it happened one day that Michael Angelo, entering the place where it was erected, found a large assemblage of strangers from Lombardy there, who were praising it highly; one of them asking who had done it, was told, 'our Hunchback of Milan'; hearing which Michael Angelo remained silent, although surprised that his work should be attributed to another. But one night he repaired to St. Peter's with a light and his chisels, to engrave his name on the figure, which seems to breathe a spirit as perfect as her form and countenance."

If his youth had been given to sculpture, his maturity to the painting of wondrous frescoes, so his old age was devoted to architecture, and as architect he rebuilt the decaying St. Peter's. In this work he felt that he partly realised his ideal. Sculpture meant more to him, "did more for the glory of God," than any other form of art. When he had finished his work on St. Peter's, he is said to have looked upon it and exclaimed: "I have hung the Pantheon in the air!"

This colossal genius died in Rome, and was carried by the light of torches from that city back to his better loved Florence, where he was buried. His tomb was made in the Santa Croce, and upon it are three female figures representing Michael Angelo's three wonderful arts: Architecture, sculpture and painting. No artist was greater than he.

His will committed "his soul to God, his body to the earth, and his property to his nearest relatives."

PLATE--DANIEL

This wonderful painting is a part of the decoration of the Sistine Chapel in Rome. The picture of the prophet tells so much in itself, that a description seems absurd. It is enough to call attention to the powerful muscles in the arm, the fall of the hand, and then to speak of the main characteristics of the artist's pictures.

It is extraordinary that there is no blade of grass to be found in any painting by Michael Angelo. He loved to paint but one thing, and that was the naked man, the powerful muscles, or the twisted limbs of those in great agony. He loved only to work upon vast spaces of ceiling or wall. Look at this picture of Daniel and see how like sculpture the pose and modelling appear to be. First of all, Michael Angelo was a sculptor, and most of the painting which fate forced him to do has the characteristics of sculpture.

One critic has remarked that he loves to think of this strange man sitting before the marble quarry of Pietra Santa and thinking upon all the beings hidden in the cliff-- beings which he should fashion from the marble.

It was said that in Michael Angelo's hands the Holy Family became a race of Titans, and where others would have put plants or foliage, Angelo placed men and naked limbs to fill the space. When his subject made some sort of herbage necessary, he invented a kind of mediæval fern in place of grass and familiar leaves. Everything appears brazen and hard and mighty, suggestive of Angelo's own throbbing spirit and maddened soul. Most of his work, when illustrated, must be shown not as a whole but in sections, but one can best mention them as entire picture themes. On the ceiling of the Sistine Chapel are nine frescoes describing "The Creation of The World," "The Fall of Man" and "The Deluge." "The Last Judgment" occupies the entire altar wall in the same chapel of the Vatican. "The Holy Family" is in the Uffizi Gallery, Florence.

III ARNOLD BÖCKLIN

(Pronounced Bek'-lin)

Modern German School (Düsseldorf)

1827-1901

This splendid artist is so lately dead that it does not seem proper yet to discuss his personal history, but we can speak understandingly of his art, for we already know it to be great art, which will stand the test of time. His imagination turned toward subjects of solemn grandeur and his work is very impressive and beautiful.

He was born in Basel, "one of the most prosaic towns in Europe." His father was a Swiss merchant, and not poor; thus the son had ordinarily good chances to make an artist of himself. He was born at a time when to be an artist had long ceased to be a reproach, and men no longer discouraged their sons who felt themselves inspired to paint great pictures.

When Böcklin was nineteen years old he took himself to Düsseldorf, with his merchant father's permission, and settled down to learn his art, but in that city he found mostly "sentimental and anecdotal" pictures being painted, which did not suit him at all. Then he took himself off to Brussels, where again he was not satisfied, and so went to Paris. But while in Brussels he had copied many old masters, and had advanced himself very much, so that he did not present himself in Paris raw and untried in art.

At first he studied in the Louvre, then went to Rome, seeking ever the best, and being hard to satisfy. He found rest and tranquillity in Zürich, a city in his native country, but it was Italy that had most influenced his work.

He loved the Campagna of Rome with its ruins and the sad grandeur of the crumbling tombs lining its way, and therefore a certain mysterious, grand, and solemn character made his pictures unlike those of any other artist. He loved to paint in vertical (up-and-down) fines, rather than with the conventional horizontal outlines that we find in most paintings. This method gives his pictures a different quality from any others in the world.

He loved best of all to paint landscape, and it is said of him that "as the Greeks peopled their streams and woods and waves with creatures of their imagination, so Böcklin makes the waterfall take shape as a nymph, or the mists which rise above the water source wreathe into forms of merry children; or in some wild spot hurls centaurs together in fierce combat, or makes the slippery, moving wave give birth to Nereids and Tritons."

Muther, art-critic and biographer, calls our attention to the similarity between Wagner's music and Böcklin's painting. While Wagner was "luring the colours of sound from music," Böcklin's "symphonies of colour streamed forth like a crashing orchestra," and he calls him the greatest colour-poet of the time.

In appearance Böcklin was fine of form, healthy and wholesome in all his thoughts and way of living. In 1848 he took part in revolutionary politics and later this did him great harm. Only the influence of his friends kept him from ruin. After the Franco-Prussian war he was made Minister of Fine Arts. In this office he rendered great service; but because he had to witness the wrecking of the Column Vendôme in order to save the Louvre and the Luxembourg from the mob, he was censured; indeed so heavy a fine was imposed that it took his whole fortune to pay it; and he was banished into the bargain. From 1892 to 1901 he lived in or near Florence, and he died at Fiesole, January 16th, 1901.

PLATE--THE ISLE OF THE DEAD

This picture is perhaps the greatest of the many great Arnold Böcklin paintings, and it is both fascinating and awe-inspiring.

It best shows his liking for vertical lines in art. The Isle of the Dead is of a rocky, shaft-like formation in which we may see hewn-out tombs; and there, tall cypress trees are growing.

The traces of man's work in the midst of this sombre, ideal, and mystic scene add to the impressiveness of the picture. The isle stands high and lonely in the midst of a sea.

The water seems silently to lap the base of the rocks and the trees are in black shadow, massed in the centre. It looks very mysterious and still. There is a stone gateway touched with the light of a dying day. It is sunset and the dead is being brought to its resting place in a tiny boat, all the smaller for its relation to the gloomy grandeur of the isle which it is approaching. One figure is standing in the boat, facing the island, and the sunlight falls full upon his back and touches the boat, making that spot stand out brilliantly from all the rest of the picture.

Among Böcklin's paintings are "Naiads at Play," which hangs in the Museum at Basel, "A Villa by the Sea," "The Sport of the Waves," "Regions of Joy," "Flora," and "Venus Dispatching Cupid."

IV MARIE-ROSA BONHEUR

(Pronounced Rosa Bon-er)

French School

1822-1895

Pupil of Raymond B. Bonheur

Rosa Bonheur, Landseer, and Murillo maybe called "Children's Painters" in this book because they painted things that children, as well as grown-ups, certainly can enjoy. To be sure, Murillo was a very different sort of artist from Rosa Bonheur or Landseer, but if the two latter painted the most beautiful, animals--dogs, sheep, and horses--Murillo painted the loveliest little children.

Rosa was the best pupil of her father; Raymond B. Bonheur. In Bordeaux they lived together the peaceful life of artists, the father being already a well known painter when his daughter was born. She became, as Mr. Hamerton, who knew her, said, "the most accomplished female painter who ever lived ... a pure, generous woman as well and can hardly be too much admired ... as a woman or an artist. She is simple in her tastes and habits of life and many stories are told of her generosity to others."

After a time the Bonheurs moved to Paris where young Rosa could have better opportunities; and there she put on man's clothing, which she wore all her life thereafter. She wore a workingman's blouse and trousers, and tramped about looking more like a man than a woman with her short hair. This, made everybody stare at her and think her very queer, but people no longer believe that she dressed herself thus in order to advertise herself and attract attention; but because it was the most convenient costume for her to get about in. She went to all sorts of places; the stockyards, slaughter houses, all about the streets of Paris, to learn of things and people, especially of animals, which she wished most to paint. She could hardly have gone about thus if she had worn women's clothing.

Rosa Bonheur exhibited her first painting at the *Salon* in 1841, and this was twelve years before her beloved father died; thus he had the happiness of knowing that the daughter whom he had taught so lovingly was on the road to success and fortune. He knew that when fortune should come to her she would use it well. The year that she exhibited her work in the *Salon* she painted only two little pictures--one of rabbits, the other of sheep and goats--but they were so splendidly done that all the critics knew a great woman artist had arrived.

It was then that her enemies, those who were becoming jealous of her work, said that she was wearing men's clothing in order to attract attention to herself.

Soon her work began to be bought by the French Government, which was a sure sign of her power. She was already much beloved by the people. In the meantime we in America and others in England had heard of Mademoiselle Bonheur, but we heard far less about her painting than we did about her masculine garb. We thought of her mostly as an eccentric woman; but one day came "The Horse Fair," and all the world heard of that, so the artist was to be no longer judged by the clothes she wore but by her art. Finally, she received the cross of the Legion of Honour, and also was made a member of the Institute of Antwerp.

She lived near Fontainebleau; her studio a peaceful retired home, till the Franco-Prussian war came about. Then she and others began to fear that her studio and pictures would be destroyed, so the artist was forced to stop her work and prepared to go elsewhere. But the Crown Prince of Prussia himself ordered that Mademoiselle Bonheur should not even be disturbed. Her work had made her belong to all the world and all the world was to protect her if need be.

Rosa Bonheur had a brother who, some critics said, was the better artist, but if that were true it is likely that his popularity would in some degree have approached that of his sister. Rosa Bonheur did not paint many large canvases, but mostly small ones, or only moderately large; but when she painted sheep it seems that one might shear the wool, it stands so fleecy and full; while her horses rampage and curvet, showing themselves off as if they were alive.

PLATE--THE HORSE FAIR

This picture was exhibited all over the world very nearly. It was carried to England and to America, and won admiration wherever it was seen. Finally it was sold in America. It was first exhibited in 1853, the year in which the artist's father died. Mr. Ernest Gambart was the first who bought the picture, and he wrote of it to his friend, Mr. S.P. Avery: "I will give you the real history of 'The Horse Fair,' now in New York. It was painted in 1852, by Rosa Bonheur, then in her thirtieth year, and exhibited in the next *Salon*. Though much admired it did not find a purchaser. It was soon after exhibited in Ghent, meeting again with much appreciation, but was not sold, as art did not flourish at the time. In 1855 the picture was sent by Rosa Bonheur to her native town of Bordeaux and exhibited there. She offered to sell it to the town at the very low price 12,000 francs ($2,400). While there, I asked her if she would sell it to me, and allow me to take it to England and have it engraved. She said: 'I wish to have my picture remain in France. I will once more impress on my countrymen, my wish to sell it to them for 12,000 francs. If they refuse, you can have it, but if you take it abroad, you must pay me 40,000 francs.' The town failing to make the purchase, I at once accepted these terms, and Rosa Bonheur then placed the picture at my disposal. I tendered her the 40,000 francs and she said: 'I am much gratified at your giving me such a noble price, but I do not like to feel that I have taken advantage of your liberality; let us see how we can combine in the matter. You will not be able to have an engraving made from so large a canvas. Suppose I paint you a small one from the same subject, of which I will make you a present.' Of course I accepted the gift, and thus it happened that the large work went travelling over the kingdom on exhibition, while Thomas Landseer was making an engraving from the quarter-size replica.

"After some time (in 1857 I think), I sold the original picture to Mr. William P. Wright, New York (whose picture gallery and residence were at Weehawken, N.J.), for the sum of 30,000 francs, but later I understood that Mr. Stewart paid a much larger price for it on the breaking up of Mr. Wright's gallery. The quarter size replica, from which the engraving was made, I finally sold to Mr. Jacob Bell, who gave it in 1859 to the nation, and it is now in the National Gallery, London. A second, still smaller replica, was painted a few years later, and was resold some time ago in London for £4,000 ($20,000). There is also a smaller water-colour drawing which was sold to Mr. Bolckow for 2,500 guineas ($12,000), and is now an heirloom belonging to the town of Middlesbrough. That is the whole history of this grand work. The Stewart canvas is the real and true original, and only large size 'Horse-Fair.'

"Once in Mr. Stewart's collection, it never left his gallery until the auction sale of his collection, March 25th, 1887, when it was purchased by Mr. Cornelius Vanderbilt for the sum of $55,000, and presented to the Metropolitan Museum of Art."

And thus we have the whole story of the "Horse-Fair." The picture is 93-1/2 inches high, and 197 inches wide, and it contains a great number of horses, some of which are ridden, while others are led, and all are crowding with wild gaiety toward the fair where it is quite plain they know they are about to be admired and their beauty shown to the best advantage. Other well-known Rosa Bonheurs are "Ploughing," "Shepherd Guarding Sheep," "Highland Sheep," "Scotch Deer," "American Mustangs," and "The Study of a Lioness."

V ALESSANDRO BOTTICELLI

(Pronounced Ah-lays-sahn'dro Bo't-te-chel'lee)

Florentine School,

1447-1510 (Vasari's dates)

Pupil of Filippo Lippi and Verrocchio

Botticelli took his name from his first master, as was the fashion in those days. The relation of master and apprentice was very close, not at all like the relation of pupil and teacher to-day.

Botticelli's father was a Florentine citizen, Mariano Filipepi, and he wished his son to become a goldsmith; hence the lad was soon apprenticed to Botticelli, the goldsmith. As a scholar, the little goldsmith had not distinguished himself. Indeed it is said that as a boy he would not "take to any sort of schooling in reading, writing, or arithmetic." It cannot be said that this failure distinguished him as a genius, or the world would be full of genius-boys; but the result was that he early began to learn his trade.

Fortunately for him and us, Botticelli, the smith, was a man of some wisdom and when he saw that the lad originated beautiful designs and had creative genius he did not treat the matter with scorn, as the master of Andrea del Sarto had done, but sent him instead to Fra Filippo (Lippo Lippi) to be taught the art of painting. So kind a deed might well establish a feeling of devotion on little Alessandro's part and make him wish to take his master's name.

Fra Filippo was a Carmelite monk, merry and kindly; simple, good, and gifted, but his temperament did not seem to influence his young pupil. Of all unhappy, morbid men, Botticelli seems to have been the most so, unless we are to except Michael Angelo.

After studying with the monk, Botticelli was summoned by Pope Sixtus IV. to Rome to decorate a new chapel in the Vatican. Before that time his whole life had been greatly influenced by the teachings of Savonarola who had preached both passionately and learnedly in Florence, advocating liberty. From the time he fell under

Savonarola's wonderful power, the artist grew more and more mystic and morbid. In Rome it was the custom to have the portraits of conspirators, or persons of high degree who were revolutionary or otherwise objectionable to the state, hung outside the Public Palace, and in Botticelli's time there was a famous disturbance among the aristocrats of the state. In 1478 the powerful Pazzi family conspired against the Medici family, which then actually had control. It was Botticelli who was engaged to paint the portraits of the Pazzi family, which to their shame and humiliation were to be displayed upon the palace walls.

One peculiarity of this artist's pictures was that he used actual goldleaf to make the high lights upon hair, leaves, and draperies. The effect of the use of this gold was very beautiful, if unusual, and it may have been that his apprenticeship as a goldsmith suggested to him such a device.

Also it was he who created certain characteristics of painting that have since been thought original with Burne-Jones. This was the use of long stiff lily-stalks or other upright details in his compositions. Examples of this idea, which produced so weird an effect, will be found in his allegory of "Spring," where stiff tree-trunks form a part of the background. In the "Madonna of the Palms" upright lily-stalks are held in pale and trembling hands. Like Michael Angelo, who came years afterward, Botticelli was a guest of the great Lorenzo the "Magnificent," in Florence. It was by Botticelli's hand that the greater painter sent a letter to Lorenzo from a duchess friend who was also his patron. This was in Angelo's youth; in Botticelli's old age.

All his life was a drama of morbid seeking after the unattainable, and finally he became so poor and helpless that in his old age he would have starved had Lorenzo de' Medici not taken care of him. Lorenzo and other friends who in spite of his gloominess admired his real piety, gathered about him and kept him from starvation.

On his "Nativity," Botticelli wrote: "This picture I, Alessandro, painted at the end of the year 1500 in the troubles of Italy, in the halftime after the time, during the fulfilment of the eleventh of John, in the second woe of the Apocalypse, in the loosing the devil for three and a half years. Afterward he shall be chained according to the twelfth of John, and see him trodden down as in this picture." All of this is interesting because Botticelli himself wrote it, but it is not very easily understood by any child, nor by many grown people.

Botticelli did some very extraordinary things, but whether they are beautiful or not one must decide for himself. They are paintings so characteristic that one must think them very beautiful or else not at all so.

PLATE--LA PRIMAVERA

(Spring)

In this picture we have the forerunner of a modern painter, because we see in it certain, qualities that we find in Böcklin. Look at the effect of vertical lines; the tree trunks, and the poses of the slender women. Over all hovers a cupid who is sending love-shafts into the hearts of all in springtime.

Notice the lacy effect of the flowers that bestar the wind-blown gown of "La Primavera," the fern-like leaves that fleck the background; the draperies that do not conceal the forms of the nymphs of the lovely springtime.

The very spirit of spring is seen in all the half-floating, half-dancing, gliding, diaphanous figures of the forest. The flowers of "La Primavera's" crown are blue and white cornflowers and primroses. She scatters over the earth tulips, anemones, and narcissus. The painting is allegorical and unique. Never were such fluttering odds and ends of draperies painted before, nor such fascinating effects had from canvas, paint, or brush. The picture hangs in Florence in the Uffizi Gallery. A German critic tells us that the "Realm of Venus," is a better title for this picture, and that it was painted after a poem of that name.

Other pictures by this artist are: "The Birth of Venus," "Pallas," "Judith," "Holofernes," "St. Augustine," "Adoration of the Magi," and "St. Sebastian."

VI WILLIAM ADOLPHE BOUGUEREAU

(Pronounced W. A'dolf Bou-gair-roh)

French (Genre) School

1825-1905
Pupil of Picot and the Ecole des Beaux-Arts

Bouguereau's business-like father meant his son also to be business-like, but he made the mistake of permitting him to go to a drawing school in Bordeaux and there, to his father's chagrin, the youngster took the annual prize. After that there seemed nothing for the father to do but grin and bear it, because the son decided to be an artist and had fairly won his right to be one.

Young Bouguereau had no money, and therefore he went to live with an uncle at Saintonge, a priest, who had much sympathy with the boy's wish to paint, and he left him free to do the best he could for himself in art. He got a chance to paint some portraits, and when he and his uncle talked the matter over It was decided that he should take the money got for them, and go to Paris. It was there that he sought Picot, his first truly helpful teacher; and there, for the first time he learned more than he already knew about art.

All Bouguereau's opportunities in life were made by himself, by his own genius. No one gave him anything; he earned all. He longed to go to Italy, and in the Ecole des Beaux-Arts he won the Prix de Rome, which made possible a journey to the land of great artists. The French Government began to buy his work, and he began to receive commissions to decorate walls in great buildings; thus, gradually, he made for himself fame and fortune.

When this artist undertook to paint sacred subjects, of great dignity, he was not at his best; but when he chose children and mothers and everyday folk engaged about their everyday business, he painted beautifully. Americans have bought many of his pictures and he has had more popularity in this country than anywhere outside of France.

Some authorities give the birthplace of Bouguereau as La Rochelle; at any rate he died there at midnight, on the nineteenth of August, 1905.

PLATE--THE VIRGIN AS CONSOLER

The main distinction about this artist's pictured faces is the peculiarly earnest expression he has given to the eyes. In this picture of the Virgin there is great genius in the pose and death-look of the little child whose mother has flung herself across the lap of Mary, abandoned to her agony. This painting is hung in the Luxembourg. Others by the same master are called "Psyche and Cupid" "Birth of Venus," "Innocence," and "At the Well."

VII SIR EDWARD BURNE-JONES

English (Pre-Raphaelite) School

1833-1898
Pupil of Rossetti

This artist has been called the most original of all contemporaneous artists. He has also been called the "lyric painter"; meaning that he is to painting what the lyric poet is to literature. His work once known can almost always be recognised wherever seen afterward. He did not slavishly follow the Pre-Raphaelite school, yet he drew most of his ideas from its methods. He was, in the use of stiff lines, a follower of Botticelli, and not original in that detail, as some have seemed to think.

PLATE--CHANT D'AMOUR

(The Love-Song)

This is a picture in the true Burne-Jones style: a beautiful woman in billowy draperies, playing upon a harp forms the central figure of the group of three--a listener on either side of her. There is the attractiveness of the Burne-Jones method about this picture, but after all there seems to be no very good reason for its having been painted. The subject thus treated has only a negative value, and little suggestion of thought or dramatic idea.

Another picture of this artist, in which his use of stiff draperies is specially shown, is that of the women at the tomb of Christ, when they find the stone rolled away and, looking around, see the Saviour's figure before them. The scene is low and cavern-like, with a brilliant light surrounding the tomb. This artist also painted "The Vestal Virgin," "King Cophetua and the Beggar Maid," "Pan and Psyche," "The Golden Stairs," and "Love Among the Ruins."

VIII JOHN CONSTABLE

English School

1776-1837

Pupil of the Royal Academy

John Constable was the son of a "yeoman farmer" who meant to make him also a yeoman farmer. Mostly we find that the fathers of our artists had no higher expectations for their sons than to have them take up their own business; to begin as they had, and to end as they expected to. But in John Constable's case, as with all the others, the father's methods of living did not at all please the son, and having most of all a liking for picture-making; young John set himself to planning his own affairs.

Nevertheless, the foundation of John's art was laid right there in the Suffolk farmer's home and conditions. He was born in East Bergholt, and the father seems to have believed in windmills, for early in life the signs of wind and weather became a part of the son's education. He learned a deal more of atmospheric conditions there on his father's windmill planted farm than he could possibly have learned shut up in a studio, French fashion. As a little boy he came to know all the signs of the heavens; the clouds gathering for storm or shine; the bending of the trees in the blast; all of these he loved, and later on made the principal subjects of his art. He learned to observe these things as a matter of business and at his father's command; thus we may say that he studied his life-work from his very infancy. All about him were beautiful hedgerows, picturesque cottages with high pitched roofs covered with thatch, and it was these beauties which bred one other great landscape painter besides Constable, of whom we shall presently speak, Gainsborough.

At last, graduating from windmills, John went to London. He had a vacation from the work set him by his father, and for two years he painted "cottages, studied anatomy," and did the drudgery of his art; but there was little money in it for him, and soon he had to go into his father's counting house, for windmills seemed to have paid the elder Constable, considerably better than painting promised to pay young John.

John doubtless liked counting-house work even less than he had done the study of windmills and weather in his father's fields. He was a most persistent fellow, however, and finally he returned to London, to study again the art he loved, this time in the Royal Academy, which meant that he had made some progress.

His father gave him very little aid to do the things he longed to do, but after his father's death he found that a little money was coming to him from the estate--£4,000. He had already triumphed over his difficulties by painting his first fine pictures; he now knew that he was to become a successful artist, and be able to take care of himself and a wife. Though in love, he had hitherto been too poor to marry. His first splendid work was "Dedham Vale."

Though things were going very well with him, it was not until Paris discovered him that he achieved great success. In 1824 he painted two large pictures which he took to Paris, and there he found fame. The best landscape painting in France dates from the time when Constable's works were hung in the Louvre, to become the delight of all art-lovers.

He received a gold medal from Charles X., and became more honoured abroad than he had ever been at home.

Constable had many enemies, and made many more after he became an Academician. Some artists, who would have liked that honour and who could not gain it for themselves, declared that Constable painted "with a palette knife," though it certainly would not have mattered if he had, since he made great pictures.

He painted things exactly as he saw them, and was not a popular artist. Most of all, he loved to paint the scenes that he had known so well in his youth, and he did them over and over again, as if the subject was one in which he wished to reach perfection.

When he died he left a picture, "Arundel Castle and Mill," standing with its paint wet upon his easel for he passed away very suddenly, on April 1st, leaving behind him many unsold paintings.

He was a sensitive chap, and throughout his youth was greatly distressed by the differences of opinion between himself and his father. He was torn asunder between a sense of duty and his own wish to be an artist; and his greatest consolation in this situation was in the friendship he had formed for a plumber, who, like himself, dearly loved art. The plumber's name was John Dunthorne, and the two men wandered about the country, when not employed at their regular work, and together, by streams and in fields, painted the same scenes. At one time they hired a little room in the neighbouring village which they made into a studio. Constable was a handsome fellow in his youth and was known to all as the "handsome miller." His father, the yeoman farmer with the windmills, was also a miller.

In London he became acquainted with one John Smith, known as "Antiquity Smith," who taught him something of etching. After he was recalled to his father's business, his mother wrote to "Antiquity Smith," that she hoped John "would now attend to business, by which he will please me and his father, and ensure his own respectability and comfort"--a complete expression of the middle-class British mind. Her satisfaction was short-lived, for her son soon returned to London.

When his first pictures were rejected by the Royal Academy he showed one of them to Sir Benjamin West, who said hopefully: "Don't be disheartened, young man, we shall hear of you again; you must have loved nature very much before you could have painted this."

About that time he tried to paint many kinds of pictures, such as portraits and sacred subjects, but he did not seem to succeed in anything except the scenes of his boyhood, which he truly loved. Hence he gave up attempting that which he could do only passably, and kept to what he could do supremely well.

When his friends wished him to continue portrait painting, the only thing that was well paid at that time, Constable wrote: "You know I have always succeeded best with my native scenes. They have always charmed me, and I hope they always will. I have now a path marked out very distinctly for myself, and I am desirous of pursuing it uninterruptedly."

About the time he fell in love and before his father's death, his health began to fail, and the young woman's mother would have none of him. Her father was in favour of Constable, but he could not hold out against the chance of his daughter losing her grandfather's fortune by marrying the wrong man.

The lady was not so distractingly in love as young Constable was, and she did not entirely like the idea of poverty, even with John, so she held off, and with so much anxiety Constable became downright ill. For five years the pair lived apart, and then the artist and the young woman, whose name was Maria Bicknell, lost their mothers about the same time, This drew them very closely together; and to help the matter on,

John's attendance upon his father in his last illness brought him to the same town as Miss Bicknell. After his father's death, he urged the young lady so strongly to be his wife that she consented They were married and her father soon forgave her, but not so her grandfather, who declared that he never would forgive her, but he really must have done so from the first, for when he died it was found that he had left her a little fortune of £4,000. This was about the same amount the artist had received from his father, so that they were able to get on very well.

After Constable's marriage he went on a visit to Sir George Beaumont, and there an amusing incident occurred which is known to-day as the story of Sir George's "brown tree." It seems that Constable's ideas of colour for his landscapes were so true to nature that a good many people did not approve of them, and one day while painting, Sir George declared that the colour of an old Cremona fiddle was the best model of colour tone that a landscape could have. Constable's only answer was to place the fiddle on the green lawn in front of the house. At another time his host asked the artist, "Do you not find it very difficult to determine where to place your brown tree?" "Not at all," was Constable's reply, "for I never put such a thing into a picture in my life."

In painting one picture many times he declared, "Its light cannot be put out because it is the light of nature." A Frenchman called attention to one of his pictures thus: "Look at these landscapes by an Englishman. The ground appears to be covered with dew."

Notwithstanding the little fortune of his wife and himself, Constable was not quite carefree, because he had to raise a good sized family of six children so that when his wife's father died and left his daughter £20,000 he said to a friend: "Now I shall stand before a six-foot canvas with a mind at ease, thank God!" In the very midst of this happiness, his beloved wife became ill with consumption, and was certain to die. He no longer cared very much for life and wrote very sadly:

"I have been ill, but am endeavouring to get work again, and could I get afloat upon a canvas of six feet, I might have a chance of being carried from myself." When he became a member of the Royal Academy, he said: "It has been delayed until I am solitary and cannot impart it," meaning that without his dear wife to share his good fortune, it seemed an empty honour to him.

Strange things are told which show how little his work was valued by his countrymen. After he had become a member of the Academy one of his small pictures was entered but rejected; nobody knowing anything about it. It was put on one side among the "outsiders." Finally, one of his fellow members glancing at it was attracted.

"Stop a bit! I rather like that. Why not say 'doubtful'?" Later Constable acknowledged the picture as his, and then they wished to hang it, but he refused to let them. Another Academy story is about his picture "Hadleigh Castle." On Varnishing Day, Chartney, a brilliant critic, told Constable that the foreground of the picture was "too cold," and so he undertook to "warm it," by giving it a strong glaze with asphaltum with Constable's brush which he snatched from the artist's hand. Constable gazed at him in horror. "Oh! there goes all my dew," he cried, and when Chartney's back was turned he hurriedly wiped the "warmth" all away and got back his "dew."

Even the amusing things that happened to him, seem to have a little sadness about them. He wrote to a friend: "Beechey was here yesterday, and said: 'Why d--n it Constable, what a d--n fine picture you are making; but you look d--n ill, and you've got a d--n bad cold!' so," added Constable, "you have evidence on oath of my being about a fine picture and that I am looking ill."

An illustration of his painstaking and truthfulness to nature is that he once took home with him from a visit bottles of coloured sand and fragments of stone which he meant to introduce into a picture; and on passing some slimy posts near a mill, he said to his host, "I wish you could cut those off and send their tops to me."

Constable was a loyal friend, the most persistent of men, and several anecdotes are told of his characteristics. His friend Fisher said to him:

"Where real business is to be done, you are the most energetic and punctual of men. In smaller matters, such as putting on your breeches, you are apt to lose time in deciding which leg shall go in first."

PLATE--THE HAY WAIN

This picture was first called "Landscape," and it was painted in 1821. In his letters about it, however, Constable also called it "Noon," and others wrote of it as "Midsummer Noon." This tells us what a wealth of hot sunlight is suggested by the painting.

It shows a little farmhouse upon the bank of a stream, a spot well known as "Willy Lott's Cottage." The owner had been born there and he died there eighty-eight years later, without ever having left his cottage for four whole days in all those years. Upon the tombstone of Lott, which is in the Bergholt burial ground, his epitaph calls the house "Gibeon Farm." It was a favourite scene with Constable, and he painted it many times from every side. It is the same house we see in the "Mill Stream," another Constable painting, and again in "Valley Farm." In this last picture he painted the side opposite to the one shown in the "Hay Wain."

The stream near which the house stands spreads out into a ford, and in the picture the hay cart, with two men upon it, is passing through the ford. The horses are decked out with red tassels. On the right of the stream there is a broad meadow, golden green in the sunlight, "with groups of trees casting cool shadows on the grass, and backed by a distant belt of woodland of rich blues and greens." On the right is a fisherman, half hidden by a bush, standing near his punt.

Constable wrote to his friend, Fisher, "My picture goes to the Academy on the tenth." This was written on April 1st, 1821. "It is not so grand as Tinney's." This shows us, that Constable had not vanity enough to interfere with his self-criticism. Again in a letter written to him by a friend: "How does the 'Hay Wain' look now it has got into your own room again?" adding that he wished to see it there, away from the Academy which to him was always "like a great pot of boiling varnish."

Later Fisher wrote: "I have a great desire to possess your 'Wain,' but I cannot now reach what it is worth;" and he begged Constable not to sell it without giving him a chance to try once more to raise the money to buy it. He wrote that the picture would become of greater value to his children if the artist left it hanging upon the walls of the Academy, "till you join the society of Ruysdael, Wilson, and Claude. As praise and money will then be of no value to you, the world will liberally bestow both."

Later a Frenchman wished to buy it for exhibition purposes, and when Constable wrote to Fisher of this, his friend replied that he had better sell it to the Frenchman "for the sake of the *éclat* it may give you. The stupid English public, which has no judgment of its own, will begin to think there is something in it if the French make your works national property. You have long lain under a mistake; men do not purchase pictures because they admire them, but because others covet them."

Finally, the "Hay Wain" was sold to the French dealer for £250, and Constable threw in a picture of Yarmouth for good measure. Later a friend declared that he had created a good deal of argument about landscape painting, and that there had come to be two divisions, for he had practically founded a new school. He received a gold medal for the "Hay Wain," and the French nation tried to buy it. In the Louvre are "The Cottage," "Weymouth Bay," and "The Glebe Farm." Elsewhere are "Hampstead Heath," "Salisbury Cathedral," "The Lock on the Stour," "Dedham Mill," "The Valley Farm," "Gillingham Mill," "The Cornfield," "Boat-Building," "Flatford Mill on the River Stour," besides many others.

IX JOHN SINGLETON COPLEY

English School

1737-1815

A little boy with a squirrel was the first picture that pointed this artist toward fame and that was painted in England and exhibited at the Society of Arts.

This American-born Irishman had no family or ancestry of account, but he himself was to become the father of Lord Chancellor Lyndhurst, and he did some truly fine things in art.

About the same time America had another painter, Benjamin West, marked out for fame, but he got his start in Europe while Copley had already become a successful artist before he left Boston, his native place.

He liked best to paint "interiors"--rooms with fine furniture and curtains, women in fine clothing and men in embroidered waistcoats and bejewelled buckles.

In 1777 he got into the Royal Academy, and on the whole had considerable influence on European art. If we study the portraits that he painted while in Boston, we can get a very complete idea of the surroundings of the "Royalists" at the time of our colonial history.

PLATE--THE COPLEY FAMILY GROUP

In this picture there are seven figures with an open landscape forming the background. The baby of the family plays, with uplifted arms, upon grandfather's knee. The mother on the couch, surrounded by her three other children, is kissing one while another clings to her. Before her stands a prim little maid, gowned in the fashion of grown-folks of her day. A little lock of hair falling upon her forehead suggests that when she was good she was very, very good, and when she was bad she was horrid! She wears a little cap. At the back is the artist himself in a wig and other fashions of the time. A great column rises behind him, forming a part of the architecture or the landscape, one hardly knows which in so artificially constructed a picture.

Copley painted also John Hancock, Judge Graham, Jeremiah Lee, and General Joseph Warren.

X JEAN BAPTISTE CAMILLE COROT

(Pronounced Zhahn Bah-teest' Cah-mee'yel Coh'roh)

Fontainebleau-Barbizon School

1796-1875
Pupil of Michallon

About three hundred years before Corot's time there was a Fontainebleau school of artists, made up of the pathetic Andrea del Sarto, the wonderful Leonardo da Vinci, and Cellini. These painters had been summoned from their Italian homes by Francis I., to decorate the Palace of Fontainebleau. The second great group of painters who had studios in the forest and beside the stream were Rousseau, Dupré, Diaz, and Daubigny; Troyon, Van Marcke, Jacque; then Millet, the painter of peasants.

Corot was born in Paris and received what education the ordinary school at Rouen could give him. He was intended by his parents for something besides art, as it would seem that every artist in the world was intended. Corot was to grow up and become a respectable draper; at any rate a draper.

The young chap did as his father wished, until he was twenty-six years old, and dreary years those must have been to him. He did not get on well with his master, nor did the world treat him very well. He found neither riches nor the fame that was his due till he was an old man of seventy. At that age he had become as rich a man as he might have been had he remained a sensible draper.

Best of all, Corot loved to paint clouds and dewy nights, pale moons and early day, and of all amusements in the world, he preferred the theatre. There he would sit; gay or sad as the play might make him, weeping or laughing and as interested as a little child.

After he had anything to give away, Corot was the most madly generous of men. It was he who gave a pension to the widow of his brother artist, Millet, on which she lived all the rest of her days. He gave money to his brother painters and to all who went to him for aid; and he always gave gaily, freely, as if giving were the greatest joy, outside of the theatre, a man could have. Everyone who knew him loved him, and there was no note of sadness in his daily life, though there seems to be one in his poetical pictures. Because of his generous ways he was known as "Pere Corot." He sang as he worked, and loved his fellowmen all the time; but most of all, he loved his sister.

"Rousseau is an eagle," he used to say in speaking of his fellow artist. "As for me, I am only a lark, putting forth some little songs in my gray clouds."

It has been noted that most great landscape painters have been city-bred, a remarkable fact. Constable and Gainsborough were born and bred in the country, but they are exceptions to the rule. Corot's parents were Parisians of the purest dye, having been court-dressmakers to Napoleon I.; and when Corot finally determined to leave the draper's shop and become a painter, his father said: "You shall have a yearly allowance of 1,200 francs, and if you can live on that, you can do as you please." When his son was made a member of the Legion of Honour, after twenty-three years of earnest work, his father thought the matter over, and presently doubled the allowance, "for Camille seems to have some talent after all," he remarked as an excuse for his generosity.

It is told that when he first went to study in Italy, Corot longed to transfer the moving scenes before him to canvas; but people moved too quickly for him, so he methodically set about learning how to do with a few strokes what he would otherwise have laboured over. So he reduced his sketching to such a science that he became able to sketch a ballet in full movement; and it is remarked that this practice trained him for presenting the tremulousness of leaves of trees, which he did so exquisitely.

One learns something of this painter of early dawn and soft evening from a letter he wrote to his friend Dupré:

One gets up at three in the morning, before the sun; one goes and sits at the foot of a tree; one watches and waits. One sees nothing much at first. Nature resembles a whitish canvas on which are sketched scarcely the profiles of some masses; everything is perfumed, and shines in the fresh breath of dawn. Bing! the sun grows bright but has not yet torn aside the veil behind which lie concealed the meadows, the dale, and hills of the horizon. The vapours of night still creep, like silvery flakes over the numbed-green vegetation. Bing! bing!--a first ray of sunlight--a second ray of sunlight--the little flowers seem to wake up joyously. They all have their drop of dew which trembles--the chilly leaves are stirred with the breath of morning--in the foliage the birds sing unseen--all the flowers seem to be saying their prayers. Loves on butterfly wings frolic over the meadows and make the tall plants wave--one sees nothing--yet everything is there--the landscape is entirely behind the veil of mist, which mounts, mounts, sucked up by the sun; and as it rises, reveals the river, plated with silver, the meadow, the trees, cottages, the receding distance--one distinguishes at last everything that one had divined at first.

In all the world there can hardly be a more exquisite story of daybreak than this; and so beautiful was the mood into which Corot fell at eventime, as he himself describes it, that it would be a mistake to leave it out. This is his story of the night:

Nature drowses--the fresh air, however, sighs among the leaves--the dew decks the velvety grass with pearls. The nymphs fly--hide themselves--and desire to be seen. Bing! a star in the sky which pricks its image on the pool. Charming star--whose brilliance is increased by the quivering of the water, thou watchest me--thou smilest to me with half-closed eye! Bing!--a second star appears in the water, a second eye opens. Be the harbingers of welcome, fresh and charming stars. Bing! Bing! Bing!--three, six, twenty stars. All the stars in the sky are keeping tryst in this happy pool. Everything darkens, the pool alone sparkles. There is a swarm of stars--all yields to illusion. The sun being gone to bed, the inner sun of the soul, the sun of art awakens. Bon! there is my picture done!

In writing those letters, Corot made literature as well as pictures. That little word "bing!" appears also in his paintings, as little leaves or bits of tree-trunk, some small detail which, high-lightened, accents the whole.

PLATE--DANCE OF THE NYMPHS

There could hardly be a more charming painting than this which hangs in the Louvre. It is of a half-shut-in landscape of tall trees, their branches mingling; and all the atmospheric effects that belong to Corot's work can here be seen.

On the open greensward is a group of nymphs dancing gaily, while over all the scene is the veil of fairy-land or of something quite mysterious. At the back and side, satyrs can be seen watching the nymphs. There is here less of the blur of leaves than that seen in later pictures, but the same soft effect is found, and the little "bings" are the accents of light placed upon a leaf, a nymph's shoulder, or a tree-trunk.

This picture was painted in 1851, when Corot had not yet developed that style which was to mark all his later work.

Besides this picture he painted "Paysage," "The Bathers" "Ville d'Arvay," "Willows near Arras," "The Bent Tree," "A Gust of Wind," and others.

XI CORREGGIO (ANTONIO ALLEGRI)

(Pronounced Cor-rage'jyo Ahl-lay'gree)

School of Parma

1494(?)-1534
Pupil of Mantegna

When Correggio was a little boy, he lived in the odour of spices, which were kept upon his father's shop-shelves. He was a highly-spiced little boy and man, although the most timid and shrinking. His imagination was the liveliest possible.

The spice merchant lived in the town of Correggio, and thus the artist got his name. Correggio knew what should be inside the lovely flesh of his painted figures before he began to paint them, because he studied anatomy in a truly scientific manner before he studied painting. Probably no other artist up to that time, had ever begun with the bare bones of his models, but Correggio may be said to have worked from the inside out. He learned about the structure of the human frame from Dr. Giovanni Battista Lombardi, and showed his gratitude to his teacher by painting a picture "Il Medico del Correggio" (Correggio's Physician), and presenting it to Doctor Lombardi.

Now Correggio's childhood, or at least his early manhood, could not have been spent in poverty, because it is known that he used the most expensive colours to paint with, painted upon the finest of canvas, while greater artists had often to be content with boards. He also painted upon copper plates, and it is said that he hired Begarelli, a sculptor of much fame, to make models in relief for him to copy for the pictures he painted on the cupolas of the churches in Parma. That sculptor's services must have been expensive.

On the lovely island of Capri, in the Franciscan convent, will be found one of his first pictures, painted when Correggio was about nineteen years old.

He was highly original in many ways. Although he had never seen the work of any great artist, he painted the most extraordinary fore-shortened pictures; and fore-shortening was a technicality in art then uncommon. He also was the first to paint church cupolas. Fore-shortening produces some peculiar as well as great results, and being a feature of art with which people were not then familiar, Correggio's work did not go uncriticised. Indeed one artist, gazing up into one of the cupolas where Correggio's fore-shortened figures were placed, remarked that to him it appeared a "hash of frogs."

But when Titian saw that cupola, he said: "Reverse the cupola, fill it with gold, and even then that will not be its money's worth."

Correggio did not receive very large sums for his work, and since he was married and took good care of his family, he must have had some source of income besides his brush. He received some interesting rewards for his paintings. For example, for "St. Jerome," called "Il Giorno," he was given "400 gold imperials, some cartloads of faggots and measures of wheat, and a fat pig." That picture is in the Parma Gallery, and all the cupolas which he painted are in Parma churches.

Some of his pictures are signed; "Leito," a synonym for his name, "Allegri." This indicates his style of art.

There is an interesting story told of how Correggio stood entranced before a picture of Raphael's, and after long study of it he exclaimed: "I too, am a painter!" showing at once his appreciation of Raphael's greatness and satisfaction at his own genius.

Doubtless a good share of Correggio's comfortable living came from the lady he married, since she was considered a rich woman for those times and in that locality. Her name was Girolama Merlini, and she lived in Mantua, the place where the Montagues and Capulets lived of whom Shakespeare wrote the most wonderful love story ever imagined. This young woman was only sixteen years old when Correggio met and loved her, and very beautiful and later on he painted a picture, "Zingarella," for which his wife is said to have been the model. It seems to have been a stroke of economy and enterprise for painters to marry, since we read of so many who made fame and fortune through the beauty of their wives.

They were very happy together, Correggio and his wife, and they had four children. Their happiness was not for long, because Correggio seems to have been but thirty-four years old when she died, nor did he live to be old. There is a most curious tale of his death which is probably not true, but it is worth telling since many have believed it. He is supposed to have died in Correggio, of pleurisy, but the story is that he had made a picture for one who had some grudge against him, and who in order to irritate him paid him in copper, fifty scudi. This was a considerable burden, and in order to save expense and time, it is said that Correggio undertook to carry it home alone. It was a very hot day, and he became so overheated and exhausted with his heavy load that he took ill and died, and he may be said literally to have been killed by "too much money," if this were true. Vasari, a biographer to be generally believed, says it is a fact.

Correggio said that he always had his "thoughts at the end of his pencil," and there are those who impudently declare that is the only place he *did* have them, but that is a carping criticism, because he was a very great artist, his greatest power being the presentation of soft blendings of light and shade. There seem to have been few unusual events in Correggio's life; very little that helps us to judge the man, but there is a general opinion that he was a kind and devoted father and husband, as well as a good citizen. With little demand upon his moral character, he did his work, did it well, and his work alone gave him place and fame.

He became the head of a school of painting and had many imitators, but we hear little of his pupils, except that one of them was his own son, Pompino, who lived to be very old, and in his turn was successful as an artist.

Correggio was buried with honours in the Arrivabene Chapel, in the Franciscan church at Correggio.

PLATE--THE HOLY NIGHT

This painting is not characteristic of Correggio's work, but nevertheless it is very beautiful. The brilliant warm light which comes from the Infant Jesus in His mother's arms is reflected upon the faces of those gathered about, and even illuminates the angelic group hovering above him. The slight landscape forming the background is also suggestive, and the conditions of the birth are indicated by the ass which may be seen in the middle distance. The faces of all are joyous yet full of wonderment, the whole scene intimate and human.

The picture is also called the "Adoration of the Shepherds," and that title best tells the story. See the shepherdess shading her face with one hand and offering two turtle-doves with the other. The ass in the distance is the one on which Mary rode to Bethlehem, and Joseph is caring for it. Even the cold light of the dawning day is softened by the beauty of the group below. This picture is in the Royal Gallery in Dresden.

PLATE--THE MYSTIC MARRIAGE OF ST. CATHERINE

The Infant Jesus sits upon His mother's lap, and places the ring upon St. Catherine's finger, while Mary's hand helps to guide that of her Child. This action brings the three hands close together and adds to the beauty of the composition. All of the faces are full of pleasure and kindliness, while that of St. Sebastian fairly glows with happy emotion. The light is concentrated upon the body of the Child and is reflected upon the faces of the women. This painting hangs in the Louvre.

Other great Correggio pictures are the "School of Cupid," which is more characteristic of his work; "Antiope," "Leda," "Danae," and "Ecce Homo."

XII PAUL GUSTAVE DORÉ

French School

1833-1883

This artist died in Paris twenty-five years ago, but there is little as yet to be told of his life history. He was educated in Paris at the Lycée Charlemagne, having gone there from Strasburg, where he was born.

He was a painter of fantastic and grotesque subjects, and as far as we know, he began his career when a boy. He made sketches before his eighth year which attracted much attention, and he earned considerable money while still at school. He was at that time engaged to illustrate for journals, at a good round sum, and before he left the Lycée he had made hundreds of drawings, somewhat after the satirical fashion of Hogarth.

His work is very characteristic and once seen is likely to be always recognised.

He first worked for the *Journal Pour Rire*, but then he undertook to illustrate the work of Rabelais, the great satirist, whose text just suited Doré's pencil. After Rabelais he illustrated Balzac, also the "Wandering Jew," "Don Quixote," and Dante's "Divine Comedy."

He undertook to do things which he could not do well, simply for the money there was in the commissions. He had but a poor idea of colour and his work was coarse, but it had such marked peculiarities that it became famous. He did a little sculpture as well, and even that showed his eccentricities of thought.

PLATE--MOSES BREAKING THE TABLETS OF THE LAW

This is one of the illustrations of the Doré Bible, published in 1865-66. The story is well known of how Moses went up into the Mount of the Lord to receive the laws for the Israelites, which were written upon tables of stone. Upon his descent from the Mount he found that his followers had set up a golden calf, which they were worshipping; and in his wrath Moses broke the tablets on which the Law was inscribed. The power shown in his attitude, the affrighted faces of the cowering Jews, the thunder and lightning as an expression of the wrath of the Almighty are all painted in Doré's best manner.

XIII ALBRECHT DÜRER

(Pronounced Dooer-rer')

Nuremberg School

1471-1528

Pupil of Wolgemuth and Schongauer

Albrecht Dürer by nationality was a Hungarian, but he was born in the city of Nuremberg. His father had come from the little Hungarian town of Eytas to Nuremberg that he might practise the craft of a goldsmith. Notwithstanding his Hungarian origin, the name is German and the family "bearing," or sign, is the open door. This device suggests that the name was first formed from "Thurer," which means "carpenter," maker of doors.

The father became the goldworker for a master goldsmith of Nuremberg named Hieronymus Holper, and very soon the new employee had fallen in love with his master's daughter. The daughter was very young and very beautiful; her name was Barbara, and as Herr Dürer was quite forty years of age, while she was but fifteen, the match seemed most unlikely, but they married and had eighteen children! The great painter was one of them.

Albrecht loved his parents most tenderly, and from first to last we hear no word of disagreement among any members of that immense household. Young Albrecht was especially the companion of his father, being brilliant, generous, and hard-working in a family where everyone needed to do his best to help along. This love and companionship never ceased until death, and after his parents died Albrecht wrote in a touching manner of their death, describing his love for them, and their many virtues. He was an author and a poet as well as a painter, and only Leonardo da Vinci matched him for greatness and versatility. We may know what Dürer's father looked like, since the son made two portraits of him; one is to be seen in the Uffizi Gallery at Florence and the other belongs to the Duke of Northumberland's collection. The latter portrait has been reproduced in an engraving, so that it is familiar to most people.

In the days when the great artist was growing up, Nuremberg was the centre of all intellectuality and art in the North. The city of Augsburg also followed art fashions, but it was far less important than Nuremberg, because in the latter city every sort of art-craft was followed in sincerity and with great originality.

In those days, the craft of the goldsmith was closely allied with the profession of the painter, because the smith had to create his own designs, and that called for much talent. Thus it was but a step from designing in precious metals to the use of colour, and to engraving. In making wood engravings, however, the drudgery of it was left almost entirely to workmen, not artists. Nuremberg was also the seat of musical learning. Wagner makes this fact pathetic, comical, and altogether charming in his "Mastersingers of Nuremberg."

Till Dürer's time, however, there had been little painting that could be regarded as art, and when he came to study it there was but little opportunity in his own land, but Dürer was destined to bring art to Nuremberg. If he went elsewhere to study, it was only for a little time, because he was above all things patriotic and dearly loved his home.

With seventeen brothers and sisters, young Dürer's problem was a serious one. His father not only meant him to become a goldsmith like himself--a craft in which there was much money to be made at a time when people dressed with great ornamentation and used gold to decorate with--it was highly necessary with so large a family that he should learn to do that which could make him helpful to his father. Hence the young boy entered his father's shop. If he had not been handicapped with so many to help to maintain, he would have laid up a considerable fortune, because from the very beginning he was master of all that he undertook; doing the least thing better than any other did it, putting conscience and painstaking into all.

"My father took special delight in me," the son said, "seeing that I was industrious in working and learning, he put me to school; and when I had learned to read and write, he took me home from my school and taught me the goldsmith's trade."

The family were good and kind; excellent neighbours, deeply religious, and little Albrecht certainly was comely. He was beautiful as a little child, and as a man was very handsome, with long light hair sweeping his shoulders, and gentle eyes. He was very tall, stately, and full of dignity.

In his father's shop he made little clay figures which were afterward moulded in metal; also he learned to carve wood and ivory, and he added the touch of originality to all that he did. He was the Leonardo da Vinci of Germany, an intellectual man, a poet, painter, sculptor, engraver, and engineer. He approached everything that he did from an intellectual point of view, looking for the reasons of things.

After a while in his father's shop, he found mere craftsmanship irksome, and he begged to be allowed to enter a studio. This was a great disappointment to the father, even a distress, because he could see no very quick nor large returns in money for an artist, and he sorely needed the help of his son; but being kind and reasonable, he consented Albrecht was apprenticed to the only artist of any repute then in Nuremberg, Wolgemuth.

To his studio Albrecht went, at the age of fifteen, and if he did not learn much more of painting, under that artist's direction, than his own genius had already taught him, he learned the drudgery of his work; how to grind colours and to mix them, and he studied wood engraving also.

In Wolgemuth's studio he remained for the three years of his apprenticeship, and then he fled to better things. For a time he followed the methods of another German artist, Schongauer, but finally he went forth to try his luck alone. He wandered from place to place, practising all his trades, goldsmithing, engraving, whatever would support him, yet always and everywhere painting.

It is thought that he may have gone as far as Italy, but it is not certain whether he went there in his first wanderings or later on. However, he was soon recalled home, for his father had found a suitable wife for him. She was the daughter of a rich citizen and her name was Agnes Frey. She was pretty as well as rich, but had she been neither Albrecht would have returned at his father's bidding. There was never any resistance to the fine and proper things of life on Albrecht Dürer's part. He was the well balanced, reasonable man from youth up.

There have been extraordinary tales told of the artist's wife. She has been called hateful and spiteful as Xantippe, the wife of Socrates, but we think this is calumny. The stories came about in this way: Dürer had a life-long friend, Wilibald Pirkheimer, who in his old age became the most malicious and quarrelsome of old fellows. He lived longer than Dürer did, and Dürer's wife also outlived her husband. Pirkheimer wanted a set of antlers which had belonged to Dürer and which he thought the wife should give him after Dürer was dead, but Agnes thought otherwise and would not give them up. Then, full of rage, the old man wrote the most outrageous letters about poor Agnes, saying that she was a shrew and had compelled Dürer to work himself to death; that she was a miser and had led the artist an awful dance through life. This is the only evidence against her, and that so sane and sensible a man as the artist lived with her all his life and cherished her, is evidence enough that Pirkheimer didn't tell the truth. When Dürer died he was in good circumstances and instead of being overworked, he for many years had done no "pot-boiling," but had followed investigations along lines that pleased him. After his death, the widow treated his brothers and sisters generously, giving them properties of Dürer's and being of much help to them. During the artist's life he and she had travelled everywhere together and had appeared to love each other tenderly; hence we may conclude that the old Pirkheimer was simply a disgruntled, gouty old man without a good word for anybody.

If Dürer's father and mother had eighteen children, Albrecht and Agnes struck a balance, for they had none. Whether or not Dürer went to Italy before his marriage in 1494, certain it is that he was in Venice, the home of Titian, in 1506. Titian was six years younger than Dürer, who was then about thirty-five years old. It is said that he started for Italy in 1505 and that he went the whole of the way, over the Alps, through forests and streams, on horseback. Who knows but it was during that very journey, while travelling alone, often finding himself in lonely ways, and full of the speculative thoughts that were characteristic of him, that he did not think first of his subject, "Knight, Death, and the Devil," which helped make his fame. In that picture we have a knight, helmeted, carrying his lance, mounted upon his horse, riding in a lonely forest, with death upon a "pale horse" by his side, holding an hour glass to remind the knight of the fleeting of time. Behind comes the devil, with trident and horn, represented as a frightful and disgusting beast, which follows hot-foot after the lonely knight, who looks neither to right nor left, but persistently goes his way.

Titian's teacher, Bellini, was still living, and he was one of Dürer's greatest admirers. Especially did he believe that he could paint the finest hair of any artist in the world. One day, while studying Dürer's work, and being especially fascinated by the hair of one of his figures, the old man took Dürer's brush and tried to reproduce as beautiful a tress. Presently he put down the brush in despair, but the younger artist took it up, still wet with the same colours, and in a few brilliant strokes produced a lovely lock of woman's hair.

While luxuriating in Venetian heat, Dürer wrote home to his friend Pirkheimer: "Oh, how I shall freeze after this sunshine!" He was a lover of warm, beautiful colour, gay and tender life. Most of all he loved the fatherland, and all the honours paid him and all the invitations pressed upon him could not keep him long from Nuremberg. The journey homeward was not uneventful because he was taken ill, and had to stop at a house on his way, where he was cared for till he was strong enough to proceed. Before he went his way he painted upon the wall of that house a fine picture, to show his gratitude for the kind treatment he had received. Imagine a people so settled in their homes that it would be worth while for an artist who came along to leave a picture upon the walls to-day--we should have moved to a new house or a new flat almost before Dürer could have washed his brushes and turned the corner.

Back in Nuremberg, he settled down into the life of a responsible citizen, lived in a fine new house, in time became a member of the council, and his studio was a veritable workshop. Studios were quite different from those of to-day. Then the pupils turned to and ground colours, did much of their own manufacturing, engaged at first in such commonplace occupations, which were nevertheless teaching them the foundation of their art, while they watched the work of the master. Such a studio as Dürer's must have been full of young men coming and going, not all working at the art of painting, but engraving, preparing materials for such work, designing, and executing many other details of art work.

After this time Dürer made his smallest picture, which is hardly more than an inch in diameter. On that tiny surface he painted the whole story of the crucifixion, and it is now in the Dresden Gallery. To those of us who see little mentality in the faces of the Italian subjects, the German art of Dürer, often ugly in the choice of models, and so exact as to bring out unpleasing details, is nevertheless the greater; because in all cases, the faces have sincere expressions. They exhibit human purposes and emotions which we can understand, and despise or love as the case may be.

They say that his Madonna is generally a "much-dressed round-faced German mother, holding a merry little German boy." That may be true; but at any rate, she is every inch a mother and he a well-beloved little boy, which is considerably more than can be said of some Italian performances.

Dürer made a painting of "Praying Hands," a queer subject for a picture, but those hands are nothing *but* praying hands. The story of them is touching. It is said that for several years Dürer had won a prize for which a friend of his had also competed, and upon losing the prize the last time he tried for it, the friend raised his hands and prayed for the power to accept his failure with resignation and humility. Dürer, looking at him, was impressed with the eloquence of the gesture; thus the "Praying Hands" was conceived.

Dürer was also called the *Father of Picture Books*, because he designed so many woodcuts that he first made possible the illustration of stories.

He printed his own illustrations in his own house, and was well paid for it. The Emperor Maximillian visited Nuremberg, and wishing to honour Dürer, commanded him to make a triumphal arch.

"It was not to be fashioned in stone like the arches given to the victorious Roman Emperors; but instead it was to be composed of engravings. Dürer made for this purpose ninety-two separate blocks of woodcuts. On these were represented Maximillian's genealogical tree and the principal events of his life. All these were arranged in the form of an arch, 9 feet wide and 10-1/2 feet high. It took Dürer three years to do this work, and he was never well paid," so says one who has compiled many incidents of his life.

"While the artist worked, the Emperor often visited his studio; and as Dürer's pet cats often visited it at the same time, the expression arose, 'a cat may look at a King!'"

On the occasion of one of these kingly visits, Maximillian tried to do a little artwork on his own account. Taking a piece of charcoal he tried to sketch, but the charcoal kept breaking and he asked Dürer why it did so.

"That is my sceptre; your Majesty has other and greater work to do," was the tactful reply. It is a question with us to-day whether the King ever did a greater work than Albrecht Dürer, king of painters, was doing.

After this, Maximillian gave Dürer a pension, but when the Emperor died the artist found it necessary to apply to the monarch who came after him, in order to have the gift confirmed. This was the occasion for his journey to the Low Countries, and he took his wife Agnes with him. In the Netherlands he was received with much honour and was invited to become court painter; and what was more, his pension was fixed upon him for life. The great work of his life was his illustration of the Apocalypse. For this he made sixteen extraordinary woodcuts, of great size.

On his journey to see Charles V., Maximillian's successor, Dürer kept a diary in which he noted the minutest details of all that happened to him. He told of the coronation of Charles; of hearing about a whale that had been cast upon the shore; of his disappointment that it had been removed before he had reached the place. He wrote with great indignation about the supposed kidnapping of Martin Luther, while he was on his way home from the Diet of Worms.

While Dürer was in the Low Countries, a fever came upon him, and when he returned home, it still followed him. Indeed, although he lived for seven years after his return, he was never well again. Among his effects there was a sketch made to indicate to his physician the seat of his illness.

Dürer did not paint great frescoes upon walls as did Raphael, Michael Angelo, and all great Italian artists; but instead he painted on wood, canvas, and in oils.

In all the civilised world Dürer was honoured equally with the great Italian painters of his time. He was a man of much conscientiousness, dignity, and tenderness. He was devoted to his home and country, and regarded the problems of life intellectually. When he came to die, his end was so unexpected that those dearest to him could not reach his bedside. He was buried in St. John's cemetery in Nuremberg. After his death, Martin Luther wrote as follows to their mutual friend, Eoban Hesse:

"As for Dürer; assuredly affection bids us mourn for one who was the best of men, yet you may well hold him happy that he has made so good an end, and that Christ has taken him from the midst of this time of troubles, and from yet greater troubles in store, lest he, that deserved to behold nothing but the best, should be compelled to behold the worst. Therefore may he rest in peace with his fathers, Amen."

PLATE--THE NATIVITY

Our description of this painting calls attention to the fact that the columns and arches of the picturesque ruin belong to a much later period in history than the birth of Christ. Dürer was not acquainted with any earlier style of architecture than the Romanesque and therefore he used it here. "The ruin serves as a stable. A roof of board is built out in front of the side-room which shelters the ox and ass, and under this lean-to lies the new born babe surrounded by angels who express their childish joy. Mary kneels and contemplates her child with glad emotion. Joseph, also deeply moved, kneels down on the other side of the child, outside the shelter of the roof. Some shepherds to whom the angel, who is still seen hovering in the air, has announced the tidings, are already entering from without the walls." (Knackfuss). The picture is the central panel of an altar-piece now in the Old Pinakothek at Munich. Dürer's oil painting of the four apostles--John, Peter, Mark, and Paul--is in the same gallery. Other Dürer pictures are: "The Knight, Death and the Devil," "The Adoration of the Magi," "Melancholy," and portraits of himself.

XIV MARIANO FORTUNY

(Pronounced Mah-ree-ah-no' For-tu'ne)

Spanish School

1838-1874

Pupil of Claudio Lorenzalez

Fortuny won his own opportunities. He took a prize, while still very young, which made it possible for him to go to Rome where he wished to study art. He did not spend his time studying and copying the old masters as did most artists who went there, but, instead, he studied the life of the Roman streets.

He had already been at the Academy of Barcelona, but he did not follow his first master; instead, he struck out a line of art for himself. After a year in Rome the artist went to war; but he did not go to fight men, he was still fighting fate, and his weapon was his sketch book. He went with General Prim, and he filled his book with warlike scenes and the brilliant skies of Morocco. From that time his work was inspired by his Moorish experiences.

After going to war without becoming a soldier, Fortuny returned to Paris and there he became fast friends with Meissonier, so that a good deal of his work was influenced by that artist's genius. After a time Fortuny's paintings came into great vogue and far-off Americans began buying them, as well as Europeans. There was a certain rich dry-goods merchant in the United States who had made a large fortune for those days, and while he knew nothing about art, he wanted to spend his money for fine things. So he employed people who did understand the matter to buy for him many pictures whose excellence he, himself, could not understand, but which were to become a fine possession for succeeding generations. This was about 1860, and this man, A.T. Stewart, bought two of Fortuny's pictures at high prices. "The Serpent Charmer," and "A Fantasy of Morocco."

When Fortuny was thirty years old he married the daughter of a Spaniard called Madrazo, director of the Royal Museum. His wife's family had several well known artists in it, and the marriage was a very happy one. Because of this, Fortuny was inspired to paint one of the greatest of his pictures, "The Spanish Marriage." In it are to be seen the portraits of his wife and his friend Regnault. After a time he went to live in Granada; but he could never forget the beautiful, barbaric scenes in Morocco, and so he returned there. Afterward he went with his wife to live in Rome, and there they had a fine home and everything exquisite about them, while fortune and favour showered upon them; but he fell ill with Roman fever, because of working in the open air, and he died while he was comparatively a young man.

PLATE--THE SPANISH MARRIAGE

Fortuny is said to "split the light into a thousand particles, till his pictures sparkle like jewels and are as brilliant as a kaleidoscope.... He set the fashion for a class of pictures, filled with silks and satins, bric-à-brac and elegant trifling."

Look at the brilliant scene in this picture! The priest rising from his chair and leaning over the table is watching the bridegroom sign his name. This chap is an old fop, bedecked in lilac satin, while the bride is a dainty young woman, without much interest in her husband, for she is fingering her beautiful fan and gossiping with one of her girl friends. She wears orange-blossoms in her black hair and is in full bridal array. One couple, two men, sit on an elegantly carved seat and are looking at the goings-on with amusement, while an old gentleman sits quite apart, disgusted with the whole unimpressive scene. Everybody is trifling, and no one is serious for the occasion. The furnishings of the room are beautiful, delicate, almost frivolous. People are strewn about like flowers, and the whole effect is airy and inconsequent. Fortuny painted also "The Praying Arab," "A Fantasy of Morocco," "Snake Charmers," "Camels at Rest," etc.

XV THOMAS GAINSBOROUGH

English School

1727-1788

Pupil of Gravelot and of Hayman

There seems to have been no artist, with the extraordinary exceptions of Dürer and Leonardo, who learned his lessons while at school. Little painters have uniformly begun as bad spellers.

Gainsborough's father was in the business of woolen-crape making, while his mother painted flowers, very nicely, and it was she who taught the small Thomas. There were nine little Gainsboroughs and, shocking to relate, the artist of the family was so ready with his pencil that when he was ten years old he forged his father's name to a note which he took to the schoolmaster, and thereby gained himself a holiday. There is no account of any other wicked use to which he put his talent. It is said that he could copy any writing that he saw, and his ready pencil covered all his copy-books with sketches of his schoolmasters. It was thought better for him finally to follow his own ideas of education, namely, to roam the woodlands and make beautiful pictures.

His father's heart was not softened till one day little Gainsborough brought home a sketch of the orchard into which the head of a man had thrust itself, painted with great ability. This man was a poacher, and father Gainsborough recognised him by the portrait. There seemed to be utility in art of this kind, and before long the boy found himself apprenticed to a silversmith.

Through the silversmith the artist got admission to an art school and began his studies; but his master was a dissolute fellow, and before long the pupil left him.

Gainsborough was born in the town of Sudbury on the River Stour, the same which inspired another great painter half a century later. Gainsborough is best known by his portraits, in particular as the inventor of "the Gainsborough hat," but he was first of all a truly great landscape painter, and learned his art as Constable did after him, along the beautiful shores of the river that flowed past his native town.

The old Black Horse Inn is still to be seen, and it was in the orchard behind it that he studied nature, the same in which he made the first of his famous portraits, that of the poacher. It is known to this day as the portrait of "Tom Pear-tree." That picture was copied on a piece of wood cut into the shape of a man, and it is in the possession of Mr. Jackson, who lent it for the exhibition of Gainsborough's work held at the Grosvenor Gallery, in 1885.

While Thomas was with his first master, by no means a good companion for a lad of fifteen, he lived a busy, self-respecting life, since he was devoted to his home and to his parents. Only three years after he set out to learn his art he married a young lady of Sudbury. The pair were by no means rich, Gainsborough having only eighteen years of experience in this world, besides his brush, and a maker of woolen-crape shrouds for a father--who was not over pleased to have an artist for a son. The lady had two hundred pounds but this did not promise a very luxurious living, so they took a house for six pounds a year, at Ipswich. Thus the two young lovers began their life together. There was a good deal of romance in the story of his wife, whose name was supposed to be Margaret Burr. The two hundred pounds that helped to pay the Ipswich rent did not come from the man accepted as her father, but from her real father, who was either the Duke of Bedford, or an exiled prince. This would seem to be just the sort of story that should surround a great painter and his affairs.

While he lived at Ipswich Gainsborough used to say of himself that he was "chiefly in the face-way" meaning that for the most part he made portraits. He loved best to paint the scenes of his boyhood, as Constable afterward did, but he soon found there was more money in portraits, and so he decided to go to live in Bath, the fashionable resort of English people in that day, where he was likely to find rich folk who wanted to see themselves on canvas. He settled down there with his wife, whom he loved dearly, and his two daughters and at once began to make money. It is said he painted five hours a day and all the rest of the time studied music. As the theatre was Corot's greatest happiness, so did music most delight Gainsborough, and he could play well on nearly every known instrument; he became so excellent a musician that he even gave concerts. He had the most delightful people about him, people who loved art and who appreciated him, and then there were the other people who paid for having themselves painted. Altogether it was an ideal situation.

His studio was in the place known as the "Circus" at Bath, and people came and went all day, for it became the fashionable resort for all the fine folks.

From five guineas for half length portraits, he soon raised his price to forty; he had charged eight for full length portraits, but now they went for one hundred. He painted some famous men of the time. The very thought is inspiring of such a company of geniuses with Gainsborough in the centre of the group. He painted Laurence Sterne, who wrote "The Sentimental Journey," and a few other delightful things; also Garrick, the renowned actor.

Even the encyclopædia reads thrillingly upon this subject and one can afford to quote it, with the feeling that the quotation will be read: "His house harboured Italian, German, French and English musicians. He haunted the green room of Palmer's Theatre, and painted gratuitously the portraits of many of the actors. He gave away his sketches and landscapes to any one who had taste or assurance enough to ask for them." This sounds royal and exciting.

After that Gainsborough went up to London with plenty of money and plenty of confidence and instead of six pounds a year for his house, he paid three hundred pounds, which suggests much more comfort.

There were two other great painters of the time in London, Sir Benjamin West--an American, by the way--and Sir Joshua Reynolds. West was court favourite, but Gainsborough too was called upon to paint royalty, and share West's honours. Reynolds was the favourite of the town, but he too had to divide honours with Gainsborough when the latter painted Richard Brinsley Sheridan, Edmund Burke and Sir William Blackstone.

Notwithstanding, his landscapes, for which he should have been most famous, did not sell. Everybody approved of them, but it is said they were returned to him till they "stood ranged in long lines from his hall to his painting room" Gainsborough was a member of the Royal Academy and also a true Bohemian. He cared little for elegant society, but made his friends among men of genius of all sorts. He was very handsome and impulsive, tall and fair, and generous in his ways; but he had much sorrow on account of one of his daughters, Mary, who married Fischer, a hautboy player, against her father's wishes. The girl became demented--at least she had spells of madness.

When Mary Gainsborough married, her father wrote the following letter to his sister, which shows that he was a man of tender feeling for those whom he truly loved:

" ... I had not the least suspicion of the attachment being so long and deeply seated; and as it was too late for me to alter anything without being the cause of total unhappiness on both sides, my consent ... I needs must give ... and accordingly they were married last Monday and settled for the present in a ready-furnished little house in Curzon Street, Mayfair ... I can't say I have any reason to doubt the man's honesty or goodness of heart, as I never heard anyone speak anything amiss of him, and as to his oddities and temper, she must learn to like them as she likes his person ... Peggy has been very unhappy about it, but I endeavour to comfort her." Peggy was his wife.

The abominable Fischer died twenty-years before Mary did--she lived to be an old, old woman.

Among those whom Gainsborough loved best was the man called Wiltshire who carried his pictures to and from London. He was a public "carrier" but would never take any money for his services to the artist, because he loved his work. All he asked was "a little picture"--and he got so many of these, given in purest affection, that he might have gone out of business as a carrier, had he chosen to sell them. Four of those little pictures are now very great ones worth thousands of pounds and known everywhere to fame. They are "The Parish Clerk," "Portrait of Quin," "A Landscape with Cattle," and "The Harvest Waggon."

We have a good many stories of Gainsborough's bad manners. The artists of his day tried to treat him with every consideration, but in return he treated them very badly, especially Sir Joshua Reynolds. Reynolds, who was then President of the Academy greatly admired Gainsborough but the latter would not return Sir Joshua's call, and when Reynolds asked him to paint his portrait for him, Gainsborough undertook it thanklessly. Sir Joshua left town for Bath for a time, and when he returned he tried to learn how soon the portrait would be finished, but Gainsborough would not even reply to his inquiry. There seems to have been no reason for this behaviour unless it was jealousy, but it made a most uncomfortable situation between fellow artists.

Gainsborough has told some not very pleasing stories about himself, but one of them shows us what a knack he had for seeing the comic side of things, and perhaps for seeing comedy where it never existed. Upon one occasion he was invited to a friend's house where the family were in the habit of assembling for prayers, and he had no sooner got inside, than he began to fear he should laugh, when prayer time came, at the chaplain. In a rush of shyness he fled, leaving his host to look for him, till he stumbled over a servant who said that Mr. Gainsborough had charged him to say he had gone to breakfast at Salisbury. Even respect for the customs of others could not make him control himself.

It was through his intimacy with King George's family that his quarrel with the Royal Academy came about. He had painted the three princesses--the Princess Royal, Princesses Augusta and Elizabeth, and these were to be hung at a certain height in Carlton House, but when he sent the first to the Academy he asked it to be specially hung and his request was refused. Then he sent a note as follows:

"He begs pardon for giving them so much trouble, but he has painted the picture of the princesses in so tender a light that, notwithstanding he approves very much of the established line for strong effects, he cannot possibly consent to have it placed higher than eight feet and a half, because the likeness and the work of the picture will not be seen any higher, therefore at a word he will not trouble the gentlemen against their inclination, but will beg the best of his pictures back again." Immediately, the Academy returned his pictures, although it would seem that they might better have accommodated Gainsborough than have lost such a fine exhibition. He never again would send anything to them.

He was inclined to be irritated by inartistic points in his sitters, and is said to have muttered when he was painting the portrait of Mrs. Siddons, the great actress: "Damn your nose madam; there is no end to it." The nose in question must have been an "eyesore" to more than Gainsborough, for a famous critic is said to have declared that "Mrs. Siddons, with all her beauty was a kind of female Johnson ... her nose was not too long for nothing."

Notwithstanding that his landscapes were not popular, he used to go off into the country to indulge his taste for painting them, and once he wrote to a friend that he meant to mount "all the Lakes at the next Exhibition in the great style, and you know, if people don't like them, it's only jumping into one of the deepest of them from off a wooded island and my reputation will be fixed forever." An old lady, whose guest he was, down in the country, told how he was "gay, very gay, and good looking, creating a great sensation, in a rich suit of drab with laced ruffles and cocked hat."

One of the boys he saw in the country he delighted to paint, and he also grew so much attached to him that he took him to London and kept him with him as his own son. That boy's name was Jack Hill and he did not care for city life, nor maybe for Gainsborough's eccentricities, so he ran away. He was found again and again, till one day he got away for good, and never came back.

All his later life Gainsborough was happy. His daughter, who had married Fischer, the hautboy-player, came back home to live, and her disorder was not bad enough to prevent her being a cause of great happiness to her father. The other daughter never married. Gainsborough says that he spent a thousand pounds a year, but he also gave to everybody who asked of him, and to many who asked nothing, so that he must have made a great deal of money during his lifetime, by his art. It is said that the "Boy at the Stile" was bestowed on Colonel Hamilton for his fine playing of a solo on the violin. A lady who had done the artist some trifling service received twenty drawings as a reward, which she pasted on the walls of her rooms without the slightest idea of their value.

Gainsborough got up early in the morning, but did not work more than five hours. He liked his friends, his music, and his wife, and spent much time with them. He was witty, and while he sketched pictures in the evening, with his wife and daughters at his side, he kept them laughing with his droll sayings.

The last days of Gainsborough showed him to be a hero. He died of cancer, and some time before he knew what his disease was he must have suffered a great deal. There is a story that is very pathetic of a dinner with his friends, Beaumont and Sheridan. Usually, he was the gayest of the gay, but of late all his friends had noticed that gaiety came to him with effort. Upon the night of this dinner, Sheridan had been his wittiest, and had tried his hardest to make Gainsborough cheer up, till finally, the artist, finding it impossible to get out of his sad mood, asked Sheridan if he would leave the table and speak with him alone. The two friends went out together. "Now don't laugh, but listen," Gainsborough said; "I shall soon die. I know it; I feel it. I have less time to live than my looks infer, but I do not fear death. What oppresses my mind is this: I have many acquaintances, few friends; and as I wish to have one worthy man to accompany me to the grave, I am desirous of bespeaking you. Will you come? Aye or no!" At that Sheridan, who was greatly shocked, tried to cheer him, but Gainsborough would not return to the table, till he got the promise, which of course Sheridan made.

It was not very long after this that a famous trial took place--that of Warren Hastings. It was in Westminster Hall, and Gainsborough went to listen several times. On the last occasion, he became so interested in what was happening that he did not notice a window open at his back. After a little he said to a friend that he "felt something inexpressibly cold" touch his neck. On his return home he told of the strange feeling to his wife. Then he sent for a doctor, and there was found a little swelling. The doctor said it was not serious and that when the weather grew warmer it would disappear; but all the while Gainsborough felt certain that it would mean his death. A short time after that he told his sister that he knew himself to have a cancer, and that was true.

When he felt that he must die, he fell to thinking of many things in the past, and wished to right certain mistakes of his behaviour as far as possible.

He sent to Sir Joshua Reynolds and asked him to come and see him, since he could not go to see Sir Joshua. Reynolds went and then Gainsborough told him of his regret that he had shown so much ill-will and jealousy toward so great and worthy a rival. Reynolds was very generous and tried to make Gainsborough understand that all was forgiven and forgotten. He left his brother artist much relieved and happier, and he afterward said: "The impression on my mind was that his regret at losing life was principally the regret of leaving his art." As Reynolds left the dying man's room, Gainsborough called after him: "We are all going to heaven--and Van Dyck is of the company."

He was buried in Kew Churchyard and the ceremonies were followed by Reynolds and five of the Royal Academicians, who forgot all Gainsborough's eccentricities of conduct toward them in their honest grief over his death. He was one of the first three dozen original members of the Royal Academy.

PLATE--PORTRAIT OF MRS. RICHARD BRINSLEY SHERIDAN

This picture is now in the collection of Lord Rothschild, London. Mrs. Sheridan was the loveliest lady of her time. She was the daughter of Thomas Linley, and a singer.

She came from a home which was called "a nest of nightingales," because all in it were musicians. The father had a large family and made up his mind to become the best musician of his time in his locality in order to support them. He was successful, and in turn most of his children became musicians. His lovely daughter, Eliza (Mrs. Sheridan), he bound to himself as an apprentice and taught her till she was twenty-one, insisting that she "serve out her time" to him, that she might become a perfect singer. The story of this beautiful lady seems to belong to the story of Gainsborough's portrait and shall be told here.

When she was a very little girl, no more than eight years old, she was so beautiful that as she stood at the door of the pump room in Bath to sell tickets for her father's concerts, everyone bought them from her. When she was a very young woman her father engaged her to marry a Mr. Long, sixty years old. She did not seem to mind what arrangements her father made for her, but continued to sing and attend to her business, till after the wedding gowns were all made and everything ready for the marriage, when she happened to meet the brilliant Richard Brinsley Sheridan, whose plays were so fashionable, and she fell deeply in love with him. She told Mr. Long she would not marry him, and without much objection he gave her up, but her father was very angry and he threatened to sue Mr. Long for letting his daughter go. Then the beautiful lady ran away to Calais and married Mr. Sheridan without her father's permission; but she came home again and said nothing of what she had done, kept on singing and helping her father earn money for his family. One day, Mr. Sheridan was wounded in a duel which he had fought with one of his wife's admirers, and when she heard the news she screamed, "my husband, my husband," so that everybody knew she was married to the fascinating playwright. Sheridan for some reason did not at once come and get her, nor arrange for them to have a home together. For a good while she continued to sing; and once hearing her in oratorio, Sheridan fell in love with his wife all over again. He took her from her home and would never let her sing again in public. They remarried publicly and went to live in London. He was not at all a rich and famous man at that time--only a poor law-student--but he would not let his wife make the fortune she might easily have made, by singing.

This must have made his beautiful wife very sad, but she made no complaint at giving up her music and letting him silence her lovely voice, but turned all her attention to advancing his fortunes. She worked for him even harder than she had for her father, and that was saying a great deal. When he became a great writer of plays his wife took charge of all the accounts of his Drury Lane Theatre, and when he was in the House of Commons she acted as his secretary. Sheridan died in great poverty and wretchedness, and it is believed had his self-sacrificing wife not died before him she would have looked after his affairs so well that he would not have lost his fortune.

Gainsborough painted the portraits of Sheridan's father-in-law, and of Samuel Linley; and it was said that this last portrait was painted in forty-eight minutes. Among his other portraits are: eight of George III., Sir John Skynner, Admiral Hood, Colonel St. Leger, and "The Blue Boy"; but he was first and last a landscape painter of highest genius.

XVI JEAN LEON GEROME

(Pronounced Zhahn Lay'on Zhay-rome)

French, Semi-classical School

1824-1904
Pupil of Delaroche

One cannot write much more than the date of birth and death of a man who lived until three or four years of the time of writing, so we may only say that Gérôme was one of the most brilliant of modern French painters. He was born at Vesoul and his father was a goldsmith. Thus he probably had no very great difficulty in getting a start in his work. The prejudice against having an artist in the family was dying out, and as a prosperous goldsmith we may believe that his father had means enough to give his son good opportunities.

Gérôme, like Millet, studied under Delaroche, but became no such characteristic painter as he. While studying with Delaroche he also was taking the course in l'Ecole des Beaux-Arts.

His first exhibited picture was "The Cock Fight," and he won a third class medal by it.

Almost always this painter has chosen his subjects from ancient or classic life, and his pictures are not always decent, but he painted with much care, the details of his work are very finely done and their vivid colour is fascinating.

PLATE--THE SWORD DANCE

This painting may be seen in the Metropolitan Museum of Art in New York City. The scene is full of action and interest, but perhaps the details of dress, mosaic decoration upon the walls, patterns of the rugs, the coloured and jewelled lamps and windows are the most splendidly painted of all.

The central figure is a dancing girl, only partly draped, balancing a sword on her head, while a brilliant green veil flies from head and face. Other Oriental women squat upon the floor watching her with a half indolent expression, while their Oriental masters and their friends sit in pomp at one side, absorbed in the dance and in the girl.

The expressions upon all the faces are excellent and, the jewelled light that falls upon the group, the rich clothing, the grace of the dancer--all make a fascinating picture of a genre type. Other Gérômes are "Daphnis and Chloe," "Leda," and "The Duel after the Masked Ball."

XVII GHIRLANDAJO

(Pronounced Geer-lan-da'yo)

Florentine School

1449-1494

Pupil of Fra Bartolommeo

It is a good deal of a name--Domenico di Tommaso di Currado Bigordi--and it would appear that the child who bore it was under obligation to become a good deal of a something before he died.

Italian and Spanish painters generally had large names to live up to, and the one known as Ghirlandajo did nobly.

His father was a goldsmith and a popular part of his work was the making of golden garlands for the hair of rich Italian ladies. His work was so beautiful that it gained for him the name of Ghirlandajo, meaning the garland-twiner, a name that lived after him, in the great art of his son. Domenico began as a worker in mosaic, a maker of pictures or designs with many coloured pieces of glass or stone.

Ghirlandajo's art was no improvement on that of his teacher, but he in turn became the teacher of Michael Angelo.

The Florentine school of painting, to which Ghirlandajo belonged, was not so famous for colour as the Venetian school, but it had many other elements to commend it. One cannot expect Ghirlandajo to rank with Titian, Rubens, or other "colourists" of his own and later periods, but he did the very best work of his day and school. He attained to fame through his choice of types of faces for his models, and by his excellent grouping of figures.

Until his day, the faces introduced into paintings were likely to be unattractive, but he chose pleasing ones, and he painted the folds of garments beautifully. He was not entirely original in his ideas, but he carried out those which others had thus far failed to make interesting.

Often, in his wish to paint exactly what he saw, he softened nothing and therefore his figures were repulsive, but Fra Bartolommeo's pupil gave promise of what Michael Angelo was to fulfill.

Ghirlandajo and Michael Angelo were a good deal alike in their emotional natures. Both sought great spaces in which to paint, and both chose to paint great frescoes. Indeed Ghirlandajo had the extraordinary ambition to put frescoes on all the fortification walls about Florence. It certainly would have made the city a great picture gallery to have had its walls forever hung with the pictures of one master. Had he painted them, inside and out, when such an enemy as Napoleon came along, with his love of art, and his fashion of taking all that he saw to Paris, he would likely enough have camped outside the walls while he decided what part of the gallery he would transfer to the Louvre.

One of the reasons that Ghirlandajo is famous is that he often chose well known personages for his models, and as he painted just what he saw, did not idealise his subject, he gave to the world amazing portraits, as well as fine paintings. The same thing was done by painters of a far different school, at another period. The Dutch and Flemish painters were in the habit of using their neighbours as models.

Ghirlandajo is classed among religious painters, but let us compare some of his "religious" paintings with those of Raphael or Murillo, and see the result.

He painted seven frescos on the walls of the Santa Maria Novella in Florence, all scenes of Biblical history, as Ghirlandajo imagined them. They show him to have been a fine artist, but to have had not much idea of history, and to have had little sense of fitness.

Ghirlandajo's seven subjects are taken from legends of the Virgin, and the greatest represents Mary's visit to Elizabeth; it is called "The Visitation," and it is a fresco about eighteen feet long painted on the choir wall.

Let us imagine the possible scene. The Virgin Mary came from Cana, a little town in Galilee placed in the hills about nine miles from Nazareth, the home of the lowliest and the poorest, of a kindly pastoral people living in the open air, needing and wanting very little, simple in their habits. Elizabeth, Mary's old cousin, lived in Judea, and St. Luke writes thus: "Mary arose in those days and went into the hill country with haste, into a city of Judea; and entered into the house of Zacharias" (Elizabeth's husband) "and saluted Elizabeth."

This record had been made at least eleven hundred years before Ghirlandajo painted in the Santa Maria Novella, and from it one cannot imagine that Mary made any preparation for her journey, nor does it suggest that Elizabeth had any chance to arrange a reception for her. Even had she done so, it must have been of the simplest description, at that time among those people. One can imagine a lowly home; an aged woman coming out to meet her young relative either at her door or in the high road.

There may have been surroundings of fruit and flowers, a stretch of highroad or a hospitable doorway; but the wildest imagination could not picture what Ghirlandajo did.

He paints Elizabeth flanked with handmaidens, as if she were some royal personage, instead of a priest's wife in fairly comfortable circumstances where comfort was easily obtained. Mary appears to be escorted by ladies-in-waiting, hardly a likely circumstance since she was affianced to no richer or more important person than a carpenter of Galilee. Possibly the three ladies that stand behind Mary in, the picture are merely lookers-on, but in that case the visit of Mary would seem to have been of public importance, especially as there are youths near by who are also much interested in one woman's hasty visit to another. The rich brocades worn by Elizabeth's waiting ladies are splendid indeed and the landscape is fine--a rich Italian landscape with architecture of the most up-to-date sort--showing, in short, that the artist lacked historical imagination. He found some models, made a purely decorative painting with an Italian setting and called it "The Visitation." The doorway on the right is distinctly renaissance.

Such a painting as this is not "religious," nor is it historic, nor does it suggest a subject; it is merely a fine picture better coloured than most of those of the Florentine school. There is another painting of this same subject by Ghirlandajo in the Louvre, but it is no nearer truth than the one in the Santa Maria.

Ghirlandajo painted other than religious subjects, and one of them, at least, is quite repulsive. It is the picture of an old man, with a beautiful little child embracing him. The old man may have tenderness and love in his face, but his heavy features, his warty nose, do not make one think of pleasant things and one does not care to imagine the dear little child kissing the grotesque old fellow.

It was before Ghirlandajo's time that another painter had discovered the use of oil in mixing paints. Previously colours had been mixed in water with some gelatinous substance, such as the white and yolk of an egg, to give the paint a proper texture or consistency. This preparation was called "distemper," and frescoes were made by using this upon plaster while it was still wet. Plaster and colours dried together, and the painting became a part of the wall, not to be removed except by taking the plaster with it.

The different gluey substances used had often the effect of making the colours lose their tone and they presented a glazed surface when used upon wood, a favourite material with artists.

There are numberless anecdotes written of this artist and his brother, and one of these shows he had a temper. The brothers were engaged in a monastery at Passignano painting a picture of the "Last Supper." While at work upon it, they lived in the house. The coarse fare did not suit Ghirlandajo, and one night he could endure it no longer. Springing from his seat in the refectory he flung the soup all over the monk who had served it, and taking a great loaf of bread he beat him with it so hard that the poor monk was carried to his cell, nearly dead. The abbot had gone to bed, but hearing the rumpus he thought it was nothing less than the roof falling in, and he hurried to the room where he found the brothers still raging over their dinner. David shouted out to him, when the abbot tried to reprove the artist, that his brother was worth more than any "pig of an abbot who ever lived!"

It is recorded in the documents found in the Confraternity of St. Paul that:

Domenico de Ghurrado Bighordi, painter, called del Grillandaio, died on Saturday morning, on the 11th day of January, 1493 (o.s.), of a pestilential fever, and the overseers allowed no one to see the dead man, and would not have him buried by day. So he was buried, in Santa Maria Novella, on Saturday night after sunset, and may God forgive him! This was a very great loss for he was highly esteemed for his many qualities, and is universally lamented.

The artist left nine children behind him.

Ghirlandajo's pictures may be found in the Louvre, the Berlin Museum, the Dresden, Munich, and London galleries. Most children will find it hard to see their beauty.

Great men are likely to come in groups, and with Ghirlandajo there are associated Botticelli and Fra Filippo Lippi.

PLATE--PORTRAIT OF GIOVANNA DEGLI ALBIZI

This lovely lady was the wife of one of the painter's patrons, Giovanni Tornabuoni, through whom he received the commission for a series of frescoes in the choir of the Santa Maria Novella, Florence. The subjects chosen were sacred, but since Ghirlandajo, no more than his neighbours, knew what the Virgin or her contemporaries looked like, he saw no reason why he should not compliment some of the great ones of his own city and his own time by painting them in to represent the different characters of Holy Writ. So, as one of the ladies attendant upon Elizabeth when Mary comes to visit her, we have this signora of the fifteenth century. The artist made another picture of her, the one here shown, but in the same dress and posed the same as she had been for the church fresco. This accounts for its dignity and simplicity. It would seem like a bas-relief cut out of marble were it not for its wonderful colouring. It is in the Rudolf Kann Collection, Paris. This artist's other pictures are "Adoration of the Shepherds," "Adoration of the Magi," "Madonna and Child with Saints," "Three Saints and God the Father," "Coronation of the Virgin," and "Portrait of Old Man and Boy."

XVIII GIOTTO (DI BORDONE)

(Pronounced Jot-to)

Florentine School

1276-1337
Pupil of Cimabue

Giotto painted upon wood, and in "distemper"--the mixture of colour with egg or some other jelly-like substance. We know nothing of his childhood except that he was a shepherd, as we learn from a story told of him and his teacher, Cimabue.

The story runs that one day while Giotto was watching his sheep, high up on a mountain, Cimabue was walking abroad to study nature, and he ran across a shepherd boy who was drawing the figure of a sheep, with a piece of slate upon a stone. In those days we can imagine how rare it was to find one who could draw anything, ever so rudely. Immediately Cimabue saw a chance to make an artist and he asked the little shepherd if he would like to be taught art in his studio. Giotto was overjoyed at the opportunity, and at once he left the mountains for the town, the shepherd's crook for the brush.

In those days the studio of one like Cimabue was really a workshop. Artists had to grind their own colours, prepare their own panels upon which to paint, and do a hundred other things of a workman rather than an artist kind in connection with their painting. Such a studio was crowded with apprentices--boys who did these jobs while learning from the master. Their teaching consisted in watching the artist and now and then receiving advice from him.

It was into such a shop as this, in Florence, that Giotto went, and soon he was to become greater than his master. Even so, we cannot think him great, excepting for his time, because his pictures, compared with later art, are crude, stiff, and strange.

No pupil was permitted to use a brush till he had learned all the craft of colour grinding and the like, and this was supposed to take about six years. These workshops were likely to be dull, gloomy places, and only a strong desire to do such things as they saw their master doing, would induce a boy to persevere through the first drudgery of the work. Giotto persevered, and not only became an original painter, at a time when even Cimabue hardly made figures appear human in outline, but he designed the great Campanile in Florence, and he saw it partly finished before he died. The Campanile is a wonder of architecture, but Giotto's Madonnas had to be improved upon, as certainly as he had improved upon those of Cimabue.

There are many amusing stories of Giotto, mainly telling of his good nature, and his ugly appearance, which everyone forgot in appreciation of his truly kind heart. Once a visit was made to his studio by the King of Naples, after the artist had become famous. Giotto was painting busily, though the day was very hot. The King entered, and bade Giotto not to be disturbed but to continue his work, adding: "Still, if I were you, I should not paint in such hot weather." Giotto looked up with a laugh in his eye: "Neither would I--if I were you, Sire!" he answered.

There is a famous saying: "As round as Giotto's "O," and this is how it came about. The pope wanted the best of the Florentine artists to do some work in Rome for him and he sent out to them for examples of their work. When the pope's messenger came to Giotto the artist was very busy. When asked for some of his work to show the pope, he paused, snatched a piece of paper and with the brush he had been using, which was full of red paint, he hurriedly drew a circle and gave it to the messenger who stared at him.

"But--is this *all*?" he asked.

"All--yes--and too much. Put it with the others." This perfect circle and the account the messenger gave of his visit so delighted the pope that Giotto was chosen from all the Florentine artists to decorate the Roman buildings.

Thus Giotto worked till he was fifty-seven or eight years old when he put aside his brush and turned to sculpture and architecture. Meantime he had far outstripped his master in art. The arrangement of the groups is about the same, but the figures look human and the draperies are more natural, while he gives the appearance of length, breadth, and thickness to his thrones and enclosures. We shall not choose a Madonna for illustration, but another of Giotto's masterpieces, remembering that good as he was in his time, he seems amazingly bad compared with those who came after him.

PLATE--THE MEETING OF ST. JOHN AND ST. ANNA AT JERUSALEM.

In 1303 a certain Enrico Scrovegno had a private chapel built in the Arena at Padua and he sent for Giotto to come there and adorn the whole of its walls and ceiling with frescoes. These remain, though the chapel is now emptied of all else, and they suffice to bring scores of art-lovers to Padua. The picture here reproduced represents the meeting and reconciliation between the father and mother of the Virgin before her birth. The peculiarly shaped eyes and eyebrows that Giotto gives to all his characters are specially noteworthy here as in every one of the thirty-eight frescoes. There are three rows of pictures, one above the other and in them are portrayed the principal scenes in the lives of Christ and the Virgin. The painter here reached his high-water mark, showed the very best he could produce in sincere, restrained art.

XIX FRANZ HALS

Dutch School

1580-04-1666
Pupil of Karel Van Mander

Franz Hals belonged to a family which for two hundred years had been highly respected in Haarlem in the Netherlands. The father of the painter left that town for political reasons in 1579, and it was at Antwerp that Franz was born sometime between that date and 1585. His parents took him back to Haarlem as an infant, and that is the town with which his name and fame are most closely associated.

Little is known of his early life except that he began his studies with Karel Van Mander and Cornelis Cornelissen. What we know of his family life is not to his credit. In the parish register of 1611 is recorded the birth of a son to Franz Hals and five years later he is on the public records for abusing his wife, who died shortly afterward. He married again within a year and the second wife bore him many children and survived him ten years. Five of his seven sons became painters.

Franz Hals drank too much and mixed too freely with the kind of disreputable people he loved to paint, but he never became so degraded that his hand lost its cunning, or his eye its keen vision for that which he wished to portray. In 1644, he was made a director of the Guild of St. Lucas, an institution for the protection of arts and crafts in Haarlem, but from that time onward he sank in popular esteem, deservedly. He fell into debt, then into pauperism, and when he died, about the age of eighty-six, he was buried at public expense in the choir of St. Bavon Church in Haarlem.

It was in the year 1616 that Hals first became known as a master of his art by the painting of the St. Jovis Shooting Company, one of the clubs composed of volunteers banded together for the defence of the town should occasion arise. Such guilds were common throughout Holland, and they became a favourite subject with Hals, as with other painters of the time, who vied with one another in portraiture of the different members. These groups were hung upon the walls of the chambers where meetings were held for social purposes in times of peace. The men of highest rank are always given the most conspicuous places in the pictures. The flag is generally the one bit of gorgeous colour in the scene; but Franz Hals seized the opportunity to show his wonderful skill in detail while painting the cuffs and ruffs worn by these grandees. In all his work there is an impression of strength rather than of beauty; it is the charm of expressiveness he is aiming at, rather than the charm of grace and colour to which the Italian school was devoted. He differed from that school, also, in his choice of subjects, for he was distinctly and almost entirely a portrait painter, and within his own limited range he is unsurpassed. A wonderful collection of his works is to be seen in the Haarlem Town Hall.

PLATE--THE NURSE AND THE CHILD

Considering the woeful life that Franz Hals led, it is amazing to think that he of all artists is the best painter of good humour. He puts a smile on the face of nearly every one of his "leading characters," whether it be a modest young girl, a hideous old woman, a strolling musician, or a riotous soldier, and in every case the laugh suits the subject. It may have been his own easygoing shiftlessness, his way of casting care aside with a jest that enabled him to live so long and to accomplish so much in spite of his poverty and other misfortunes.

The roguish look upon the face of this baby of the house of Ilpenstein makes it appear older than the pleasant faced nurse. The dress of the child is such as Hals delighted to spend his talents upon. The picture is in the Berlin Gallery.

Among his best known paintings are "The Laughing Cavalier," "The Fool," "The Man with the Sword," and "Hille Bobbe. the Witch of Haarlem."

XX MEYNDERT HOBBEMA

Dutch School

1637-1709
Pupil of Jacob van Ruisdael

When a man becomes famous many people claim his acquaintance, and often many places his birthplace. In Hobbema's case it has never been decided whether he was born in the little town of Koeverdam, or in the city of Haarlem or in Amsterdam. Nor is it quite certain when he was born; but what he did afterward, we are all acquainted with.

No one knows much about the life of this artist, but his master was doubtless his uncle, van Ruisdael. Hobbema was dead a hundred years before the world acknowledged his genius, thus he reaped no reward for hard work and ambition. He, like Rembrandt, died in great poverty, and with nearly the same surroundings. Rembrandt died forsaken in Roosegraft Street, Amsterdam, and Hobbema died in the same locality. We must speak chiefly about his work, since we know little of his personality or affairs.

If Böcklin's pictures seem to be composed of vertical lines, Hobbema's are as startling in their positive vertical and horizontal lines combined. We are not likely to find elevations or gentle, gradual depressions in his landscapes, but straight horizons, long trunked, straight limbed trees; and the landscape seems to be punctured here and there by an upright house or a spire. It is startlingly beautiful, and so characteristic that after seeing one or two of Hobbema's pictures we are likely to know his work again wherever we may find it.

Hobbema got at the soul of a landscape. It was as if one painted a face that was dear to one, and not only made it a good likeness but also painted the person as one felt him to be--all the tenderness, or maybe all the sternness.

It may be that Hobbema's failure to get money and honours, or at the very least, kind recognition as a great artist, while he lived, influenced his painting, and made him see mostly the sad side of beauty, nor it is certain that his landscapes give one a strange feeling of sadness and desolation, even when he paints a scene of plenty and fulness.

The French have made a phrase for his kind of work, *paysage intime*--meaning the beloved country--the one best known. It is a fine phrase, and it was first used to describe Rousseau's and Corot's work; but it especially applies to Hobbema's.

While this artist was not yet recognised, his uncle van Ruisdael was known as a great artist. The family must have been rich in spirit that gave so much genius to the world. Hobbema certainly loved his art above all things, for he had no return during his lifetime, save what was given by the joy of work. There are those who complain that Hobbema was a poor colourist. True, he used little besides grays and a peculiar green, which seemed especially to please him; but since that colouring belonged to the subjects he chose, one cannot complain on the ground that what he did was unsatisfying. For lack of knowledge about him we can think of him as a man of moods, sad, desolate ones at that; because his work is too extreme and uniform in its character for us to believe his method was affected.

PLATE--THE AVENUE, MIDDELHARNIS, HOLLAND

This perhaps is one of the most characteristic of Hobbema's pictures. Note a strange hopelessness in the scene, as well as beauty. The tall and solemn trees, the high light upon the road, suggesting to us all sorts of joys struggling through the cheerlessness of life. What other artist would have chosen such a corner of nature for a subject to paint? To quote a fine description:

"He loved the country-side, studied it as a lover, and has depicted it with such intimacy of truth that the road to Middelharnis seems as real to-day as it did over a hundred years ago to the artist. We see the poplars, with their lopped stems, lifting their bushy tops against that wide, high sky which floats over a flat country, full of billowy clouds as the sky near the North Sea is apt to be. Deep ditches skirt the road, which drain and collect the water for purposes of irrigation, and later on will join some deeper, wider canal, for purposes of navigation. We get a glimpse on the right, of patient perfection of gardening, where a man is pruning his grafted fruit trees; farther on a group of substantial farm buildings. On the opposite side of the road stretches a long, flat meadow, or "polder," up to the little village which nestles so snugly around its tall church tower; the latter fulfilling also the purpose of a beacon, lit by night, to guide the wayfarer on sea and land; scene of tireless industry, comfortable prosperity, and smiling peace. ... Pride and love of country breathe through the whole scene. To many of us the picture smiles less than it thrills with sadness. Perhaps it speaks thus only to those who find a kind of hurt in the revival of the spring, which promises so much and may fulfill so little."

Hobbema's "Watermill" is very well-known and so are his "Wooded Landscape," and "Haarlem's Little Forest."

XXI WILLIAM HOGARTH

School of Hogarth (English)

1697-1764

William Hogarth, like Watteau, originated his own school; in short there never was anybody like him. He was an editorial writer in charcoal and paint, or in other words he had a story to tell every time he made a picture, and there was an argument in it, a right and a wrong, and he presented his point of view by making pictures.

English artists in literature and in painting have done some great reformatory work. Charles Dickens overthrew some dreadful abuses by writing certain novels. The one which has most interest for children is the awful story of Dotheboys' Hall, which exposed the ill treatment of pupils in a certain class of English schools. What Dickens and Charles Reade did in literature, Hogarth undertook to do in painting. He described social shams; painted things as they were, thus making many people ashamed and possibly better.

Italians had always painted saints and Madonnas, but Hogarth pretended to despise that sort of work, and painted only human beings. He did not really despise Raphael, Titian, and their brother artists, but he was so disgusted with the use that had been made of them and their schools of art, to the entire exclusion of more familiar subjects, that he turned satirist and ridiculed everything.

First of all, Hogarth was an engraver. He was born in London on the 10th December, 1697, and eighteen days later was baptised in the church of St. Bartholemew the Great. His father was a school teacher and a "literary hack," which means that in literature he did whatever he could find to do, reporting, editing, and so on.

Hogarth must early have known something of vagabond life, for his father's life during his own youth must have brought him into association with all sorts of people. He knew how madhouses were run, how kings dined, how beggars slept in goods boxes, and many other useful items.

Hogarth said of himself: "Shows of all sorts gave me uncommon pleasure when an infant, and mimicry, common to all children, was remarkable in me.... My exercises, when at school, were more remarkable for the ornaments which adorned them, than for the exercises themselves." He became an engraver or silver-plater, being apprenticed to Mr. Ellis Gamble, at the sign of the "Golden Angel," Cranbourne Alley, Leicester Fields.

Engraving on silver plate was all well enough, but Hogarth aspired to become an engraver on copper, and he has said that this was about the highest ambition he had while he was in Cranbourne Alley.

The shop-card which he engraved for Mr. Ellis Gamble may have been the first significant piece of work he undertook. The card is still among the Hogarth relics. He set up as an engraver on his own account, though he did study a little in Sir James Thornhill's art school; but whatever he learned he turned to characteristic account.

He continued to make shop-cards, shop-bills, and book-plates. Finally, in 1727, a maker of tapestry engaged Hogarth to sketch him a design end he set to work ambitiously He worked throughout that year upon the design, but when he took it to the man it was refused. The truth was that the man who had commissioned the work had heard that Hogarth was "an engraver and no painter," and he had so little intelligence that he did not intend to accept his design, however much it might have pleased him. Hogarth sued the man for his refusal and he won the suit. He next began to make what he called "conversation pieces," little paintings about a foot high of groups of people, the figures being all portraits. These were very fashionable for a time and made some money for the artist. Both he and Watteau were fond of the stage, and both painted scenes from operas and plays.

In time he moved into lodgings at the "Golden Head," in Leicester Fields, and there he made his home. He had already begun the great paintings which were to make him famous among artists. These were a series of pictures, telling stories of fashionable and other life. His own story of how he came to think of the picture series was that he had always wished to present dramatic stories--present them in scenes as he saw them on the stage.

He had married the daughter of Sir James Thornhill, and had never been thought of kindly by his father-in-law till he made so much stir with his first series. Then Sir James approved of him, and Hogarth found life more pleasing.

There are very few anecdotes to tell of the artist's life, and the story of his pictures is much more amusing. One of his first satires was made into a pantomime by Theophilus Gibber, and another person made it into an opera. Many pamphlets and poems were written about it, and finally china was painted with its scenes and figures. There was as much to cry as to laugh over in Hogarth's pieces and that is what made them so truly great. One of his great picture series was called the "Rake's Progress" and it was a warning to all young men against leading too gay a life. It showed the "Rake" at the beginning of his misfortunes, gambling, and in the last reaping the reward of his follies in a debtor's prison and the madhouse. There are eight pictures in that set.

In this series, especially in the fifth picture, there are extraordinary proofs of Hogarth's completeness of ideas. Upon the wall in the room wherein the "Rake" marries an old woman for her money, the Ten Commandments are hung, all cracked, and the Creed also is cracked and nearly smudged out; while the poor-box is covered with cobwebs. The eight pictures brought to Hogarth only seventy guineas.

One of his pictures was suggested to him by an incident which greatly angered him. He had started for France on some errand of his own, and was in the very act of sketching the old gate at Calais, when he was arrested as a spy. Now Hogarth was a hard-headed Englishman, and when he was hustled back to England without being given time for argument, he was so enraged that he made his picture as grotesque as possible, to the lasting chagrin of France. He painted the French soldiers as the most absurd, thin little fellows imaginable, and that picture has largely influenced people's idea of the French soldier all over the English-speaking world.

As Hogarth grew old he grew also a little bitter and revengeful toward his enemies, often taking his revenge in the ordinary way of belittling the people he disliked, in his paintings.

Hogarth came before Reynolds or Gainsborough; in short, was the first great English artist, and his chief power lay in being able instantly to catch a fleeting expression, and to interpret it. An incident of Hogarth's youth illustrates this. He had got into a row in a pot-house with one of the hangers-on, and when someone struck the brawler over the head with a pewter pot, there, in the midst of excitement and rioting, Hogarth whipped out his pencil and hastily sketched the expression of the chap who had been hit.

Hogarth was friends with most of the theatre managers, and one of his souvenirs was a gold pass given him by Tyers, the director of Vauxhall Gardens, which entitled Hogarth and his family to entrance during their lives. This was in return for some "passes," which Hogarth had engraved for Tyer.

Upon one occasion Hogarth set off with some companions for a trip to the Isle of Sheppey. Incidentally Forest wrote a sketch of their journey and Hogarth illustrated it. That work is to be found, carefully preserved, in the British Museum. The repeated copying and reproduction for sale of his pictures brought about the first effort to protect his works of art by copyright. But it was not till he had done the "Rake's Progress" that he was able to protect himself at all, and even then not completely.

Just before his death he was staying at Chiswick, but the day before he died he was removed to his house in Leicester Fields. He was buried in the Chiswick churchyard; and in that suburb of London may still be seen his old house and a mulberry tree where he often sat amusing children for whom he cared very much. Garrick wrote the following epitaph for his tomb:

Farewell, great Painter of Mankind!
Who reached the noblest point of art,
Whose pictured Morals charm the Mind
And through the Eye correct the Heart.

If Genius fire thee, Reader, stay;
If Nature touch thee, drop a tear;
If neither move thee, turn away,
For Hogarth's honour'd dust lies here.

PLATE--THE MARRIAGE CONTRACT

The picture used in illustration here is part of probably the very greatest art-sermon ever painted, called "Marriage à la Mode." The story of it is worth telling:

"The first act is laid in the drawing-room of the Viscount Squanderfield"--is not that a fine name for the character? "On the left, his lordship is seated, pointing with complacent pride to his family tree, which has its roots in William the Conqueror. But his rent roll had been squandered, the gouty foot suggesting whither some of it has gone; and to restore his fortunes he is about to marry his heir to the daughter of a rich alderman. The latter is seated awkwardly at the table, holding the marriage contract duly sealed, signed and delivered; the price paid for it, being shown by the pile of money on the table and the bunch of cancelled mortgages which the lawyer is presenting to the nobleman, who refuses to soil his elegant fingers with them. Over on the left is his weakling son, helping himself at this critical turn of his affairs, to a pinch of snuff while he gazes admiringly at his own figure in the mirror. The lady is equally indifferent; she has strung the ring on to her finger and is toying with it, while she listens to the compliments being paid to her by Counsellor Silver-tongue. Through an open window another lawyer is comparing his lordship's new house, that is in the course of building, with the plan in his hand. A marriage so begun could only end in misery." This is the first act, and the pictures that follow show all the steps of unhappiness which the couple take. There are five more acts to that painted drama, which is in the National Gallery, London.

XXII HANS HOLBEIN, THE YOUNGER

(Pronounced Hahntz Hol'bine)

German School

1497-1543
Pupil of Holbein, the Elder

There were three generations of painters in the Holbein family, and the Hans of whom we speak was of the third. His grandfather was called "old Holbein," and when more painters of the same name and family came along it became necessary to distinguish them from each other thus: "old Holbein," the "elder Holbein," and "young Holbein." The first one was not much of an artist; still, in a locality where at best there was not much art he was good enough to be remembered.

"Young Holbein" was born in Augsburg, which is in Swabia, in southern Germany; "elder Holbein" and his father, Michael, "old Holbein," had moved there from Schonenfeld, a neighbouring village, about forty three years before little Hans was born, the old Michael bringing his family to the larger town where it was easier to make a living.

The "elder Holbein" was a really good artist and well thought of in Augsburg, and when little Hans's turn came he had no teacher but his father, unless indeed we were to call him also a pupil of his elder brother, Ambrosius. His uncle Sigismund, too, taught him something of art, for the whole Holbein family seem to have been artists. Young Holbein was never regularly apprenticed to any outsider.

Art was not then taught as it is now. The work of a beginner was often to paint for his master certain details which it was thought that he might handle properly, while the master occupied himself with what he thought to be some more important part of the picture. It is said that Hans often painted the draperies of his father's figures when his father was engaged upon the altar pieces so fashionable at the time. The Holbeins one and all must have been bad managers or improvident; at any rate, Hans did not turn out well as a man and we read that his father was always in debt and difficulty although he received much money for his work and was not handicapped, like Dürer's father, by a family of eighteen children.

The story of the Holbeins is quite unlike that of the Dürers, and not nearly so attractive.

Some time before Hans was twenty years of age, the entire family had packed up and gone to live in Lucerne, while Hans and his brother, Ambrosius, went travelling together, as most young Germans went at that time before they settled down to the serious work of life. The last we hear of Ambrosius he had joined the painters' guild in Basel, and probably he died not long afterward, or at any rate while he was still young. There was in Basel a certain Hans Bar, for whose wedding occasion Hans Holbein designed a table, on which he pictured an allegory of "St. Nobody." This was very likely such work as our cartoonists do to-day, but being the work of Holbein, it had great artistic value. Besides that, he painted a schoolmaster's sign to be hung outside the door.

As an illustrator, Holbein made the acquaintance of several authors about that time and started on the high road to fame. He was a man of very little conscience or fine feeling, and there could hardly be a greater contrast than that between the clean sweet life of Dürer and the brawling, unfeeling one that Hans Holbein led.

Dürer married, had no children, but tenderly loved and cared for his wife, taking her with him upon his journeys and making her happy.

Holbein married and beat his wife; had several children and took care of none of them. His wife grew to look old and worn while he remained a gay looking sport, quite tired of one whom he had had on his hands for ten years. He wandered everywhere and left his family to shift for itself. One writer in speaking of the two men says:

"Dürer would never have deserted his wife whom he took with him even on his journey to the Netherlands; and he was bound by the same tenderness to his native town. However much he rejoiced to receive a visit from Bellini at Venice, or when at Antwerp, the artists instituted, a torch-light procession in his honour, nothing could have moved him to leave Nuremberg." Dürer loved his home; Holbein hated his.

Holbein had a cold, light-blue eye; Dürer a soft and tender glance. While Dürer lived he was the mainstay of his family--father and brothers. Holbein's father died in misery and his brother's life was disastrous, Hans doing nothing to serve them and looking on at their sufferings indifferently.

There is a court document in existence which tells the particulars of Hans Holbein's arrest for getting into a brawl with a lot of goldsmiths' apprentices during a night of carousal. The court warned him that he would be more severely punished if he did not cease his lawless life and he was made to promise not to "jostle, pinch, nor beat his lawful spouse." When he died he made no provision in his will for his family. There is a picture of his wife, Elizabeth Schmidt, to be seen in his "Madonna" at Solothurn Holbein used her for the model. She then was young and blooming and the model for the child was his own baby; at that time he found them useful.

His life of folly can hardly be excused by impulsiveness or emotion, for his pictures show little of either. He was best at portrait painting. At that time guilds and town councils wanted the portraits of their members preserved in some way, and it was the habit of painters like Holbein to form picturesque groups and give to such dramatic groupings the features of townsmen. Rembrandt did this much later than Holbein, when he painted the "Night Watch," or as it is more properly called, "The Sortie."

Probably Holbein's first important work was to make title pages for the second edition of Martin Luther's translation of the New Testament. This MS. was made about the time that Holbein's work began to be of interest to the public, and so the commission was given to him.

After a time this artist went to England with letters of introduction to Sir Thomas More, Chancellor to King Henry VIII. Sir Thomas treated him very kindly and set him to work making portraits of his own family. During the time he was living at More's home in Chelsea, the King himself, used frequently to visit there, and on one occasion he saw the brilliant portraits of the More family and inquired about the artist. Sir Thomas offered the King any of the pictures he liked, but Henry VIII. asked to see the artist. When brought before him, Holbein's fortune seemed to be made for the King asked him to go to court and paint for him, remarking that "now he had the artist he did not care about the pictures."

Holbein seems to have been a favourite with Henry and many anecdotes are told of his life at Whitehall, where he went to live. Once while Holbein was engaged upon a portrait, a nobleman insisted upon entering his studio, after the artist had told him that he was painting the portrait of a lady, by order of the King. The nobleman insisted upon seeing it, but Holbein seized him and threw him down the Stairs; then he rushed to the King and told what had happened. He had no sooner finished than the nobleman appeared and told his story. The King blamed the nobleman for his rudeness.

"You have not to do with Holbein," he said, "but with me. I tell you, of seven peasants I can make seven lords, but of seven lords I cannot make one Holbein. Begone! and remember that if you ever attempt to avenge yourself, I shall look upon any injury offered to the painter as done to myself."

It was Holbein who, visiting a brother artist and finding a picture on the easel, painted a fly upon it. When the artist returned he tried to brush the fly off, then set about looking for the one who had deceived him.

His portrait painting was so superb that he received many commissions.

Meantime, Sir Thomas More had fallen into disfavour with the King and was to lose his head, but it is written that the artist's portraits "betray nothing of this tragedy." He was as ready to climb to fame by the favour of his generous patron's enemies as he had been to accept the offices of Sir Thomas More. He painted the portraits of several of the wives of Henry VIII., and it may be said that there was a good deal of that monarch's temperament to be found in Holbein himself. Take him all in all, Hans was as detestable as a man as he was excellent as a painter.

In his adopted home in Lucerne, Holbein had painted frescoes, both on the inside and the outside of a citizen's house, and this house stood until 1824, when it was torn down to make way for street improvements, but several artists hastily copied the frescoes so that they are not entirely lost.

Before he left Germany for England, Holbein had been commissioned to decorate the town hall in Basel, and a certain amount of money was voted for the work, but after he had finished three walls, he decided that the money was only enough to pay him for what he had already done. The councillors agreed with him, but as money was a little "close" in Basel at that time, they felt unable to give him more, and so voted to "let the back wall alone, till further notice."

He painted one Madonna whom he surrounded with the entire family of Burgomaster Meyer, including even the burgomaster's first wife, who was dead. This work is called the "Meyer Madonna."

It is said that after Holbein's return to Basel he, with others, was persecuted for his "religious principles," but if this were true, his persecutors went to considerable pains for nothing, because Holbein was never known to have any sort of principles, religious or otherwise. He was neither a Protestant, nor a Catholic but a painter, a man without convictions and without thought. He did not care for family, country, friends, politics, religion, nor for anything else, so far as any one knows.

When he was asked why he had not partaken of the Sacrament, he answered that he wanted to understand the matter better before he did so. Thus he escaped punishment, and when matters were explained to him, he did whatever seemed safest and most convenient under the circumstances.

On his return to England, he settled among the colony of German and Netherland merchants, who were in the habit of meeting at a place called "The Steelyard," as their home and warehouses were grouped in that locality, with a guild hall and a wineshop they alone patronised.

While associated with his compatriots Holbein made portraits of many of them, and these are magnificent works of art. He painted them separately or in groups; in their offices and in their guild hall, as the case might be. The men whom he thus painted were: Gorg Gisze, Hans of Antwerp, Derich Berck, Geryck Tybis, Ambrose Fallen, and many others. He designed the arch which the guild erected upon the occasion of Anne Boleyn's coronation, and he painted Henry's next Queen, Jane Seymour.

Holbein painted many portraits of Henry VIII. and probably all those dated after 1537 were either copies or founded upon the portrait which Holbein made and which was destroyed with Whitehall.

While he painted for Henry, Holbein received a sort of retainer's fee of thirty pounds a year, but he may have received sums for outside commissions which he undertook. On one occasion, when he took a journey to Upper Burgundy to paint a portrait of the Duchess whom Henry contemplated making his next wife, the King gave him ten pounds out of his own purse. We have no record of vast sums such as Raphael received.

Henry did not succeed in making the Duchess his wife, so Holbein was sent to paint another--Anne of Cleves--that Henry might see what he thought of her before he undertook to make her his queen. Holbein did a disastrous deed, for he made Anne a very acceptable looking woman, (the portrait hangs in the Louvre) and Henry negotiated for her on the strength of that portrait. Later, when he saw her, he was utterly disgusted and disappointed.

Holbein, notwithstanding this trick, was employed to paint the next wife of Henry, and doubtless he also made the miniature of Catherine Howard which is in Windsor Castle. Holbein finally died of the plague and no one knows where he was buried. His wife died later, and it was left for his son, Philip, who was said to be "a good well-behaved lad," to bring honours to the family. He was apprenticed in Paris, and, settling later in Augsburg, he founded a branch of the Holbein family on which the Emperor Matthias conferred a patent of nobility, making them the Holbeins of Holbeinsberg.

PLATE--ROBERT CHESEMAN WITH HIS FALCON

This is one of the best of the many splendid portraits Holbein painted. It hangs in The Hague gallery. The gentleman was forty-eight years old and in the portrait he wears a purplish-red doublet of silk and a black overcoat, which was the fashion of the day, all trimmed with fur. He has curly hair, just turning gray. His left hand is gloved and on it he holds his falcon, while with the other hand he strokes its feathers.

Of all sports at that time, falconry was the most fashionable and every fine gentleman had his sporting birds. Robert Cheseman lived in Essex. He was rich and a leader in English politics. His father was "keeper of the wardrobe to Henry VIII." and he himself served in many public offices. He was one of the gentleman chosen to welcome Anne of Cleves when she landed on English soil to marry Henry VIII. These details were first published by Mr. ArthurChamberlain and are taken from his sketch of Holbein and his works.

Among Holbein's other famous pictures are: "The Ambassadors," "Hans of Antwerp," "Christina of Denmark," "Jane Seymour," "Anne of Cleves," and "St. George and the Dragon."

XXIII WILLIAM HOLMAN HUNT

English (Pre-Raphaelite) School

1827--
Pupil of Academy School

The story of the Pre-Raphaelites is all by itself a story of art. Holman Hunt was one of three who formed this "brotherhood"; and he, with one other, are the only ones whom some of us think worthy of giving a place in art. This is to be the story of the brotherhood rather than a story of one man.

The last great artist England had had before this extraordinary group, was J. M. W. Turner, truly a wonderful man, but after him England's painters became more and more commonplace, drawing further and further away from truth, There was one, J. F. Lewis, who went away to Syria and lived a lonely and studious life, trying to paint with fidelity sacred scenes, but he was not great enough to do what his conscience and desires demanded of him; and, finally, Constable declared that the end of art in England had come. But it had not, for up in London, in the very heart of the city, in Cheapside (Wood Street) there was born, in April, 1827, a child destined to be a brilliant and wonderful man, who was actually to rescue English art from death. Many do not think thus, but enough of us do to warrant the statement.

The new artist was Holman Hunt. He was the son of a London warehouseman, with no inclination whatever for learning, so that it seemed simply a waste of time to send him to school. This continually repeated history of artists who seem to know nothing outside their brushes and colours, is astonishing, but it is true that artists for the most part must be regarded as artists, pure and simple, and not as men of even reasonably good intellectual attainments, and more or less this accounts for their low estate centuries ago. One does not associate "learning" and the artist. When we have such splendid examples as Dürer and two or three others we discuss their intellectuality because they are so unusual.

Holman Hunt was like most of his brother artists in all but his art. He hated school and at twelve years of age was taken from it. His father wanted him to become a warehouse merchant like himself, and he began life as clerk or apprentice to an auctioneer. He next went into the employment of some calico-printers of Manchester.

The designing of calicoes can hardly be called art, even if the department of design had fallen to Holman Hunt's lot and we have no evidence that it did, but he started to be an artist nevertheless, there in the print-shop. He found in his new place another clerk who cared for art; and this sympathy encouraged him to fix his mind upon painting more than ever. He used to draw such natural flies upon the window panes that his employer tried one day to "shoo away a whole colony of flies that seemed miraculously to have settled." This gave the clerks much amusement, and also attracted attention to Holman Hunt's genius.

His very small salary was spent, not on his support, but in lessons from a portrait painter of the city. His parents did not like this, but they could not help themselves, and thus this greatest of the Pre-Raphaelites began his work.

The Pre-Raphaelites were a little group of men who believed that artists were drawing too much on their imaginations, not painting things as they saw them, and that the painter had become incapable of close observation. He worked in his studio, did not get near enough to nature, and instead of trying to follow along this line, this group of men, with their new and partly correct ideas, meant to go back further than the great masters themselves and present an elemental art. This was a part of their scheme and partly it was justified, but of all the men who undertook to make a new school, Holman Hunt was the only one who remained, and will remain forever, a representative. He alone stuck to the original purpose of the group and developed it into a truly great school; so that it is he alone we need to know.

After he began to take lessons of the portrait painter in London, he developed so quickly that he found by painting portraits three days a week, he could pay his own expenses, and the rest of the time he devoted to study. He tried to be admitted to the Academy schools twice and was twice refused before they would receive him.

It was there in the Academy the three original Pre-Raphaelites met for the first ti- me; they were Holman Hunt, Dante Gabriel Rossetti, and Millais. After entering the school Hunt painted and sold four excellent pictures, but they all seem to have been lost; nobody can trace them. He was not yet a "Pre-Raphaelite."

All this time Hunt was half ill because he knew that he was grieving his father of whom he was devotedly fond, and the strain of trying to work while he was unhappy nearly destroyed him. The pictures that he exhibited at the Royal Academy were so poor that the commission declared they should not only be removed but that Hunt ought really to be forbidden to exhibit any more. This must have been a great blow to the young and struggling artist, and to add to this trouble, his father was being jeered at for having such a good-for-nothing son. Hunt's pictures in the Academy were so much despised that his father was told his son was a disgrace to him, and we may be sure that did not help the young fellow, who meantime was earning a living, not by painting pictures, but by cleaning up those of another man. Dyce, who had painted on the walls of Trinity House, engaged him to clean and restore those paintings, and Hunt was doing this for his bread and butter.

At that time he became so downhearted and discouraged that he almost decided to leave England altogether and go to live in Canada away from his friends who jeered, and his family who reproached him; but just then Millais, one of the successful painters whom he had met in the Academy school, who could afford to be generous, came to Hunt's aid and gave him the means of living while he painted "The Hireling Shepherd." This was destined to be the turning point in Hunt's luck, for that painting was properly hung at the exhibition, and it received recognition. After that he painted a picture which he sold on the installment plan--being paid by the purchaser so much a month.

Meantime he owed his landlady a large sum, and he says himself that he "suffered almost unbearable pain at passing her and her husband week after week without being able to even talk of annulling his debts." In time he not only settled that bill which distressed him, but paid back his friend Millais the money loaned by him.

Hunt rarely took a commission, because to do so meant that he must paint a picture after the manner his employer wished, and Hunt had certain ideas of art in which he believed and therefore would not bind himself to depart from them; but after a little success, which enabled him to pay his bills, he did undertake a commission from Sir Thomas Fairbairn, and it was called "The Awakened Conscience." He finished this picture on a January day late in the afternoon, and that very night he left England, setting out upon a longed-for journey to the Holy Land, where he meant to study the country and people till he believed himself able to paint a truthful picture of sacred scenes. He refused to paint pictures of Eastern Jews who should look like Parisians, with Venetian backgrounds. He meant to paint Oriental scenes as nearly as he could, as they might have taken place.

He came back to his English home just two years and one month from the time he had left it, and he brought back a picture of the goat upon which the Jews loaded their sins and then turned loose in waste-places to wander and die. "The Scapegoat" was a great picture, but before he left England he had painted a greater--the one we see here--"The Light of the World."

He had depended upon the sale of the "Scapegoat" to pay his way for a time after his return home, and alas, it did not sell. More than that, his beloved father died and this added to his sense of desolation, for he had not been sufficiently successful before his death to justify himself in his father's eyes. These things so overwhelmed his sensitive mind with trouble, that his condition became very serious, and if certain good friends had not stood by him loyally, he would probably never have painted again.

He began at last another ambitious picture--"Finding of Christ in the Temple"--but while he was engaged upon this, he had to paint mere pot-boilers also in order to get on at all, and he says that half the time the great picture "stood with its face to the wall" while he was trying merely to earn bread and butter. The wonderful Louis Blanc tried once to plan a way by which all deserving people should have in this world equal opportunity to try. This has never been "worked out." It never will be, but Holman Hunt reminds us how much the world loses by not providing that "equal opportunity." No one deserves more than his chance; but such struggles of genius tell us that all is not fair.

Hunt persevered with this Christ in the Temple and when finished he sold it for 5,500 guineas--a larger sum than he had ever before been given for a painting.

He no sooner received his money for this great picture than off he went once more to the Holy Land. He was conscientious in everything he did, and never before had an artist painted scenes of Christ that carried such a sense of truth with them. The set haloes seen about the heads of the saints and of holy people even in Raphael's pictures and in those of the very greatest artists of his time, disappeared with Holman Hunt's coming. In the "Light of the World," the halo is an accident--the great white moon, happening to rise behind the Christ's head--and there we have the halo, simple, natural, only suggestive, not artificial. Then, too, in the "Shadow of Death," there is a menacing shadow of the cross--made upon the wall by Christ's body, as he naturally stretches out his arms, after his work in the carpenter shop.

There is not one false note that shocks us, or makes us feel that after all the story itself is affected and artificial. Everything that is symbolical is brought about naturally. They are sincere, truthful pictures that speak to the mind as well as to the eye.

Hunt's colouring and many other technical matters are often far from perfect, but there is something besides technicality to be considered in judging a picture.

For a time, while the three men, Hunt, Rossetti, and Millais, kept together, their pictures were signed P. R. B., as a sign of their league; but this did not last very long, and afterward Hunt signed his pictures independently.

After the "Brotherhood" had worked against the greatest discouragements for a long time, and felt nearly hopeless of success, John Ruskin, one of the greatest of critics and most fearless of men, who was so much respected that his words had great influence, suddenly published a defence of these Pre-Raphaelites. He declared that they were the greatest artists of the time, and while scorning their critics he applauded those three young men, till he turned the tide, and everybody began to know what truly brilliant work they were doing. Ruskin's words came, Hunt said, "as thunder out of a clear sky."

When the "Brotherhood" was formed the three young men thought they should have a paper--a periodical of some sort, in which they might tell of their purposes and express their ideas; and so Rossetti, who wrote as well as painted, proposed that they print such a periodical once a month, and call it the *Germ*; and the P. R. B's. were to be joint proprietors. Rossetti had first thought of a different title, *Thoughts Toward Nature*, and his brother, W. M. Rossetti, who was going to take charge of the monthly, thought that expressed the Pre-Raphaelites' idea; but it was finally agreed to call it the *Germ*. Only two numbers could be published by the Pre-Raphaelites, because nobody bought it and the young men's money gave out, but the printers came to the rescue, and put up the money to issue two or three more *Germs*.

Although that journal failed utterly, its four numbers were worth publishing, and are to-day worth reading. They were truly valuable, for they contained a story and poem by Dante Gabriel Rossetti, besides work of the other P. R. B's.

Above all things Hunt was conscientious in his work, trying with all his might to represent things as be believed them to be. When he made his "Scapegoat," he went to the shores of the Dead Sea to paint, accompanied only by Arab guides, and there he found the desolate, hard landscape for his picture. The hardships he experienced were very many. The wretched goat he took with him died in the desert of that dreary place after it had been no more than sketched in, but back in Jerusalem Hunt finished the goat. Ruskin's description of the picture helps one to feel all the desolation of the subject: "The salt sand of the wilderness of Ziph, where the weary goat is dying. The neighbourhood is stagnant and pestiferous, polluted by the decaying vegetables brought down by the Jordan in its floods, and the bones of the beasts of burden that have died by the way of the sea, lie like wrecks upon its edge, bared by the vultures and bleached by the salt ooze."

Even the superstitious Arabs would not go near the spot which Hunt chose as the scene of his picture, but Hunt endured all things, believing it due to his art.

When he painted "Christ in the Temple," he needed Jewish models, and it was almost impossible for him to get them. He could not let them know what they were to represent, or they would not have sat for him at all but he succeeded in painting the "first Semitic presentment of the Semitic Scriptures." In Jerusalem the Jews heard that he had come "to traffic with the souls of the faithful," and they forbade him to have any Jews come into his studio; so that he could not finish the picture there. Back in London he had to find his models in the Jewish school. He left the figures of Christ and the Virgin till the last and then painted them "from a lady of the ancient race, distinguished alike for her amiability and beauty, and a lad in one of the Jewish schools, to which the husband of the lady furnished a friendly introduction."

Thus, step by step, through the greatest difficulties, Holman Hunt established a new school of painting--allegory with a modern treatment which all could understand.

PLATE--THE LIGHT OF THE WORLD

This is the most popular picture of a sacred subject, ever painted; and John Ruskin's description of it, here quoted, is the best ever written or that can be written. "On the left of the picture is seen the door of the human soul. It is fast barred, its bars and nails are rusty; it is knitted and bound to its stanchions by creeping tendrils of ivy, showing that it has never been opened. A bat hovers over it; its threshold is overgrown with brambles, nettles and fruitless corn.... Christ approaches in the night time, ... he wears the white robe, representing the power of the Spirit upon Him; the jewelled robe and breastplate, representing the sacredotal investiture; the rayed crown of gold, interwoven with the crown of thorns; not dead thorns, but now bearing soft leaves, for the healing of the nations.... The lantern carried in Christ's left hand is the light of conscience.... Its fire is red and fierce; it falls only on the closed door, on the weeds that encumber it, and on an apple shaken from one of the trees of the orchard, thus marking that the entire awakening of the conscience is not to one's own guilt alone, but to the guilt of the world, or, 'hereditary guilt.'...

"This light is suspended by a chain, wrapt around the wrist of the figure, showing that the light which reveals sin to the sinner appears also to chain the hand of Christ. The light which proceeds from the head of the figure--is that of the hope of salvation; it springs from the crown of thorns, and, though itself sad, subdued and full of softness, is yet so powerful, that it entirely melts into the glow of it the forms of the leaves and boughs which it crosses, showing that every earthly object must be hidden by this light, where its sphere extends."

If you will study every detail of this reproduction, finding all the objects--the apple, the rusty bolts--noting how the full risen moon has formed a natural nimbus for the sacred head, and then re-read what Ruskin has said, you will discover the rarest truths in Holman Hunt's picture. The several pictures which he painted, but which cannot now be found are: "Hark!" which was first exhibited in the Royal Academy; "Scene from Woodstock," "The Eve of St. Agnes," "Jerusalem by Moonlight," "The King of Hearts," "Moonlight at Salerno," "Interior of the Mosque of Omar," "The Pathless Water," "Winter," "Afternoon," "Sussex Downs," "Penzance," "The Archipelago," "Will-o'-the-Wisp," "Ivybridge," "The Foal of an Ass," "Road over the Downs," "The Haunt of the Gazelle," "'Oh, Pearl,' Quoth I," "Miss Flamborough," "The School-girl's Hymn." Portraits: Mr. Martineau; Mr. J. B. Brice. Small sketch of the "Scapegoat," "Sunset on the Sea," "Morning Prayer," "Bianca," "Past and Present," and "Dead Mallard."

Should you ever find one of these pictures bearing the initials P. R. B. or those of Holman Hunt, you will have made an interesting discovery and should make it known to others.

XXIV GEORGE INNESS

American

1825-1897

Pupil of Regis Gignoux

George Inness was destined to keep a grocery store as his father had kept one before him, and had grown rich in it. When George was a young man he was given a grocery store in Newark, New Jersey, a very small store indeed, and it is not surprising that the young man preferred art to butter and eggs. The Inness family had just moved from Newburg, probably the elder Innes seeking in Newark a good location for his son's beginning.

The first art-work Inness did was engraving; as he had been apprenticed to that business, but afterward he studied with Gignoux, a pupil of Delaroche.

At that time there was what is known as the Hudson River School. Its ideas were set and formal, and not very inspiring, aside from the subjects treated. Church was then a young man like Inness, and he was studying in the Hudson River School, but the young grocer struck out a line for himself.

He was forty years old before he got to Paris, but once there, he turned to the men at Barbizon--Rousseau, Millet, Corot, and the rest--for inspiration, and began to do beautiful things indeed. Rousseau became his friend, and the art of Inness grew large and rich through such influences.

Inness had inherited much religious feeling from his Scotch ancestors, and all his work was conscientious, very carefully done.

When Inness returned from Paris he was not yet well known. He went to Montclair, New Jersey, to live and it was there that he did his best work. Finally, after he was fifty years old, he became known as a truly splendid painter. He loved best to paint quiet scenes of morning, evening sunset, and the like. His pictures began to gain value, and one that he had sold for three hundred dollars jumped in price to ten thousand and more. His work is not equally good, because his moods greatly influenced him.

PLATE--BERKSHIRE HILLS

This picture in the George A. Hearn collection is full of the sense of restfulness that the works of this artist always convey. The trees are as motionless as the distant hills, and if the oxen are moving at all it is but slowly.

Some other Inness paintings are the "Georgia Pines," "Sunset on the Passaic," "The Wood Gatherers" and "After a Summer Shower."

XXV SIR EDWIN HENRY LANDSEER

English School

1802-1873
Pupil of his father, John Landseer

It is pleasant to speak of one artist whose good work began in the companionship of his father; the case of Edwin Landseer is most unusual.

His father was a skilful engraver who loved art, and encouraged the cultivation of it in his son, as other fathers of painters encouraged them to become priests or haberdashers or bakers, as the case might be. Little Landseer's beginning has been described by his father as he and a friend stood looking upon one of the scenes of his childhood:

"These two fields were Edwin's first studio. Many a time have I lifted him over this very stile. I then lived in Foley Street, and nearly all the way between Marylebone and Hampstead was open fields. It was a favourite walk with my boys; and one day when I had accompanied them, Edwin stopped by this stile to admire some sheep and cows which were quietly grazing. At his request I lifted him over, and finding a scrap of paper and a pencil in my pocket, I made him sketch the cow. He was very young indeed, then--not more than six or seven years old.

"After this we came on several occasions, and as he grew older this was one of his favourite spots for sketching. He would start off alone, or with John (Thomas?) or Charles, and remain till I fetched him in the afternoon. I would then criticise his work, and make him correct defects before we left the spot. Sometimes he would sketch in one field, sometimes in the other, but generally in the one beyond the old oak we see there, as it was more pleasant and sunny."

All the Landseer men were gifted, and the mother was the beautiful woman whom Reynolds painted as a gleaner, carrying a bundle of wheat upon her head.

There were seven little Landseers, the oldest of them being Thomas, the famous engraver, whose reproduction of his brother's works will preserve them to us always, even after the originals are gone. The first of Edwin's drawings which seemed to his family worthy of publishing was a great St. Bernard dog, such a wonderful performance for a little fellow of thirteen that Thomas engraved it and distributed it all over England. Little Edwin had seen this beautiful dog one day in the streets of London in a servant's charge, and he was so delighted with its beauty, that he followed the two home and asked the dog's owner if he might sketch him. The St. Bernard was six feet four inches long "and at the middle of his back, stood two feet seven inches in height." A great critic said that this drawing was one of the very finest that any master of art had ever made, though it was done by a little child of thirteen years and it is also said that Landseer himself never did anything better than that little-boy work. A live dog who was let into the room with it--as critic, maybe--proved to be the most flattering of such, because he bristled instantly for a fight.

While the boy was still thirteen--which seems to have been a magic and not a tragic number to him--he exhibited pictures in the Royal Academy. These were a mule, and a dog with a puppy. In the stories of "Famous Artists" we are told that he was a fine, manly little chap with light curly hair and very well behaved. When he became a student of the Academy the keeper, Fuseli, used to look about among the students and cry: "Where is my little dog boy?" if Landseer was not in his place. The little chap's favourite dog was his own Brutus, which he painted lying at full length; and though the picture was small, it sold for seventy guineas. This means an earning capacity indeed, for a small boy.

When he was but seven years old he had made pictures of lions and tigers, each with a different expression from the other and each with a character of its own. Critics spoke specially of the tiger's whiskers as "admirable in the rendering of foreshortened curves." Tigers' whiskers were thought to be most difficult things to make, but in Landseer's pictures, they were as "natural as life." The great success of the artist's animal pictures was that he made them seem to have human intelligence, and it was also said that if one only saw the dog's collar, as Landseer painted it, he would know it to be the work of a great artist, that a great dog-picture must be attached to it.

At least one of his pictures had a remarkable history. He had been commissioned by the Hon. H. Pierrpont to paint a "white horse in a stable." After the painting was ready for delivery it disappeared, and for twenty-four years it could not be found. At last it was discovered in a hay-loft! It had been stolen by a servant and hidden there. In spite of the long years that had passed, Landseer sent it at once to the man for whom it had been made, with the message that he had not retouched it nor changed it in the least, "because," said he, "I thought it better not to mingle the style of my youth with that of my old age."

One of Landseer's early advisers had told him he must dissect animals to get the proper effects in painting them, as it was necessary for him to understand their construction. So, one time, when a famous old lion died in the Exeter Exchange menagerie Landseer got its body and dissected it, and immediately afterward he painted three great lion pictures: "The Lion Disturbed at His Repast," "A Lion Enjoying His Repast," and "A Prowling Lion."

Sir Walter Scott became so enchanted with Landseer's pictures that the great novelist came to London to take the young artist to his home at Abbotsford. "His dogs are the most magnificent things I ever saw," said Scott, "leaping and bounding and grinning all over the canvas."

Landseer lived in the centre of London till he was more than thirty years old, and then, looking for more quiet and space he bought a very small house and garden at No. 1, St. John's Wood. There was not much room in the house but it had a stable attached which made a fine studio, and there Landseer lived with a sister of his, for nearly fifty years. When he first wished to rent the house, the landlord asked him a hundred pounds premium which Landseer felt that he could not pay and he was about to give it up, when a friend declared that if the matter of money was all that prevented him, he was to rent it immediately, and he could repay him as he chose. Landseer then took the house, his friend paying down the premium, and Landseer returned the money twenty-pounds at a time, till all the debt was paid.

Landseer made this a famous and hospitable house, and it is said that more great people gathered under his roof than had ever gathered about any other artist with the exception of Sir Joshua Reynolds. That was the house in which Landseer's loving old father spent his last days and finally died. A story is told of the witty D'Orsay, who would call out at the door, when he went to visit the artist: "Landseer, keep de dogs off me, I want to come in and some of dem will bite me--and dat fellow in de corner is growling furiously."

On one of his several visits to Abbotsford, where he went many times after his first invitation, to enjoy Scott's delightful hospitality, he painted a famous dog of Sir Walter's called Maida, which died six weeks afterward.

There are several such stories about dogs who died rather tragically and were also painted by Landseer. The two King Charles spaniels which he painted both died soon after sitting to the great painter. They had been pets of Mr. Vernon, who commissioned the painting, and the white Blenheim spaniel fell from a table and was killed, while the King Charles fell through the railings of a staircase and was picked up dead. The great bloodhound, Countess, belonging to Mr. Bell who gave her picture to the Academy, was watching for her master's return one dark night and when she heard the wheels of his carriage, then his voice, she leaped from the balcony, but missed her footing and fell nearly dead at Mr. Bell's feet. That gentleman loved the dog so much that he was distracted, and taking her into his gig, knowing that she must die, he raced in to London again that same night, and rousing Sir Edwin, begged him to paint the dog before it was too late. Then and there was the sketch of the dying animal made.

Sir Edwin Landseer was the most versatile and entertaining of artists. He was a wit, and could also perform all sorts of sleight of hand tricks, besides being so quick with his pencil that his doings seemed miraculous. One evening, during a conversation with many friends, someone declared that in point of time Sir Edwin could do a record-sketch. One young woman spoke up and said: "There is one thing that even he cannot do--he cannot make two different pictures at the same time."

"Think not?" cried Sir Edwin. "Let us see!" Gaily taking two pencils, he rapidly drew a stag's head with one hand and a horse's head with the other.

Landseer became the guest of royalty, a favourite of Queen Victoria, whose dog Dash was one of the many famous dogs painted by him. Dash was the favourite spaniel of the Duchess of Kent, Victoria's mother; and the Queen's biographer says that she too loved him very much. On Coronation Day she had been away from him longer than usual, and when the great state coach rolled up to the palace steps she could hear Dash barking for her in the hall. "Oh," she exclaimed, "there's Dash," and throwing aside the ball and sceptre which she carried, she hurried to change her fine robes, in order to wash the dog. This is a very homelike and picturesque story, but it is possibly not true. Doubtless the little Queen heard the dog bark--and was glad to see him.

At Windsor Landseer painted another royal dog, Islay, the pet terrier of Victoria; also Dandie Dinmont, belonging to the Princess Alice; then Eos, who was Prince Albert's--King Edward's--dog. All the last years of Sir Edwin Landseer' life, the royal family were his devoted and comforting friends. The painter suffered much and during his visits to Balmoral he wrote to his sister how the Queen used to go several times a day to his room, to look after his comfort and to inquire about his condition. He wrote:

"The Queen kindly commands me to get well here. She has to-day been twice to my room to show additions recently added to her already rich collection of photographs. Why, I know not, but since I have been in the High lands I have for the first time felt wretchedly weak, without appetite. The easterly winds, and now again the unceasing cold rain, may possibly account for my condition, but I can't get out. Drawing tires me; however, I have done a little better to-day. The doctor residing in the castle has taken me in hand, and gives me leave to dine to-day with the Queen and the rest of the royal family.... Flogging would be mild compared with my sufferings. No sleep, fearful cramp at night, accompanied by a feeling of faintness and distressful feebleness."

When he was well, he was gay and cheerful; and Dickens, Thackeray, and many other noted men were his friends. We are told that above all things. Sir Edwin was a great mimic and that one night at dinner he threw everybody into fits of laughter by imitating his friend the sculptor Sir Francis Chantry. It was at the sculptor's table, where a large party was assembled. Chantry called Sir Edwin's attention, when the cloth was removed, to the reflection of light in the highly polished table.

"Come here and sit in my place," said Chantry, "and see the perspective you can get." Then he went and stood by the fire, while Landseer sat in his place. Seated then in Chantry's chair, Landseer called out in perfect imitation of his host: "Come, young man, you think yourself ornamental; now make yourself useful, and ring the bell." Chantry did so, and when the butler came in he was confused and amazed to hear his master's voice from where Landseer sat in Chantry's place at the table. The voice of his master from the head of the table ordered claret, while his master really stood before the fire with his hands under his coat-tails.

We are told that Landseer stood his pictures on their heads, or upon one corner or looked at them from between his legs, any way, every way, to get a complete view of them from all quarters. He went to bed very late and got up very late, but in the mornings, while lying in bed he mostly thought out the subjects of his pictures.

He was not much of a sportsman, preferring to paint animals rather than to kill them, and one day when hunting, he saw a fine stag before him. Instead of firing at it, he thrust his gun into a gillie's hands, crying: "Hold that! hold that!" and whipping out his pencil and pad he began to sketch the stag. Whereupon the gillies were disgusted that he should miss so fine a shot, and they said something to each other in Gaelic, which Sir Edwin must have understood, for he became very angry.

"It was a pity," wrote one who knew all his qualities, "that Landseer, who might have done so much for the good of the animal kind, never wrote on the subject of their treatment. He had a strong feeling against the way some dogs are tied up, only allowed their freedom now and then. He used to say a man would fare better tied up than a dog, because the former can take his coat off, but a dog lives in his forever. He declared a tied-up dog, without daily exercise, goes mad, or dies, in three years."

He had a wonderful power over dogs, and he told one lady it was because he had "peeped into their hearts." A great mastiff rushed delightedly upon him one day and someone remarked how the dog loved him. "I never saw the dog before in my life," the artist said.

While teaching some horses tricks for Astley's, he showed his friends some sugar in his hand and said: "Here is my whip." His studio was full of pets, and one dog used as a model used to bring the master's hat and lay it at his feet when he got tired of posing.

This charming man suffered a great deal before his death, and had dreadful fits of depression. During one of these he wrote: "I have got trouble enough; ten or twelve pictures about which I am tortured, and a large national monument to complete." That monument was the one in Trafalgar Square, for which he designed the lions at the base. "If I am bothered about anything and everything, no matter what, I know my head will not stand it much longer." Later he wrote: "My health (or rather condition), is a mystery beyond human intelligence. I sleep seven hours, and awake tired and jaded, and do not rally till after luncheon. J. L. came down yesterday and did her best to cheer me... I return to my own home in spite of kind invitations from Mr. and Mrs. Gladstone to meet Princess Louise at breakfast." Of the many anecdotes told of this great man, his introduction to the King of Portugal furnishes the most amusing. "I am delighted to make your acquaintance," the King said, "I am so fond of beasts."

Before he died he had made a large fortune from his work, and during his illness he was tended most lovingly by his friends and sister. One day, walking in his garden, much depressed, he said sadly: "I shall never see the green leaves again," but he did live through other seasons. He wished to die in his studio, and at one time when he was much distracted the Queen wrote him not to fear, but to trust those who were doing all they could for him, that her confidence in his physicians and nurses was complete. At last with brother, sister, friends and fortune about him the great animal painter died, and on October 11, 1873, and was buried with great honours in St. Paul's Cathedral.

PLATE--THE OLD SHEPHERD'S CHIEF MOURNER

Of all the dogs Landseer loved to paint, the sheep collie has the most character; and here he shows us one expressing in every line of his face and form the most profound grief. The Glengarry bonnet on the floor beside the shepherd's staff, the spectacles lying on the Bible, the ram's horn, the vacant chair, the black and white shawl known as a "Shepherd's plaid"--all these things have failed to comfort this humble follower. We can imagine him, not bounding ahead with a joyous bark, but walking staidly behind the coffin when it is borne away and laying himself down upon his master's grave, perhaps to die of starvation, as some of his kind have been known to do. The painting is one of the Sheepshanks Collection in the South Kensington Museum.

Among Landseer's other famous dog pictures are "Low Life and High Life," "Dignity and Impudence" and "The Sleeping Bloodhound," all in the National Gallery.

XXVI CLAUDE LORRAIN (GELLEE)

Classical French School

1600-1689
Pupil of Godfrey Wals

Of all the contrasts between the early and later lives of great artists, Claude Lorrain gives us the most complete.

He was born to make pastry. His family may have been all pastry cooks, because people of Lorrain were famous for that work; anyway as a little chap he was apprenticed to one. His parents were poor, lived in the Duchy of Lorrain and from that political division the Artist was named.

The town in which he was born was Chamagne, and his real name was Gellée. As a pastry cook's apprentice he served his time, and then, without any thought of becoming anything else in the world, he set off with several other pastry cooks to go to Rome, where their talents were to be well rewarded.

But how strangely things fall out! In Rome he was engaged to make tarts for Agostine Tassi, a landscape painter. His work was not simply to furnish his master with desserts, but to do general housekeeping, and it fell to his lot to clean Tassi's paint brushes. So far as we know, this was the first introduction of Claude Lorrain to art other than culinary.

From cleaning brushes it was but a step to trying to use them upon canvas, and Tassi being a good-natured man, began to give Lorrain instruction, till the pastry cook became his master's assistant in the studio. This led to a larger and larger life for the young Frenchman, and he copied great masters, did original things, and finally in his twenty-fifth year returned to France a full-fledged artist. He remained there two years, and then went back to Italy, where he lived till he died. The visit to France turned out fortunately because on his way back he fell in with one of the original twelve members of the French Academy, Charles Errard, who became the first director of the Academy in Rome. A warm friendship sprang up between the men, and Errard was very helpful to the young artist.

Nevertheless, Lorrain did not gain much fame till about his fortieth year, when he was noticed by Cardinal Bentivoglio, and was given certain commissions by him. He grew in Bentivoglio's favour so much that the Cardinal introduced him to the pope. The Catholic Church set the fashions in art, politics, and history of all sorts at that time, so that Lorrain could not have had better luck than to become its favourite. The pope was Urban VIII., whose main business was to hold the power of the Church and make it stronger if he could, so that he was continually building fortresses and other fortifications, and he had use for artists and decorators. Lorrain's fame outlasted the life of Urban VIII., and he became a favourite in turn with each of the three succeeding popes. All this time he was doing fine work in Italy and for Italy, besides receiving orders for pictures from France, Holland, Germany, Spain, and England, for his fame had reached throughout the world.

Besides leaving many paintings behind him when he died, he left half a hundred etchings; also a more precise record of his work than most artists have left. He executed two hundred sketches in pen or pencil, washed in with brown or India ink, the high lights being brought out with touches of white. On the backs of them the artist noted the date on which the sketch was developed into a picture, and for whom the latter was intended. The story is that his popularity produced many imitators, and that he adopted this means to establish the identity of his own work and distinguish it from the many copies made.

These sketches were collected in a volume by Lorrain and called "Liber Veritatis," and for more than a hundred years the Dukes of Westminster have owned this.

PLATE--ACIS AND GALATEA

This picture in the Dresden Gallery is a scene from the mythical story of a goddess who fell in love with the youthful son of a faun and a naiad. Thus she excited the jealous fury of the cyclops, Polythemus, who is seen in the picture herding his flock of sheep upon the high cliff at the right. Soon he will rise and hurl a rock upon Acis, crushing the life out of him, so that there will be nothing left for Galatea to do but to turn him into the River Acis, but meanwhile the lovers are unconscious and happy. Venus is reposing near them on the waves and Cupid is closer still, while the sea in the background seems to be stirred with a fresh morning breeze.

Some of the famous Lorrains in the Louvre are: "Seaport at Sunset," "Cleopatra Landing at Tarsus," and "The Village Festival."

XXVII MASACCIO (TOMMASO GUIDI)

(Pronounced Tome-mah'so Mah'sahch'cheeo)

Florentine School

1401-1428
Pupil of Ghibertio, Donatello, and Brunellesco

This artist, who lived and died within the century that witnessed the discovery of America, was famous for more than his painting. He was the original inventor who first learned and taught the mixing of colours with oils, thus making the peculiar "distemper" unnecessary.

The story of Italian artists includes a history of their names, for the Italians seem to have had most remarkable reasons for naming children. For example, this artist, Masaccio, was born on St. Thomas's day, hence, his name of Tommaso. Presently, for short, or for love, he was called Maso, and to cap all, being a careless lad, his friends added the derogatory "accio," and there we have the artist completely named. He owed nothing of this to his father, who was plain, or ornamentally, Ser Giovanni di Simone Guidi, of Castello San Giovanni, in the Valdamo.

As a very little boy, it was plain to be seen that slovenly Thomas was going to be a great artist, and no time was lost in putting him to work with the best of masters.

He was a veritable inventive genius. Until his time difficulties in drawing had been overcome mostly by ignoring them. Since no artist had been able to draw a foreshortened foot, it had been the fashion in art to paint people standing upon their tiptoes, to make it possible for an artist to paint the foot. The enterprising Thomas came along and he decided that feet must be painted both flat and crossed, on tiptoe or otherwise; in short he did not mean to lose by a foot.

He worked at this problem day and night, till at last the naturally poised foot came into existence for the artist. Never after Masaccio's time did an artist paint the foot stretched upon the toes. Moreover, until his time flesh had never been painted of a remotely natural colour, so Masaccio set about combining colours till he made one that had the tint of real flesh. Thus he was the first to overcome the difficulties of drawing and the first to discover a mixture that would not leave a glazed, hard, unnatural appearance and be likely to crack and destroy the finest effort of an artist.

He worked during his youth in Pisa, where the "leaning tower" stands; then he worked in Florence, finally in Rome, but those early pictures are long since gone. It was a century of adventure and discovery as well as of art, and with so much change, so many wars and rumours of wars, many great art works were lost. Besides, the horrible plague swept Italy east, west, north, and south. Who was to concern himself with saving works of art, when human life was going out wholesale all over the land?

Masaccio was certainly very poor most of his life. He lived with his mother and his brother Giovanni, an artist like himself, but not nearly so brilliant. Masaccio could not spend his life in painting but had to eke out the family fortunes by keeping a little shop near the old Badia, and being pestered day and night by his creditors he was forced again and again to go to the pawn shop.

Somewhere about 1422, careless Thomas painted his greatest picture which was doomed to destruction too early for us to know much about it; but it was named "San Paolo" and it was painted in the bell-room of the Church of the Carmine in Florence. The figure for his model was an illustrious personage, Bartoli d'Angiolini, who had held many honourable offices in Florence for many years. A critic and friend of artists tells us that the portrait was so great it lacked only the power of speech.

In this picture Masaccio made his first great triumph in the foreshortening of feet.

He undertook to celebrate the consecration Of the Church of the Carmine, and for this he made many frescoes, among which was a correct painting of the procession as it entered from the cloisters of the church. "Among the citizens who followed in its wake, portraits are introduced of Brunellesco, Donatello, Masolino, Felice Brancacci (the founder of the chapel) Giovanni di Bicci de' Medici, and others, including the porter of the convent with the key of the door in his hand."

This work was thought to be very wonderful because the figures grew smaller in the distance, thereby giving "perspective" for the first time. Imagine how crude a thing was painting in the day of careless Thomas.

That fresco is long since gone, but drawings of it still exist which tell us something of the people of Christopher Columbus's day--previous to their appearance, and their conditions.

After Masaccio had finished the procession he went back to his painting of the chapel and in the end covered three of its four walls with his works. Many of those paintings are scenes from the life of St. Peter, and several were worked at by other artists than Masaccio.

Masaccio was greater than Raphael, greater than Michael Angelo in so far as he pointed the way that they were to go, having solved for them all the problems that had kept artists from being great before him. Sir Joshua Reynolds says that "he appeared to be the first who discovered the path that leads to every excellence to which the art afterward arrived; and may therefore be justly considered one of the great fathers of modern art."

The artist lived but a little time, and was most likely poisoned. Nobody knows, but it is said that other painters were so wildly jealous of his original genius that they wished him out of the way, and his death was at least mysterious. He drew very rapidly and let the details go, caring only to represent motion and action. Because he painted so many portraits into his pictures there was great life and animation in them, and people said of him that he painted not only the body but the soul.

PLATE--ARTIST'S PORTRAIT [Footnote: Many artists have left us portraits of themselves, painted, no doubt, with the aid of a mirror, in a group or alone. This one of Masaccio in the Naples Museum, shows him to have been a picturesque model.]

Some of his known pictures are the frescoes in the church of St. Clemente in Rome; the frescoes in the Brancacci Chapel in the Church of the Carmine, "St. Peter Baptising" and the "Madonna and Child, with St. Anne," which is in the Accademia at Florence.

XXVIII JEAN LOUIS ERNEST MEISSONIER

(Pronounced May-sohn-yay)

French School

1815-1891
Pupil of Léon Cogniet

This artist was born at Lyons. His father was a salesman and an art-training seemed impossible for the young man because the Meissoniers were poor people. Nevertheless, he was so persevering that while still a young man he got to Paris and began to paint in the Louvre. He was but nineteen at that time, and his fate seemed so hard and bitter that later in life he refused to talk of those days.

He sat for many days in the Louvre, by Daubigny's side, painting pictures for which we are told he received a dollar a yard. We can think of nothing more discouraging to a genius than having to paint by the yard. It is said that his poverty permitted him to sleep only every other night, because he must work unceasingly, and someone declares that he lived at one time on ten cents a week. This is a frightful picture of poverty and distress.

Meissonier's first paying enterprise was the painting of bon-bon boxes and the decorating of fans, and he tried to sell illustrations for children's stories, but for these he found no market. A brilliant compiler of Meissonier's life has written that "his first illustrations in some unknown journal were scenes from the life of 'The Old Bachelor.' In the first picture he is represented making his toilet before the mirror, his wig spread out on the table; in the second, dining with two friends; in the third, on his death-bed, surrounded by greedy relations and in the fifth, the servants ransacking the death chamber for the property." This was very likely a vision of his own possible fate, for Meissonier must have been at that time a lonely and unhappy man.

There are many stories of his first exhibited work, which Caffin declares was the "Visit to the Burgomaster," but Mrs. Bolton, who is almost always correct in her statements, tells us that it was called "The Visitor," and that it sold for twenty dollars. At the end of a six years struggle in Paris, his pictures were selling for no more.

Until this artist's time people had been used only to great canvases, and had grown to look for fine work, only in much space, but here was an artist who could paint exquisitely a whole interior on a space said to be no "larger than his thumb nail." His work was called "microscopic," which meant that he gave great attention to details, painting very slowly.

During the Italian war of 1859, and in the German war of 1870, this wonderful artist was on the staff of Napoleon III. During the siege of Paris he held the rank of colonel, and he lost no chance to learn details of battles which he might use later, in making great pictures. Thus he gained the knowledge and inspiration to paint his picture "Friedland," which was bought by A. T. Stewart and is now in the Metropolitan Museum. He, himself, wrote of that picture: "I did not intend to paint a battle--I wanted to paint Napoleon at the zenith of his glory; I wanted to paint the love, the adoration of the soldiers for the great captain in whom they had faith, and for whom they were ready to die.... It seemed to me I did not have colours sufficiently dazzling. No shade should be on the imperial face.... The battle already commenced, was necessary to add to the enthusiasm of the soldiers, and make the subject stand forth, but not to diminish it by saddening details. All such shadows I have avoided, and presented nothing but a dismounted cannon, and some growing wheat which should never ripen.

"This was enough.

"The men and the Emperor are in the presence of each other. The soldiers cry to him that they are his, and the impressive chief, whose imperial will directs the masses that move around, salutes his devoted army. He and they plainly comprehend each other and absolute confidence is expressed in every face."

This great work was sold at auction for $66,000 and given to the Metropolitan Museum.

It is said that when he painted the "Retreat from Russia," Meissonier obtained the coat which Napoleon had worn at the time, and had it copied, "crease for crease and button for button." He painted the picture mostly out of doors in midwinter when the ground was covered with snow, and he writes: "Sometimes I sat at my easel for five or six hours together, endeavouring to seize the exact aspect of the winter atmosphere.

My servant placed a hot foot-stove under my feet, which he renewed from time to time, but I used to get half-frozen and terribly tired."

So attentive was he to truthfulness in detail that he had a wooden horse made in imitation of the white charger of the Emperor; and seating himself on this, he studied his own figure in a mirror.

At last this conscientious man was made an officer of the Legion of Honour, having already become President of the Academy. Edmund About writes that "to cover M. Meissonier's pictures with gold pieces simply would be to buy them for nothing; and the practice has now been established of covering them with bank-notes."

Meissonier seldom painted the figure of a woman in his pictures, but all of his subjects were wholesome and fine.

One time an admirer said to him "I envy you; you can afford to own as many Meissonier pictures as you please!"

"Oh no, I can't," the distinguished artist replied. "That would ruin me. They are a good deal too dear for me."

In his maturity he became very rich, and his homes were dreams of beauty, filled with rare possessions such as bridles of black leather once owned by Murat, rare silver designed by the artist himself, great pictures, and flowers of the rarest description besides valuable dogs and horses. Yet it was said that "this man who lives in a palace is as moderate as a soldier on the march. This artist, whose canvases are valued by the half-million, is as generous as a nabob. He will give to a charity sale a picture worth the price of a house. Praised as he is by all he has less conceit in his nature than a wholesale painter."

On the 31st of January in his country house at Poissy, this great man, whose life reads like a romance, died, after a short illness. His funeral services were held in the Madeleine, and he was buried at Poissy, near Versailles, a great military procession following him to the grave.

PLATE--RETREAT FROM MOSCOW

In the painting of this picture we have already told how every detail was mastered by actual experience of most of them. Meissonier made dozens of studies for it--"a horse's head, an uplifted leg, cuirasses, helmets, models of horses in red wax, etc. He also prepared a miniature landscape, strewn with white powder resembling snow, with models of heavy wheels running through it, that he might study the furrow made in that terrible march home from burning Moscow. All this work--hard, patient, exacting work."

Some of his other pictures are "The Emperor at Solferino," "Moreau and His Staff before Hohenlinden," "A Reading at Diderot's" and the "Chess Players."

XXIX JEAN FRANÇOIS MILLET

Fontainebleau-Barbizon School

1814-1875
Pupil of Delaroche

Two great artists painted peasants and little else. One was the artist of whom we shall speak, and the other was Jules Breton. One was realistic, the other idealistic. Both did wonderful work, but Millet painted the peasant, worn, patient steadfast, overwhelmed with toil; Breton, a peasant full of energy, grace, vitality, and joy.

Millet painted peasants as he knew them, and hardly any one could have known them better, for he was himself peasant-born. His youth was hard, and the scenes of his childhood were such as in after life he became famous by painting. Millet lived in the department of Manche, in the village of Gruchy, near Cherbourg. Manche juts into the sea, at the English Channel, and whichever way Millet looked he must have seen the sea. His old grandmother looked after the household affairs, while his father and mother worked in the fields and Millet must have seen them hundreds of times, standing at evening, with bowed heads, listening to the Angelus bell. He toiled, too, as did other lads in his position. His grandmother was a religious old woman, and nearly all the pictures he ever saw in his boyhood were those in the Bible, which he copied again and again, drawing them upon the stone walls in white chalk.

The old grandmother watched him, never doubting that her boy would become an artist. It was she who had named him--François, after her favourite saint, Francis, and it was she, who, beside the evening fire, would tell him legends of St. Francis. It was she alone who had time and strength left, after the day's work, to teach him the little he learned as a boy and to fix in his mind pictures of home. His father and mother were worn, like pack-horses, after their day in the fields. The mother very likely had to hitch herself up with the donkey, or the big dog, after the fashion of these people, as she helped draw loads about the field. Who can look for Breton's ideal stage peasants from Millet who knew the truth as he saw it every day?

Many years after his life in the Gruchy home, Millet painted the portrait of the grandmother whom he had loved so much that he cried out: "I wish to paint her soul!" No one could desire a better reward than such a tribute.

Millet had an uncle who was a priest and he did what he could to give the boy a start in learning. He taught him to read Virgil and the Latin Testament; and all his life those two books were Millet's favourites. Besides drawing pictures on the walls of his home, he drew them on his sabots. Pity some one did not preserve those old wooden shoes! He did his share of the farm work, doing his drawing on rainy days.

When he was about eighteen years old, coming from mass one day, he was impressed with the figure of an old man going along the road, and taking some charcoal from his pocket he drew the picture of him on a stone wall. The villagers passing, at once knew the likeness; they were pleased and told Millet so. Old Millet, the father, also was delighted for he, too, had wished to be an artist, but fate had been against him. Seeing the wonderful things his son could do, he decided that he should become what he himself had wished to be, and that he should go to Cherbourg to study.

François set off with his father, carrying a lot of sketches to show, and upon telling the master in Cherbourg what he wanted and showing the sketches, he was encouraged to stay and begin study in earnest. So back the old father went, with the news to the mother and grandmother and the priest uncle, that François had begun his career. He stayed in Cherbourg studying till his father died, when he thought it right to go home and do the work his father had always done. He returned, but the women-folk would not agree to him staying. "You go back at once," said the grandmother, "and stick to your art. We shall manage the farm." She sewed up in his belt all the money she had saved, and started him off again, for he had then been studying only two months. Now he remained till he was twenty-three, a fine, strapping, broad-shouldered country fellow. He had long fair hair and piercing dark blue eyes. All the time he was with Delaroche he was dissatisfied with his work--and with his master's, which seemed to Millet artificial, untrue. He knew nothing of the classical figures the master painted and wished him to paint, for his heart and mind were back in Gruchy among the scenes that bore a meaning for him. He wished to study elsewhere, and by this time he had done so well that one of the artists with whom he had studied went to the mayor of Millet's home town, and begged him to furnish through the town-council money enough to send Millet to Paris. This was done, and Millet began to hope.

He was very shy and afraid of seeming awkward and out of place. The night he got to Paris was snowy, full of confusion and strange things to him, and an awful loneliness overwhelmed him. The next morning he set out to find the Louvre, but would not ask his way for fear of seeming absurd to some one, so that he rambled about alone, looking for the great gallery till he found it unaided. He spent most of the days that followed gazing in ecstasy at the pictures.

He liked Angelo, Titian, and Rubens best. He had come to Paris to enter a studio, but he put off his entrance from day to day, for his shyness was painful and he feared above all things to be laughed at by city students. At last one day, he got up enough courage to apply to Delaroche, whose studio he had decided to enter if he could, as he liked his work best. The students in that studio were full of curiosity about the new chap, with his peasant air, his bushy hair and great frame, so sturdy and awkward. They at once nicknamed him "the man of the woods," and they nagged at him and laughed at the idea that he could learn to paint, till one day, exasperated nearly to death, he shook his fist at them. From that moment he heard no more from them, for they were certain that if he could not paint he could use his fists a good deal better than any of them. Delaroche liked the peasant but did not understand him very well, and Millet was not too fond of his painting, so after two years he and a friend withdrew from that studio and set up one for themselves. Thus eight years passed, the friends living from hand to mouth, doing all sorts of things: sign-painting, advertisements, and the like; and Millet, in the midst of his poverty, got married.

He went home, returning to Paris with his wife, and after starving regularly, he became desperate enough to paint a single picture as he wished. It seemed at the time the maddest kind of thing to do. Who would see ugly, toil-worn peasants upon his *salon* walls? Paris wanted dainty, aesthetic art, and an Academy artist would have scoffed at the idea; but the Millets were starving anyway, so why not starve doing at least what one chose. So Millet painted his first wonderful peasant picture "The Winnower," and just as the family were starving he sold it--for $100. He had done at last the right thing, in doing as he pleased. This was a sign to him that there was after all a place for truth and emotion in art. But the Millets must change their place of living, and go to some place where the money made would not at once be eaten up. Jacque--the friend with whom Millet had set up shop, and who also became famous, later--advised them to go to a little place he knew about, which had a name ending in "zon." It was near the forest of Fontainebleau, he said and they could live there very cheaply, and it was quiet and decent. The Millets got into a rumbling old cart and started in search of the place which ended in "zon" near the forest of Fontainebleau. Jacque had also decided to take his family there and they all went together. When they got to Fontainebleau they got down from the car and went a-foot through the forest.

They arrived tired and hungry toward evening, and went to Ganne's Inn, where there were Rousseau, Diaz, and other artists who like themselves had come in search of a nice, clean, picturesque place in which to starve, if they had to. Those who were just sitting down to supper welcomed the newcomers, for they had been there long enough to form a colony and fraternity ways. One of these was to take a certain great pipe from the wall, and ask the newcomer to smoke; and according to the way he blew his "rings" he was pronounced a "colourist" or "classicist." The two friends blew the smoke, and at once the other artists were able to place Jacque. He was a colourist; but what were they to say about Millet who blew rings after his own fashion.

"Oh, well!" he cried. "Don't trouble about it. Just put me down in a class of my own!"

"A good answer!" Diaz answered. "And he looks strong and big enough to hold his own in it!" Thus the newcomers took their places in the life of Barbizon--the place whose name ended in "zon," and Millet's real work began. His first wife lived only two years, but he married again. All this time he was following his conscience in the matter of his work, and selling almost nothing. In a letter to a friend he tells how dreadfully poor they are, although his new wife was the most devoted helpful woman imaginable, known far and near as "Mère Millet." The artist wrote to Sensier, his friend, who aided him: "I have received the hundred francs. They came just at the right time. Neither my wife nor I had tasted food in twenty-four hours. It is a blessing that the little ones, at any rate, have not been in want."

The revolution of 1848 had come before Millet went to Barbizon, and he like other men had to go to war. Then the cholera appeared, and these things interrupted his work; and after such troubles people did not begin buying pictures at once. Rousseau was famous now, but Millet lived by the hardest toil until one day he sold the "Woodcutter" to Rousseau himself, for four hundred francs. Rousseau had been very poor, and it grieved him to see the trials and want of his friend, so he pretended that he was buying the picture for an American. That picture was later sold at the Hartmann sale for 133,000 francs. Millet was now forty years old, and had not yet been recognised as a wonderful man by any but his brother artists. He was truly "in a class of his own." He had learned to love Barbizon, and cried: "Better a thatched cottage here than a palace in Paris!" and we have the picture in our minds of Millet followed patiently and lovingly by "Mère Millet" in the peasant dress which she always wore, that she might be ready at a moment's notice to pose for his figures. Then there were his little children and his sunny, simple, fraternal surroundings, which make his life the most picturesque of all artists.

His paintings had the simplest stories with seldom more than two or three figures in them. It was said that he needed only a field and a peasant to make a great picture. When he painted the "Man with the Hoe," he did it so truthfully, in a way to make the story so well understood by all who looked upon it, that he was called a socialist. No one was so much surprised as Millet by that name. "I never dreamed of being a leader in any cause," he said. "I am a peasant--only a peasant."

Of his picture "The Reaper" a critic wrote, "He might have reaped the whole earth." All his pictures were sermons, he called them "epics of the fields." He pretended to nothing except to present things just as they were, as he writes in a letter to a friend about "The Water Carrier:"

In the woman coming from drawing water I have endeavoured that she shall be neither a water-carrier nor a servant, but the woman who has just drawn water for the house, the water for her husband's and her children's soup; that she shall seem to be carrying neither more nor less than the weight of the full buckets; that beneath the sort of grimace which is natural on account of the strain on her arms, and the blinking of her eyes caused by the light, one may see a look of rustic kindliness on her face. I have always shunned with a kind of horror everything approaching the sentimental. I have desired on the other hand, that this woman should perform simply and good-naturedly, without regarding it as irksome, an act which, like her other household duties, is one she is accustomed to perform every day of her life. Also I wanted to make people imagine the freshness of the fountain, and that its antiquated appearance should make it clear that many before her had come to draw water from it.

At forty he was in about the same condition as he had been on that evening ten or twelve years before, when he had entered Barbizon carrying his two little daughters upon his shoulders, his wife following with the servant and a basket of food, to settle themselves down to hardship made sweet by kind comradeship and hope. Now a change came. Millet painted "The Angelus." He was dreadfully poor at that time and sold the picture cheaply, but it laid the foundation of his fame and fortune. He had worked upon the canvas till he said he could hear the sound of the bell. Although its first purchaser paid very little for it, it has since been sold for one hundred and fifty thousand dollars.

At last, having struggled through his worst days, without recognition, and with nine little children to feed and clothe, he was given the white cross of the Legion of Honour; and as if to make up for the days of his starvation, he was nearly feasted to death in Paris. He was placed upon the hanging committee of the *Salon*, and took a dignified place among artists. He and Mère Millet travelled a little, but always he returned to Barbizon, till the war came and he had to move to Normandy to work. Afterward he returned to Barbizon, to the scenes and the old friends he loved so well, and there he died. He had come back ill and tired with the long struggle, and he instructed his friends to give him a simple funeral. This was done. They carried his coffin, while his wife and children walked beside him to the cemetery, and he was buried near the little church of Chailly, whose spire is seen in "The Angelas," and where Rousseau, whom he loved, had already been laid.

There in Barbizon, to-day, may be seen Rousseau's cottage and Millet's studio. "The peasants sow and reap and glean as in the days of Millet; Troyon's oxen and sheep are still standing in the meadow; Jacque's poultry are feeding in the barnyard. The leaves on Rousseau's grand old trees are trembling in the forest; Corot's misty morning is as fresh and soft as ever; while Diaz's ruddy sunsets still penetrate the branches; and the peasant pauses daily as the Angelus from the Chailly church calls him to silent prayer."

PLATE--THE ANGELUS

In "The Angelus" you may see far-off the spire of the church at Chailly, from which the bell sounds. The day's work is drawing to a close. The peasant man and woman have been digging potatoes--the man uncovering them, while his wife has been putting them in the basket. As the Angelus floats across the fields, the two pause and bow their heads in prayer. The man has dropped his fork and uncovered his head, and his wife has clasped her hands devoutly before her.

All the air seems still and full of tender sound and colour, and we, like Millet, seem "to hear the bell." This is the only picture he painted which is full of the sentimentality he so much disliked. It is a great picture, but we need to know the title in order to interpret it.

Besides this one, Millet painted "The Gleaners," "The Woodcutters," "The Sower," "The Man with the Hoe;" "The Water Carrier," "The Reaper," and many other stories of the peasant poor.

XXX CLAUDE MONET

(Pronounced Claude Mo-nay)

Impressionist School of France

1840--

Another--Manet--was the founder of this school among modern painters, but Monet is always considered his most conspicuous follower.

Monet's remarkable method of putting his colours upon canvas does not mean impressionism. He is an impressionist but also *Monet*--an artist with a method entirely different from that of any other. He belongs to what in France is called the *pointillistes*. The word means nothing more nor less than an effort to accomplish the impossible. If you stand a little way from a very hot stove you may be able to see a kind of movement in the air, a quivering of particles or molecular motion, and this is what the *pointillistes* try to show in their paintings--Monet most of all.

The theory is that by putting little dabs of primitive colours, close together upon canvas, without mixing them, just separate dabs of red, yellow, blue, etc., the effect of movement is produced. Needless to say, none of them ever have produced such an effect, but they have made such grotesque, ugly pictures that they have attracted attention even as a humpbacked person does.

The first who painted thus was a Frenchman named Seurat, who tried it after closely studying experiments made in light and colour by Professor Rood, of Columbia University. After him came Pissarro, and then Monet. America also has such a painter, Childe Hassam, but nobody is so grotesque as Monet.

He was born in Paris but spent most of his youth in Havre, where he met a painter of harbours and shipping scenes called Boudin. Through his influence Monet studied out-of-door effects, and was beginning to do fairly good work, when he was drawn as a conscript and sent to Algeria. It is written that Monet discovered that "green, seen under strong sunshine is not green, but yellow; that the shadows cast by sunlight upon snow or upon brightly lighted surfaces are not black, but blue; and that a white dress, seen under the shade of trees on a bright day, has violet or lilac tones." This only means that these things have been scientifically determined, not that the naked eye ever perceives them, and it is for the natural, unscientific eye that art exists. None of us see the separate colours of the spectrum, as we look about in every-day fashion upon every-day objects.

Professor Rood managed to produce an intelligent effect by putting separate colours on discs and whirling these round so that the colours mingled. Monet tried to do the same by dotting his original colours close together, and leaving the picture to its own destruction. It ought to revolve, if the scientific idea is to be carried out.

Nothing desirable can be made out of his pictures even when viewed from far off, while at close range they are simply grotesque, and photographs of them give the impression that the entire landscape is wabbling to the ground.

I wonder if anyone, small or grown up, can understand this: "It was indeed a higher kind of impressionism that Monet originated, one that reveals a vivid rendering, not of the natural and concrete facts, but of their influence upon the spirit when they are wrapped in the infinite diversities of that impalpable, immaterial, universal medium which we call light, when the concrete loses itself in the abstract, and what is of time and matter impinges on the eternal and the universal." Monet's pictures look just as that explanation of them sounds!

The same writer says that Monet was greater than Corot because he was more sensitive to colour; but if Monet had been as sensitive to colour as Corot, he could not have lived and looked at his own pictures.

PLATE--HAYSTACK IN SUNSHINE

The main feature of this picture is such a hay stack as never existed anywhere, of indescribable lurid colour, against a background of blue such as never was seen. All about there are violet and rose-coloured trees, and it is a picture that every child should know, because he is likely never to have another such opportunity.

Monet has made two interesting pictures of churches, one at Vernon, the other at Varangeville.

XXXI MURILLO (BARTOLOME ESTEBAN)

(Pronounced Moo-reel'oh Bar-tol-o-may' A-stay'bahn)

Andalusian School

1617-1682
Pupil of Juan del Castillo

The story of Murillo has been delightfully told by Mrs. Sarah Bolton.

Like Velasquez, he was born in Seville, a city called "the glory of the Spanish realms," and was baptised on New Year's day, 1618, in the Church of the Magdalen.

Murillo's father paid his rent in work, instead of in money. He made a bargain with the convent who owned his house that he would keep it in repair if he might have it free of rent, so there Gaspar Estéban and his wife, Maria Perez, settled. "Perez" was the family name of Murillo's mother, who had very good connections; one of her brothers, Juan del Castillo, being a man who encouraged all art and had an art school of his own. Little Murillo therefore had encouragement from the start, an unusual circumstance at a time when parents rarely wished to think of their sons as painters. As a matter of fact, his mother would have preferred that he should become a priest, but she was kind and sensible, and put no difficulties in the way of the little Murillo doing as he wished.

The story goes that the Perez family had been very rich, but, however it may have been, that was not the case when the artist was born. One day after his mother had gone to church, Murillo being left at home alone, retouched a picture that hung upon the wall. It was a picture of sacred subject--"Jesus and the Lamb." He thought he could make some improvements in it, so he painted his own hat upon the head of Jesus and changed the lamb into a little dog. His mother was a good deal shocked at what seemed to her an irreligious act, though it showed the family genius. After that the boy was found to be painting upon the walls of his schoolroom, and making sketches upon the margins of his books, though he did little else at school.

He had one sister, Therese, and they were left without father or mother before the artist was eleven years old.

It was at that time that he received the name of "Murillo" by which he is known.

It came about thus: After the death of his parents he went to live with his mother's sister, the Doña Anna Murillo, who had married a surgeon called Juan Agustin Lagares, and since the little artist was to live with his aunt, he soon became known by her family name. There, in her home, he and his sister Therese, were brought up, but he was not to become a surgeon like his uncle-in-law, but an artist like his uncle Juan, the teacher in Seville. That uncle took him in hand, taught the boy to draw, to mix colours, to stretch his canvas, and soon Murillo's genius won the love of master and pupils.

In peace and reasonable comfort he served a nine years apprenticeship, and painted his first important, if not especially great, pictures. These were two Madonnas, one of them "The Story of the Rosary." St. Dominic had instituted the rosary; using fifteen large and one hundred and fifty small beads upon which to keep record of the number of prayers he had said; the large beads representing the *Paternosters and Glorias* and the small ones, the *Aves*. This practical way of indicating duties helped the heedless to concentrate their attention, and did much to increase the number of prayers offered. Indeed, it is said that "by this single expedient Dominic did more to excite the devotion of the lower orders, especially of the women, and made more converts, than by all his orthodoxy, learning, arguments, and eloquence." It was this incident in the history of the Catholic Church that Murillo commemorated.

When the artist was twenty-two years old, his uncle, Juan del Castillo, broke up his home and went elsewhere to live, leaving the artist without home or means, and with his little sister to take care of. Without vanity or ambition, but with only the wish to care for his sister and to get food, the marvellous painter took himself to the market place, and there, wedged in between stalls, old clothes, vegetables, all sorts of wares, like a wanderer and a gypsy, he began his career.

At the weekly market--the *Feria* or fair, opposite the Church of All Saints--his brotherly, kindly feeling for the vagabonds he daily met is shown in the treatment he gives them in his wonderful pictures. During the two years that he worked in that open-air studio he had flower-girls, muleteers, hucksters all about him, and he painted dozens of rough pictures which found quick sale among the patrons of the market. What Velasquez was doing in the court of Madrid, Murillo was doing in the streets of Seville; the one painting cardinals, kings, and courtiers; the other painting beggars, *gamins*, and waifs. Between the two, the world has been shown the social history of Spain as it then existed.

Through a peculiar happening, the American Indian saw the beauties of Murillo's work before Europe was even conscious there was such a man. In his old home, his uncle's studio, Murillo had had a dear comrade, Moya. They had not met for two years or more, and when they did come together again Moya told Murillo he had been travelling, that he had been to Flanders with the Spanish army, and thence to London, in both places seeing gorgeous paintings and other inspiring things. He opened the eyes of Murillo to the splendours the world contained, and the artist became wild with desire to go and see them for himself, but he had no money. He was painting pictures in the market place of Seville and getting so little for his hasty work that he could barely support himself and little Therese. What must he do in order to get to London and see the world?

What he did do was to buy a piece of linen, cut it into six pieces and hide himself long enough to paint upon them "saints, flowers, fruit and landscapes," and then he went forth to sell them.

He actually sold those pictures to a ship-owner who was sending his ship to the West Indies. Eventually they were hung upon the walls of a mission in wild, far off America. It is said that after this Murillo made no little money by painting such pictures, destined to give the American savage an idea of the Christian religion. One cannot but wonder if there may not be, all unknown to us, Murillo pictures, made in the market-place of Seville nearly three hundred years ago, hidden away in the remains of those old Spanish missions, even to-day. Such a picture would be more rare than the greatest that he ever painted.

After selling his six pictures Murillo started a-foot, not to London but on a terrible journey across the Sierra Mountains, to Madrid--the home of Velasquez. Murillo knew that this native of Seville had become a famous artist. He was powerful and rich and at the court of Philip II., while Murillo had no place to lay his head, and besides he had left Therese behind in Seville in the care of friends. He had no claim upon the kindness of Velasquez but he determined to see him; to introduce himself and possibly to gain a friend. It was under these forlorn circumstances he made himself known to the great Spanish court painter.

The story of their meeting is a fine one. For Murillo Velasquez had a warm embrace, a kind and hospitable word. The stranger told Velasquez how he had crossed the mountains on foot, was penniless, but could use his brush. Instead of jealousy and suspicion, the young man met with nothing but the most cheerful encouragement, found the Velasquez home open to him, took up his lodging there and established his workshop with nothing around him but friendship and the sympathy his nature craved.

From the market-place to the home of Velasquez and the Palace of Philip II.! It was a beautiful dream to Murillo.

With what splendour of colour and mastery of design he illuminated the annals of the poor! Coming forth from some dim chancel or palace-hall in which he had been working on a majestic Madonna picture, he would sketch in, with the brush still loaded with the colours of celestial glory, the lineaments of the beggar crouching by the wall, or the gypsy calmly reposing in the black shadow of an archway. Such versatility had never before been seen west of the Mediterranean, and it commanded the admiration of his countrymen.

All his beggarly little children, neglected and houseless, appeared only to be full of cheer and merriment, with soft eyes and contented faces. It was a happy, care-free, gay, and kindly beggardom that he painted, with nothing in it to sadden the heart.

Thus he lived for three years; working in the galleries of the king, making friends at court, painting beautiful women, gallant cavaliers and fascinating little beggars.

In the course of time, however, he grew restless, and Velasquez wished to give him letters of introduction to Roman artists and people of quality, advising him to go to Rome to study the greatest art in the world. This was an alluring plan to Murillo, but after all he longed for his own home and chose to return there rather than go to Rome. Besides, his sister Therese was still in Seville.

Once more in his home, at one stroke of his magic brush Murillo raised himself and a monastic order from obscurity to greatness. In his native city was the order of San Francisco. The monks had long wished to have their convent decorated in a worthy manner by some artist of repute; but they were poor and had never been able to engage such a painter. When Murillo got back home, he was as badly in need of work as the Franciscans were in want of an artist. The monks held a council and finally agreed upon a price which they could pay and which Murillo could live upon. Then he began a wonderful set of eleven large paintings. Among them were many saints, dark and rich in colouring, and no sooner was it known that the paintings were being made than all the rich and powerful people of Seville flocked to the convent to see the work. They gathered about the young artist, overwhelmed him with honours and praise, and the monastery was crowded from morning till night with those who wished to study his work. From that moment Murillo's fame, if not his fortune, was made.

He married a rich and noble lady with the tremendous name of Doña Beatriz de Cabrera y Sotomayer. He had fallen in love with her while painting her as an angel.

About that time he formed a strange partnership with a landscape painter, who agreed to supply the backgrounds that his pictures needed, if Murillo would paint figures into his landscapes. This plan did very well for a little time, but it did not last long.

Murillo painted in three distinct styles, and these have come to be known as the "warm," the "cold," and the "vaporous." He painted pictures in the great cathedral of the Escorial and the "Guardian Angel" was one of them. Also, he painted "St. Anthony of Padua," and of this picture there is one of those absurd stories meant to illustrate the perfection of art. It is said that the lilies in it are so natural that the birds flew down the cathedral aisles to pluck at them. Many artists have painted this saint, but Murillo's is the best picture of all.

When the nephew of his first master, Murillo's cousin, saw that work he said: "It is all over with Castillo! Is it possible that Murillo, that servile imitator of my uncle, can be the author of all this grace and beauty of colouring?"

The Duke of Wellington offered for this picture as many gold pieces "as would cover its surface of fifteen square feet." This would have been about two hundred and forty thousand dollars; but we need not imagine that Murillo received any such sum for the work. This picture has a further interesting history. The canvas was cut from the frame by thieves in 1874, and later it was sold to Mr. Schaus, the connoisseur and picture dealer of New York. He paid $250 for it, and at once put it into the hands of the Spanish consul, who restored it to the cathedral.

The story of the saint whom Murillo painted is as interesting as Murillo's own. Among the many wonderful things said to have happened to him was that a congregation of fishes hearing his voice as he preached beside the sea, came to the top and lifted up their heads to listen.

While Murillo was doing his work, he was living a happy, domestic life. He had three children, and doubtless he used them as models for his lively cherubs, as he used his wife's face for madonnas and angels.

He founded an academy of painting in Seville, for the entrance to which a student could not qualify unless he made the following declaration: "Praised be the most Holy Sacrament and the pure conception of Our Lady."

The most delightful stories are told of Murillo's kindness and sweetness of disposition. He had a slave who loved him and who, one day while Murillo was gone from the studio, painted in the head of the Virgin which the master had left incomplete. When Murillo returned and saw the excellent work he cried: "I am fortunate, Sebastian"--the slave's name--"For I have not created only pictures but an artist!" This slave was set free by Murillo and in the course of time he painted many splendid pictures which are to-day highly prized in Seville.

This is a description of Murillo's house which is still to be seen near the Church of Santa Cruz: "The courtyard contains a marble fountain, amidst flowering shrubs, and is surrounded on three sides by an arcade upheld by marble pillars. At the rear is a pretty garden, shaded by cypress and citron trees, and terminated by a wall whereon are the remains of ancient frescoes which have been attributed to the master himself. The studio is on the upper floor, and overlooks the Moorish battlements, commanding a beautiful view to the eastward, over orange groves and rich corn-lands, out to the gray highlands about Alcala."

Murillo's fame brought fortune to his little sister, Therese. She married a nobleman of Burgos, a knight of Santiago and judge of the royal colonial court. He became the chief secretary of state for Madrid.

Murillo made money, but gave almost all that he made to the poor, though he did not make money in the service of the Church, as Velasquez made it in the service of the king.

His work of more than twenty pictures in the Capuchin Church of Seville occupied him for three years, and in that time he did not leave the convent for a single day.

Of all the charming stories told of this glorious artist, one which is connected with his work in that church is the most picturesque. It seems that every one within the walls loved him, and among others a lay brother who was cook. This man begged for some little personal token from Murillo and since there was no canvas at hand, the artist bade the cook leave the napkin which he had brought to cover his food, and during the day he painted upon it a Madonna and child, so natural that one of his biographers declares the child seems about to spring from Mary's arms. This souvenir made for the cook of the Capuchin, convent has been reproduced again and again, as one of the artist's greatest performances.

Toward the close of his happy life, he became more and more devout, spending many hours before an altar-piece in the Church of Santa Cruz where was a picture of "The Descent from the Cross," by Pedro Campana. "Why do you always tarry before 'The Descent from the Cross?'" the sacristan once asked of him.

"I am waiting till those men have brought the body of our blessed Lord down the ladder." Murillo answered. His wife had died, his daughter had become a nun, and all that was left to him was his dear son Gaspar, when in his sixty-third year he began his last work, "The Marriage of St. Catherine." He had not finished this when he fell from the scaffolding upon which he was working, and fatally hurt himself. He died, with his son beside him. He was a much loved man, and when he was buried, his bier was carried by "two marquises and four knights and followed by a great concourse of people." He chose to be buried beneath the picture he loved so much--"The Descent from the Cross," and upon his grave was laid a stone carved with his name, a skeleton and an inscription in Latin which means "Live as one who is about to die."

The church has since been destroyed, and on its site is the Plaza Santa Cruz, but Murillo's grave is marked by a tablet.

Each country seems to have had at least one man of beautiful heart and mind, to represent its art. Raphael in Italy, Murillo in Spain, were types of gentle and greatly beloved men. Leonardo in Italy and Dürer in Nuremberg, were types of forceful, intellectual men, highly respected and of great benefit to the world.

Of all the painters who ever lived, Murillo was the one who painted little children with the most loving and fascinating touch.

PLATE--THE IMMACULATE CONCEPTION

Besides the little angels in this picture, we have a bewildering choice among many other beauties.

Many pictures of this subject have been painted, and many were painted by Murillo, but the one presented here is the greatest of all. It hangs in the Louvre, Salle VI. Mary seems to be suspended in the heavens, not standing upon clouds. Under the hem of her garments is the circle of the moon, while there is the effect of hundreds of little cherub children massed about her feet, in a little swarm at the right, where the shadow falls heaviest, and still others, half lost in the vapoury background at the left, where the heavenly light streams upon them, and brilliantly lights up the Virgin's gown. In this picture are all Murillo's beloved child figures, some carrying little streamers, their tiny wings a-flutter and all crowding lovingly about Mary. Far below this gorgeous group we can imagine the dark and weary earth lost in shadow.

Among Murillo's most famous paintings are: "The Birth of the Virgin," "Two Beggar Boys," "The Madonna of the Rosary," "The Annunciation," "Adoration of the Shepherds," "Holy Family," "Education of Mary," "The Dice Players," and "The Vision of St. Anthony."

XXXII RAPHAEL (SANZIO)

(Pronounced Rah'fay-el (Sahnt'syoh))

1483-1590
Umbrian, Florentine, and Roman Schools

Pupil of Perugino

It was said of Raphael that "every evil humour vanished when his comrades saw him, every low thought fled from their minds"; and this was because they felt themselves vanquished by his pleasant ways and sweet nature.

Imagine his beautiful face, with its sunny eyes, reflecting no shadow of sadness or pain. Such a one was sure to be beloved by all.

The father of Raphael was Giovanni Santi, himself an able artist. Both he and Raphael studied in many schools and took the best from each. The son was brought up in an Italian court, that of Guidobaldo of Urbino, where the father was a favourite poet and painter, so that he had at least one generation of art-lovers behind him, at a time when learning and art were much prized. Nothing ever entered into his life that was sad or sorrowful; his whole existence was a triumph of beautiful achievements. There were three great artists of that time, the other two being Michael Angelo and Leonardo da Vinci, both of whom were absolutely unlike Raphael in their art and in their characters.

Raphael was born on April 6th at Contrada del Monte in the ducal city of Urbino. His mother's name was Magia Ciarla, and she was the daughter of an Urbino merchant. She had three children besides the great painter, all of whom died young, and when Raphael was but eight years old his mother died also. It is said that it was from her Raphael inherited his beauty, goodness, mildness, and genius. His father's patron, the Duke of Urbino, was a fine soldier, but he also cherished scholarship and art, and kept at his court not less than twenty or thirty persons at work copying Greek and Latin manuscript which he wished to add to his library.

Raphael had a stepmother, Bernardina, the daughter of a goldsmith, a good and forceful woman, but not gentle like the first wife; and when Raphael was eleven years of age his father, too, died. By his father's will Raphael became the charge of his uncle

Bartolommeo, a priest, but the property was left to the stepmother so long as she remained unmarried. Almost at once the priest and the stepmother fell to quarreling over the spoils, and thus Raphael was left pretty much to his own devices, but just when life began to look dark and sad for him, his mother's brother took a hand in the situation. He settled the dispute between the priest and the second wife, and arranged that Raphael should be placed in the studio of some great painter, for the loving lad had already worked in his father's studio, and had given promise of his wonderful gifts. So he became the pupil of Perugino, a painter noted for his fine colouring and sympathetic handling of his subjects. At that time, Italian schools were less wonderful in colouring than in other matters of technique.

"Let him become my pupil," said Perugino, when Raphael was brought to him and some of his work was exhibited; "soon he will be my master." A very different attitude from that of Ghirlandajo toward Michael Angelo.

Raphael and his master became friends and worked together for nine years.

His first work was not conceived until Raphael was seventeen. It was to be a surprise to his master who had gone to Florence. A banner was wanted for the Church of S. Trinita at Citta di Castello, and Raphael undertook it, painting the "Trinity," on one canvas and the "Creation of Man" on another. Then he painted the "Crucifixion," which was bought by Cardinal Fesch, who lived in Rome. That painting is now in a collection of the Earl of Dudley. It was sold away from Rome in 1845, for twelve thousand dollars--or a little more. No one will deny that this is an unusual sum for an artist's first work, but about the same time he did a much more wonderful thing.

He painted a little picture, six and three-quarter inches square. It was of the Virgin walking in the springtime, before the leaves had appeared upon the trees, and with snow-capped mountains behind her. She holds the infant Jesus in her arms while she reads from a small book, and the little child looks upon the page with her. This six inches of beauty sold to the Emperor of Russia, in 1871, for sixty thousand dollars.

Before Raphael was twenty-one, he had left his master's studio and had gone into the splendid world of Rome, where Angelo was straining at his bonds. But how differently each accepted his life! The gentle Raphael, who took the best of the ideas of all great painters, and gave to them his own exquisite characteristics, was beloved of all, shed light upon art and friends alike. To such a one all life was joyous. Michael Angelo, trying ever to do the impossible, betraying his hatred of limitations in all that he did, doing always that which aroused horror, distress, longing, elemental feelings, in those who studied his wonderful work, and giving hope and satisfaction and peace to none-- to such as he life must ever have been hateful and painful. These men lived at the same time, among the same people.

One of Raphael's greatest pictures came into the possession of a poor widow, who being hard pressed by poverty, sold it to a bookseller for twelve scudi. In time it was bought from the bookseller by Grand Duke Ferdinand III. of Tuscany, who prayed before it night and morning, taking it with him on his travels. That picture is now in the Pitti Palace at Florence and it is called the "Madonna del Granduca." The Berlin Museum purchased a Raphael Madonna for $34,000 which was painted about the same time as these others, but after a little the artist left Florence where he had been studying the methods of Leonardo and Angelo and returned to Urbino, the home he loved, where his conduct was such that all the world seems to have become his lover. It is written that he was "the only very distinguished man of whom we read, who lived and died without an enemy or detractor!" No better can ever be said of any one.

While he dwelt in Perugia and Urbino he had painted the "Ansidei Madonna," so called because that was the name of the family for which it was painted. That Madonna was sold in 1884 to the National Gallery, by the Duke of Marlborough for $350,000. A Madonna on a round plaque-like canvas, 42-3/4 inches in diameter, was bought by the Duke of Bridgewater for $60,000. It is the "Holy Family under a Palm Tree," painted originally for a friend, Taddeo Taddei, who was a Florentine scholar. Many of the pictures which after many vicissitudes have landed far from home and been bought for fabulous sums were painted for love of some friend, or were paid for by modest sums at the time the artist received the commissions. Lord Ellesmere in London now owns the "Holy Family under a Palm Tree."

It is said of Raphael that whenever another painter, known to him or not, requested any design or assistance of any kind at his hands, he would invariably leave his work to perform the service. He continually kept a large number of artists employed, all of whom he assisted and instructed with an affection which was rather that of a father to his children than merely of an artist to artists. From this it followed that he was never seen to go to court, except surrounded and accompanied, as he left his house, by some fifty painters, all men of ability and distinction, who attended him, thus to give evidence of the honour in which they held him. He did not, in short, live the life of a painter, but that of a prince.

There is something wonderfully inspiring about such a life. We read of emperors and the homage paid to them; of the esteem in which men who accomplish deeds of universal value are held, but nowhere do we behold the power of a beautiful and exquisite personality and character, allied with a single art, so impressively exhibited.

He urged nothing, yet won all things by the force of his loving and sympathetic mind. "How is it, dear Cesare that we live in such good friendship, but that in the art of painting we show no deference to each other?" he asked of Cesare da Sesto, who was Da Vinci's greatest pupil.

In discussing the great ones of the earth, Herman Grimm, son of the collector of fairy tales, says: "Can we mention a violent act of Raphael's, Goethe's or Shakespeare's? No, it is restful only to recall these wonderful men."

One of Raphael's most beautiful Virgins was modeled from a beautiful flower-girl whom he loved, "La Belle Jardinière."

Raphael as well as Michael Angelo was summoned by Pope Julius II., but how different were the two occasions! Michael Angelo had stood with dogged, gloomy self-assertiveness before the pope, head covered, knee unbent. Uncompromising, while yet no injury had been done him, resentful before he had received a single cause for resentment, the attitude was typical of his art and his unhappy life.

When Raphael appeared, his bent knee, his "chestnut locks falling upon his shoulders, the pope exclaimed: ' He is an innocent angel. I will give him Cardinal Bembo for a teacher, and he shall fill my walls with historical pictures.'" The artist's behaviour was no sign of servility, but the simple recognition of forms and customs which the people themselves had made and by which they had decided they should graciously be bound. The attitude of Angelo was not heroic but vulgar; that of Raphael not servile, but in good taste, showing a reasonable mind.

Pope Julius had summoned Raphael for a special reason. Alexander VI., his predecessor in the Vatican, had been a depraved man. The fair and virile Julius had a healthy sentiment against occupying rooms which must continually remind him of the notorious Alexander's mode of life. Some one suggested that he have all the portraits of the former pope removed, but Julius declared: "Even if the portraits were destroyed, the walls themselves would remind me of that Simoniac, that Jew!" The word 'Jew' was then execrated by all Christians, for the world was not yet Christian enough to know better.

Raphael was summoned to decorate the Vatican, that Julius might have a place which reminded him not at all of Alexander. It is said that when Raphael had completed one of his masterpieces the pope threw himself upon the ground and cried, "I thank Thee, God, that Thou hast sent me so great a painter!"

While at work upon his first fresco at the Vatican--"La Disputa," the dispute over the Holy Sacrament--Raphael met a woman with whom he fell deeply in love. Her father was a soda manufacturer and her name was Margherita. Missirini relates this incident in Raphael's career.

"She lived on the other side of the Tiber. A small house, No. 20, in the street of Santa Dorothea, the windows of which are decorated with a pretty frame work of earthenware, is pointed out as the house where she was born.

"The beautiful girl was very frequently in a little garden adjoining the house, where, the wall not being very high, it was easy to see her from the outside. So the young men, especially artists--always passionate admirers of beauty--did not fail to come and look at her, by climbing up above the wall.

"Raphael is said to have seen her for the first time as she was bathing her pretty feet in a little fountain in the garden. Struck by her perfect beauty, he fell deeply in love with her, and after having made acquaintance with her, and discovered that her mind was as beautiful as her body, he became so much attached as to be unable to live without her."

She is spoken of to-day as the "Fornarina," because at first she was supposed to have been the daughter of a baker (*fornajo*).

Raphael made many rough studies for his picture "La Disputa," and upon them he left three sonnets, written to the woman so dear to him. These sonnets have been translated by the librarian of l'Ecole Nationale des Beaux-Arts, as follows: "Love, thou hast bound me with the light of two eyes which torment me, with a face like snow and roses, with sweet words and tender manners. So great is my ardour that no river or sea could extinguish my fire. But I do not complain, for my ardour makes me happy.... How sweet was the chain, how light the yoke of her white arms about my neck. When these bonds were loosed, I felt a mortal grief. I will say no more; a great joy kills, and, though my thoughts turn to thee, I will keep silence."

Although he had been a man of many loves, Raphael must have found in the manufacturer's daughter his best love, because he remained faithful and devoted to her for the twelve years of life that were left to him. It was said some years later, while he was engaged upon a commission for a rich banker, that "Raphael was so much occupied with the love that he bore to the lady of his choice that he could not give sufficient attention to his work. Agostino (the banker) therefore, falling at length into despair of seeing it finished, made so many efforts by means of friends and by his own care that after much difficulty he at length prevailed on the lady to take up her abode in his house, where she was accordingly installed, in apartments near those which Raphael was painting; In this manner the work was ultimately brought to a conclusion."

Raphael painted this beautiful lady-love many times, and in a picture in which she wears a bracelet he has placed his name upon the ornament.

After this time he painted the "Madonna della Casa d'Alba," which the Duchess d'Alba gave to her physician for curing her of a grave disorder. She died soon afterward, and the physician was arrested on the charge of having poisoned her. In course of time the picture was purchased for $70,000 by the Russian Emperor, and it is now in "The Hermitage," St. Petersburg.

A writer telling of that time, relates the following anecdote: "Raphael of Urbino had painted for Agostino Chigi (the rich banker already mentioned) at Santa Maria della Pace, some prophets and sibyls, on which he had received an advance of five hundred scudi. One day he demanded of Agostino's cashier (Giulio Borghesi) the remainder of the sum at which he estimated his work. The cashier, being astounded at this demand, and thinking that the sum already paid was sufficient, did not reply. 'Cause the work to be estimated by a judge of painting,' replied Raphael, 'and you will see how moderate my demand is.'

"Giulio Borghesi thought of Michael Angelo for this valuation, and begged him to go to the church and estimate the figures of Raphael. Possibly he imagined that self-love, rivalry, and jealousy would lead the Florentine to lower the price of the pictures.

"Michael Angelo went, accompanied by the cashier, to Santa Maria della Pace, and, as he was contemplating the fresco without uttering a word, Borghesi questioned him. 'That head,' replied Michael Angelo, pointing to one of the sibyls, 'that head is worth a hundred scudi.' ... 'and the others?' asked the cashier. 'The others are not less.'

"Someone who witnessed this scene related it to Chigi. He heard every particular and, offering in addition to the five hundred scudi for five heads a hundred scudi to be paid for each of the others, he said to his cashier, 'go and give that to Raphael in payment for his heads, and behave very politely to him, so that he may be satisfied; for if he insists on my paying also for the drapery, we should probably be ruined!'"

By the time Raphael was thirty-one he was a rich man, and had built himself a beautiful house near the Vatican, on the Via di Borgo Nuova. Naught remains of that dwelling except an angle of the right basement, which has been made a part of the Accoramboni Palace. His friends wished him above all things to marry, but he was still true to Margherita though he had become engaged to the daughter of his nephew. He put the marriage off year after year, till finally the lady he was to have married died, and was buried in Raphael's chapel in the Pantheon.

Margherita was with him when he died, and it was to her that he left much of his wealth.

In the time of Raphael excavations were being made about Rome, and many beautiful statues uncovered, and he was charged with the supervision of this work in order that no art treasure should be lost or overlooked. The pope decreed that if the excavators failed to acquaint Raphael with every stone and tablet that should he unearthed, they should be fined from one to three hundred gold crowns.

Raphael had his many paintings copied under his own eye and engraved, and then distributed broadcast, so that not only men of great wealth but the common people might study them.

Henry VIII. invited him to visit England, and become court painter, and Francis I. wished him to become the court painter of France.

He loved history, and wished to write certain historical works. He loved poetry and wrote it. He loved philosophy and lived it--the philosophy of generous feeling and kindly thought for all the world. He kept poor artists in his own home and provided for them.

Raphael died on Good Friday night, April 6th, in his thirty-seventh year, and all Rome wept. He lay in state in his beautiful home, with his unfinished picture of the "Transfiguration," as background for his catafalque. That painting with its colours still wet, was carried in the procession to his burial place in the Pantheon. When his death was announced, the pope, Leo X., wept and cried *"Ora pro nobis!"* while the Ambassador from Mantua wrote home that "nothing is talked of here but the loss of the man who at the close of his six-and-thirtieth year has now ended his first life; his second, that of his posthumous fame, independent of death and transitory things, through his works, and in what the learned will write in his praise, must continue forever."

Raphael painted two hundred and eighty-seven pictures in his thirty-seven years of life.

PLATE--THE SISTINE MADONNA

It is said that the "Sistine Madonna," while painted from an Italian model-- doubtless the lady whom Raphael so dearly loved--has universal characteristics, so that she may "be understood by everyone."

He lived only three years after painting this picture and it was the last "Holy Family" painted by him. The Madonna stands upon a curve of the earth, which is scarcely to be seen, and looming mistily in front of her is a mass of white vaporous clouds. On either side are figures, St. Sixtus (for whom the picture was named) and St. Barbara. Beside St. Sixtus we see a crown or tiara; and the little tower at St. Barbara's side is a part of her story.

Barbara was the daughter of an Eastern nobleman who feared that her great beauty might lead to her being carried off; therefore he caused her to be shut up in a great tower. While thus imprisoned Barbara became a Christian through the influence of a holy man, and she begged her father to make three windows in her gloomy tower: one, to let the light of the Father stream upon her, another to admit the light of the Son, and the third that she might bathe in the light of the Holy Ghost. Both St. Barbara and St. Sixtus were martyrs for their faith.

This Madonna is painted as if enclosed by green velvet curtains, which have been drawn aside, letting the golden light of the picture blaze upon the one who looks; then upon a little ledge below, looking out from the heavens, are two little cherubs--known to all the world. They look wistful, wise, roguish, and beautiful, with fat little arms resting comfortably upon the ledge. Raphael is said to have found his models for these little angels in the street, leaning wistfully upon the ledge of a baker's window, looking at the good things to eat, which were within. Raphael took them, put wings to them, placed them at the feet of Mary, and made two little images which have brought smiles and tears to a multitude of people. The "Sistine Madonna" hangs alone in a room in the Dresden Gallery.

Among Raphael's greatest works are: The "Madonna della Sedia" (of the chair), "La Belle Jardinière," "The School of Athens," "Saint Cecilia," "The Transfiguration," "Death of Ananias" (a cartoon for a series of tapestries), "Madonna del Pesce," "La Disputa," "The Marriage of Mary and Joseph," "St. George Slaying the Dragon," "St. Michael Attacking Satan" and the "Coronation of the Virgin."

XXXIII REMBRANDT (VAN RIJN)

Dutch School

1606-1669
Pupil of Van Swanenburch

Here are a few of the titles that have been given to the greatest Dutch painter that ever lived: The Shakespeare of Painting; the Prince of Etchers; the King of Shadows; the Painter of Painters. Muther calls him a "hero from cloudland," and not only does he alone wear these titles of greatness, but he alone in his family had the name of Rembrandt.

One writer has said that the great painter was born "in a windmill," but this is not true. He was born in Leyden for certain, though not a great deal is known about his youth; and his father was a miller, his mother a baker's daughter.

When the Pilgrim Fathers, who had sought safety in Leyden, were starting for America, where they were going to oppress others as they had been oppressed, Rembrandt was just beginning his apprenticeship in art.

He was born at No. 3, Weddesteg, a house on the rampart looking out upon the Rhine whose two arms meet there. In front of it whirled the great arms of his father's windmill, though he was not born in it; and of all the women Rembrandt ever knew, it is not likely that he ever admired or loved one as passionately as he admired and loved his mother. He painted and etched her again and again, with a touch so tender that his deepest emotion is placed before us.

Rembrandt had brothers and sisters--five: Adriaen, Gerrit, Machteld, Cornelis, and Willem. Of these, Adriaen became a miller like his father, and presumably the old historic windmill fell to him; Willem became a baker, but Rembrandt, the fourth child, it was determined should be a learned man, and belong to one of the honoured professions, such as the law. So he was sent to the Leyden Academy, but here again we have an artist who decided he knew enough of all else but art before he was twelve years old. He found himself at that age in the studio of his first art-master, Jacob van Swanenburch, a relative, who had studied art in Italy, and was a good master for the lad; but Rembrandt became so brilliant a painter in three years' time, that he was sent to Amsterdam to learn of abler men.

The lad could not in those days get far from his adored mother; so he stayed only a little time, before he went back to Leyden where she was. There was his heart, and, painting or no painting, he must be near it.

Until the past thirty years no one has seemed to know a great deal of Rembrandt's early history, but much was written of him as a boorish, gross, vulgar fellow. Those stories were false. He was a devoted son, handsome, studious in art, and earnest in all that he did, and after he had made his first notable painting he was compelled by the demands of his work to move to Amsterdam for good. He hired an apartment over a shop on the Quay Bloemgracht; it is probable that his sister went with him to keep his house, and that it is her face repeated so frequently in the many pictures which he painted at that time. This does not suggest coarse doings or a careless life, but permits us to imagine a quiet, sober, unselfish existence for the young bachelor at that time.

Soon, however, he fell in love. He saw one other woman to place in his heart and memory beside his mother. His wife was Saskia van Ulenburg, the daughter of an aristocrat, refined and rich. He met her through her cousin, an art dealer, who had ordered Rembrandt to paint a portrait of his dainty cousin. Rembrandt could have been nothing but what was delightful and good, since he was loved by so charming a girl as Saskia.

He painted her sitting upon his knee, and used her as model in many pictures. First, last, and always he loved her tenderly.

In one portrait she is dressed in "red and gold-embroidered velvets"; the mantle she wore he had brought from Leyden. In another picture she is at her toilet, having her hair arranged; again she is painted in a great red velvet hat, and then as a Jewish bride, wearing pearls, and holding a shepherd's staff in her hand. Again, Rembrandt painted himself as a giant at the feet of a dainty woman, and in every way his work showed his love for her. After he married her, in June 1634, he painted the picture, "Samson's Wedding," "Saskia, dainty and serene, sitting like a princess in a circle of her relatives, he himself appearing as a crude plebeian, whose strange jokes frighten more than they amuse the distinguished company. ... The early years of his marriage were spent in joy and revelry. Surrounded by calculating business men who kept a tight grasp on their money bags, he assumed the rôle of an artist scattering money with a free hand; surrounded by small townsmen most proper in demeanour, he revealed himself as the bold lasquenet, frightening them by his cavalier manners. He brought together all manner of Oriental arms, ancient fabrics, and gleaming jewellery; and his house became one of the sights of Amsterdam." His existence reads like a fairy tale.

It is said that Saskia strutted about decked in gold and diamonds, till her relatives "shook their heads" in alarm and amazement at such wild goings on.

Before he married Saskia he had painted a remarkable picture, named the "School of Anatomy." It represents a great anatomist, the friend of Rembrandt--Nicholaus Tulp,--and a group of physicians who were members of the Guild of Surgeons of Amsterdam. It is so wonderful a picture that even the dead man, who is being used as a subject by the anatomist, does not too greatly disturb us as we look upon him. The thoughtful, interested faces of the surgeons are so strong that we half lose ourselves in their feeling, and forget to start in repulsion at sight of the dead body. A fine description of this painting can be found in Sarah K. Bolton's book "Famous Artists" and it includes the description given by another excellent authority.

The artist was twenty-six years old when he painted the "School of Anatomy." This picture is now at The Hague and two hundred years after it was painted the Dutch Government gave 30,000 florins for it.

Rembrandt painted a good many "Samsons" first and last--himself evidently being the strong man; and the pictures beyond doubt express his own mood and his idea of his relation to things. After a little son was born to the artist, he painted still another Samson--this time menacing his father-in-law but as the artist had named his son after his father-in-law,--Rombertus--we cannot believe that there was any menace in the heart of Rembrandt--Samson. Soon his son died, and Rembrandt thought he should never again know happiness, or that the world could hold a greater grief, but one day he was to learn otherwise. A little girl was born to the artist, named Cornelia, after Rembrandt's mother, and he was again very happy.

Meantime his brothers and sisters had died, and there came some trouble over Rembrandt's inheritance, but what angered him most of all, was that Saskia's relatives said she "had squandered her heritage in ornaments and ostentation." This made Rembrandt wild with rage, and he sued her slanderers, for he himself had done the squandering, buying every beautiful thing he could find or pay for, to deck Saskia in, and he meant to go on doing so.

At this time he painted a picture of "The Feast of Ahasuerus" (or the "Wedding of Samson") and he placed Saskia in the middle of the table to represent Esther or Delilah as the case might be, dressed in a way to horrify her critical relatives, for she looked like a veritable princess laden with gorgeous jewels.

One of his pictures he wished to have hung in a strong light, for he said: "Pictures are not made to be smelt. The odour of the colours is unhealthy."

The first baby girl died and on the birth of another daughter she too was named Cornelia, but that baby girl also died, and next came a son, Titus, named for Saskia's sister, Titia, and then Saskia died. Thus Rembrandt knew the deepest sorrow of his life.

He painted her portrait once again from memory, and that picture is quite unlike the others for it is no longer full of glowing life, but daintier, suggestive of a more spiritual life, as if she were growing fragile.

It is written that "from this time, while he did much remarkable work, he seemed like a man on a mountain top, looking on one side to sweet meadows filled with flowers and sunlight, and on the other to a desolate landscape over which a clouded sun is setting." With Saskia died the best of Rembrandt. He made only one more portrait of himself--before this he had made many; and in it he makes himself appear a stern and fateful man. It was after Saskia's death that he painted the "Night Watch," or more properly, "The Sortie."

Rembrandt's home, where he and Saskia were so happy, is still to be seen on a quay of the River Amstel. It is a house of brick and cut stone, four stories high. The vestibule used to have a flag-stone pavement covered with fir-wood. There were also "black-cushioned, Spanish chairs for those who wait," and all about were twenty-four busts and paintings. There was an ante-chamber, very large, with seven Spanish chairs covered with green velvet, and a walnut table covered with "a Tournay cloth"; there was a mirror with an ebony frame, and near by a marble wine-cooler. Upon the wall of this *salon* were thirty-nine pictures and most of them had beautiful frames. "There were religious scenes, landscapes, architectural sketches, works of Pinas, Brouwer, Lucas van Leyden, and other Dutch masters; sixteen pictures by Rembrandt; and costly paintings by Palma Vecchio, Bassano, and Raphael."

In the next room was a real art museum, containing splendid pictures, an oaken press and other things which suggest that this was the workroom where Rembrandt's etchings were made and printed.

In the drawing-room was a huge mirror, a great oaken table covered with a rich embroidered cloth, "six chairs with blue coverings, a bed with blue hangings, a cedar wardrobe, and a chest of the same wood." The walls were literally covered with pictures, among which was a Raphael.

Above was a sort of museum and Rembrandt's studio. There was rare glass from Venice, busts, sketches, paintings, cloths, weapons, armour, plants, stuffed birds and shells, fans, and books and globes. In short, this was a most wonderful house and no other interior can we reconstruct as we can this, because no other such detailed inventory can be found of a great man's effects as that from which these notes are taken: a legal inventory made in 1656, long after Saskia had died and possibly at a time when Rembrandt wished to close his doors forever and forget the scenes in which he had been so happy.

Holland being truly a Protestant country, its artists have given us no great Madonna pictures, although they painted loving, happy Dutch mothers and little babes, but on the whole their subjects are quite different from those of the painters of Italy, France, and Spain.

Rembrandt's studio was different from any other. When he first began to work independently and to have pupils, he fitted it up with many little cells, properly lighted, so that each student might work alone, as he knew far better work could be done in that way. It is said that his pictures of beggars would, by themselves, fill a gallery. He had a kindly sympathy for the poor and unfortunate, and tramps knew this, so that they swarmed about his studio doors, trying to get sittings.

There is a story which doubtless had for its germ a joke regarding the slowness of an errand boy in a friend's household, but which at the same time shows us how rapidly Rembrandt worked. The artist had been carried off to the country to lunch with his friend Jan Six, and as they sat down at the table, Six discovered there was no mustard. He sent his boy, Hans, for it, and as the boy went out, Rembrandt wagered that he could make an etching before the boy got back. Six took the wager, and the artist pulled a copper plate from his pocket--he always carried one--and on its waxed surface began to etch the landscape before him. Just as Hans returned, Rembrandt gleefully handed Six the completed picture.

He was a great portrait painter, but he loved certain effects of shadow so well that he often sacrificed his subject's good looks to his artistic purpose, and very naturally his sitters became displeased, so that in time he had fewer commissions than if he had been entirely accommodating.

His meals in working time were very simple, often just bread and cheese, eaten while sitting at his easel, and after Saskia died he became more and more careless of all domestic details.

Rembrandt finally married again, the second time choosing his housekeeper, a good and helpful woman, who was properly bringing up his little son, and making life better ordered for the artist, but he had grown poor by this time for he was never a very good business man. His beautiful house was at last sold to a rich shoemaker. Every picture latterly reflected his condition and mood. He chose subjects in which he imagined himself always to be the actor, and when his second wife died he painted a picture of "Youth Surprised by Death"; he had not long to live. He became more and more melancholy; and sleeping by day, would wander about the country at night, disconsolate and sad. Finally, when he died, an inventory of his effects, showed him to be possessed of only a few old woollen clothes and his brushes The miracle in Rembrandt's painting is the deep, impenetrable shadow, in which nevertheless one can see form and outline, punctuated with wonderful explosions of light. Nothing like it has ever been seen. It is the most dramatic work in the world, and the most powerful in its effect. Other men have painted light and colour; Rembrandt makes gloom and shadow living things.

This miracle-worker's funeral cost ten dollars; he died in Amsterdam and was buried in the Wester Kirk.

PLATE--THE SORTIE

This picture is generally known as "The Night Watch," but it is really "The Sortie" of a company of musketeers under the command of a standard bearer. Captain Frans Banning-Cock and all his company were to pay Rembrandt for painting their portraits in a group and in action, and they expected to see themselves in heroic and picturesque dress, in the full blaze of day, but Rembrandt had found a magnificent subject for his wonderful shadows, and the artist was not going to sacrifice it to the vanity of the archers.

This picture was called the "Patrouille de Nuit," by the French and the "Night Watch," by Sir Joshua Reynolds because upon its discovery the picture was so dimmed and defaced by time that it was almost indistinguishable and it looked quite like a night scene. After it was cleaned up, it was discovered to represent broad day--a party of archers stepping from a gloomy courtyard into the blinding sunlight. "How this different light is painted, which encircles the figures, here sunny, there gloomy!... Rembrandt runs through the entire range of his colours, from the lightest yellow through all shades of light and dark red to the gloomiest black." One writer describes it thus: "It is more than a picture; it is a spectacle, and an amazing one... A great crowd of human figures, a great light, a great darkness--at the first glance this is what strikes you, and for a moment you know not where to fix your eyes in order to comprehend that grand and splendid confusion... There are officers, halberdiers, boys running, arquebusiers loading and firing, youths beating drums, people bowing talking, calling out, gesticulating--all dressed in different costumes, with round hats, plumes, casques, morions, iron corgets, linen collars, doublets embroidered with gold, great boots, stockings of all colours, arms of every form; and all this tumultuous and glittering throng start out from the dark background of the picture and advance toward the spectator. The two first personages are Frans Banning-Cock, Lord of Furmerland and Ilpendam, captain of the company, and his lieutenant, Willem van Ruijtenberg, Lord of Vlaardingen, the two marching side by side. The only figures that are in full light are this lieutenant, dressed in a doublet of buffalo-hide, with gold ornaments, scarf, gorget, and white plume, with high boots, and a girl who comes behind, with blond hair ornamented with pearls, and a yellow satin dress; all the other figures are in deep shadow, excepting the heads, which are illuminated. By what light? Here is the enigma. Is it the light of the sun? or of the moon? or of the torches? There are gleams of gold and silver, moonlight coloured reflections, fiery lights; personages which, like the girl with blond tresses, seem to shine by a light of their own.... The more you look at it, the more it is alive and glowing; and, even seen only at a glance, it remains forever in the memory, with all its mystery and splendour, like a stupendous vision." Charles Blanc has said: "To tell the truth, this is only a dream of night, and no one can decide what the light is that falls on the groups of figures. It is neither the light of the sun or of the moon, nor does it come from the torches; it is rather the light from the genius of Rembrandt."

This wonderful picture was painted in 1642 and many of the archer's guild who gave Rembrandt the commission would not pay their share because their faces were not plainly seen. This picture which alone was enough to make him immortal, was the very last commission that any of the guilds were willing to give the artist, because he would not make their portraits beautiful or fine looking to the disadvantage of the whole picture. This work hangs in the Rijks Museum in Amsterdam. He painted more than six hundred and twenty-five pictures and some of them are: "The Anatomy Lesson," "The Syndics of the Cloth Hall," "The Descent from the Cross," "Samson Threatening His Step Father," "The Money Changer," "Holy Family," "The Presentation of Christ in the Temple," "The Marriage of Samson," "The Rape of Ganymede," "Susanna and the Elders," "Manoah's Sacrifice," "The Storm," "The Good Samaritan," "Pilate Washing His Hands," "Ecce Home," and pictures of his wife, Saskia.

XXXIV SIR JOSHUA REYNOLDS

English School

1723-1792

Pupil of Thomas Hudson

When Reynolds was "little Josh," instead of "Sir Joshua" he grew tired in church one day, and sketched upon the nail of his thumb the portrait of the Rev. Mr. Smart who was preaching. After service he ran to a boat-house near, and with ship's paint, upon an old piece of sail, he painted in full and flowing colours that reverend gentleman's portrait. After that there was not the least possible excuse for his father to deny him the right to become an artist.

The father himself was a clergyman with a good education, and he had meant that his son should also be well educated and become a physician; but a lad who at eight years of age can draw the Plympton school house--he was born at Plympton Earl, in Devonshire--has a right to choose his own profession.

At twenty-three years of age Sir Joshua was painting the portraits of great folk, and being well paid for it, as well as lavishly praised. His first real sorrow came at a Christmas time when he was summoned home from London where he was working, to his father's deathbed.

After that the artist turned his thoughts toward Italy, but where was the money to come from? Earning a living did not include travelling expenses, but a good friend, Captain Keppel, was going out to treat with the Dey of Algiers about his piracies, and learning that the artist wished to go to Italy he invited him to go with him on his own ship, the *Centurion*. So while the captain was discussing pirates with the dey, Sir Joshua stopped with the Governor of Minorca and painted many of the people of that locality. Thence on to Rome!

Strange to say, Raphael's pictures disappointed the English artist, and he said so; but Michael Angelo was to Reynolds the most wonderful of painters, and he said that his pictures influenced him all the rest of his life. He wished his name to be the last upon his lips, and while that was not so, yet it was the last he pronounced to his fellow Academicians in his final address.

It was in Italy that a distressing misfortune came upon Sir Joshua. He meant to learn all that a man could learn in a given time of the art treasures there, and while he was working in a draughty corridor of the Vatican, he caught a severe cold which rendered him deaf. He continued deaf till the end of his life and had to use an ear-trumpet when people talked with him.

When he got back to England, Hudson, his old master, said discouragingly: "Reynolds, you don't paint as well as when you left England." On the whole his reception at home, after his long absence, was not all that he could have wished, but he took a place in Leicester Square, settled down to live there for the rest of his life, and went at painting in earnest.

Although artists criticised him more or less after his return, the public appreciated him and very soon orders for portraits began to pour in upon him, and the flow of wealth never ceased so long as he lived. It was said that all the fashionables came to him that did not go to Gainsborough, but those who were partial to Sir Joshua declared that all who could not go to him went to Gainsborough. The two great artists controlled the art world in their time, dividing honours about equally. It was said that all those women and men sat to Sir Joshua for portraits "who wished to be transmitted as angels... and who wished to appear as heroes or philosophers."

Sir Joshua was a charming man, generous in feeling--as Gainsborough was not--and his closest friend was Dr. Johnson, the most different man from the artist imaginable, but Reynolds's art and Johnson's philosophy made a fine combination, each giving the other great pleasure. Besides Johnson, his friends were Goldsmith, Garrick, Bishop Percy, and other famous men of the time. These and others formed the "Literary Club" at Sir Joshua's suggestion. About that time there was the first public exhibition of the work of English artists, and Sir Benjamin West and Sir Joshua Reynolds built the Royal Academy for that first exhibition, with the help of King George's patronage. Joshua Reynolds was knighted when he was made the first president of that great body.

Soon after the Academy was established, Reynolds began a series of "discourses," which in time became famous for their splendid literary quality, and some people, knowing his close friendship with Burke and Dr. Johnson, declared that the artist got one of them to write his "discourses" for him. This threw Johnson and Burke into a fury of resentment for their friend, and the doctor declared indignantly that "Sir Joshua would as soon get me to paint for him as to write for him!" Burke denied the story no less emphatically. Besides these speeches, which were a great advantage to the members of the Academy, Sir Joshua instituted the annual banquet to the members, and King George--who just before had given the commission of court painter to one less talented than Sir Joshua--bade him paint his portrait and the queen's, to hang in the Academy. This was a great thing for the new society and advanced its fortunes very much.

Barry and Gainsborough were both churlish enough to envy Sir Joshua and to quarrel with his good feeling for them, but both men had the grace to be sorry for behaviour that had no excuse, and both made friends with him before they died-- Gainsborough on his death-bed.

Toward his last days the artist was attacked with paralysis, but grew better and was able to paint again; then he began to go blind--he was already deaf--and this affliction made painting impossible. Shortly before his death, he undertook to raise funds for a monument to his dead friend, Dr. Johnson, but he grew more and more ill, "and on the 23d February, 1792, this great artist and blameless gentleman passed peacefully away."

That he was very painstaking in his work is shown by an anecdote about his infant "Hercules." "How did you paint that part of the picture?" some one asked him. "How can I tell! There are ten pictures below this, some better, some worse"--showing that in his desire for perfection he painted and repainted.

So untiring was he in seeking out the secrets of the old masters that he bought works of Titian and Rubens, and scraped them, to learn their methods, insisting that they had some secret underlying their work. So anxious was he to get the most brilliant effects of colours that he mixed his paints with asphaltum, egg, varnish, wax, and the like, till one artist said: "The wonder is that the picture did not crack beneath the brush." Many of these great pictures did go to pieces because of the chances Sir Joshua took in mixing things that did not belong together, in order to make wonderful results.

Sir George Beaumont recommended a friend to go to Reynolds for his portrait and the friend demurred, because "his colours fade and his pictures die before the man."

"Never mind that!" Sir George declared; "a faded portrait by Reynolds is better than a fresh one by anybody else."

The same tender, sensitive and devoted nature which caused Sir Joshua's mother to weep herself blind upon her husband's death, belonged to the artist. All of his life he was surrounded by loving friends, and his devotion to them was conspicuous. He, like Dürer and several other painters, was a seventh son, and his father's disappointment was keen when he took to art instead of to medicine. So little did his father realise what his future might be, that he wrote under the sketch of a wall with a window in it, drawn upon a Latin exercise book: "This is drawn by Joshua in school, out of pure idleness."

But by the time Joshua was eight years old and had drawn a fine "sketch of the grammar-school with its cloister... the astonished father said: 'Now, this exemplifies what the author of "perspective" says in his preface: "that, by observing the rules laid down in this book, a man may do wonders"--for this is wonderful.'"

Sir Joshua laid down--even wrote out--a great many rules of conduct for himself. Some of these were: "The great principle of being happy in this world is not to mind or be affected with small things." Also: "If you take too much care of yourself, nature will cease to take care of you."

When Samuel Reynolds, Joshua's father, consulted with his friend Mr. Craunch, as to whether a boy who made wonderful paintings at twelve years of age, would be likely to be a successful apothecary, he told Craunch that Joshua himself had declared that he would rather be a good apothecary than a poor artist, but if he could be bound to a good master of painting he would prefer that above everything in the world. This was how he came to be apprenticed to Hudson, the painter. Young Reynolds's sister paid for his instruction at first--or for half of it, with the understanding that Reynolds was to pay her back when he was earning. At that time Reynolds wrote to his father: "While I am doing this I am the happiest creature alive."

One day, while in an art store, buying something for Hudson, Reynolds saw Alexander Pope, the poet, come in, and every one bowed to him and made way for him as if for a prince. Pope shook hands with young Reynolds, and in writing home, describing the poet, the artist said that he was "about four feet six inches high; very humpbacked and deformed. He wore a black coat and according to the fashion of that time, had on a little sword. He had a large and very fine eye, and a long handsome nose; his mouth had those peculiar marks which are always found in the mouths of crooked persons, and the muscles which run across the cheeks were so strongly marked that they seemed like small cords." This is a masterly description of one famous man by another.

He finally was dismissed from his master's studio on the ground that he had neglected to carry a picture to its owner at the time set by Hudson, but the fact was the older artist had become jealous of the work of his pupil, and would no longer have him in his studio.

Afterwards, while he was painting down in Devonshire--thirty portraits of country squires for fifteen dollars apiece--he said: "Those who are determined to excel must go to their work whether willing or unwilling, morning, noon, and night, and they will find it to be no play, but, on the contrary, very hard labour." This shows that Reynolds's idea of genius was "an infinite capacity for hard work."

While Reynolds was on his memorable journey to Rome, he made several volumes of notes about the pictures of great Italian artists--Raphael, Titian, etc. And one of those volumes is in the Lenox Library, New York City. He made a most characteristic and delightful remark in regard to his disappointment in Raphael's pictures. "I did not for a moment conceive or suppose that the name of Raphael, and those admirable paintings in particular, owed their reputation to the *ignorance* ... of mankind; on the contrary, my not relishing them, as I was conscious I ought to have done was one of the most humiliating things that ever happened to me."

He loved home and country so much that while in Venice he heard a familiar ballad sung in an opera, and it brought the tears to his eyes because of its association with "home."

His young sister, was so undecided in her ways and opinions as to make it impossible for Reynolds long to live with her, but she undertook to be his housekeeper when he returned to London, and she also tried to copy his pictures Reynolds said the results "made other people laugh, but they made me cry."

Reynolds painted the portraits of two Irish sisters--the Countess of Coventry and the Duchess of Hamilton--two of the most beautiful women in all the British Empire. "Seven hundred people sat up all night, in and about a Yorkshire inn, to see the Duchess of Hamilton get into her postchaise in the morning, while a Worcester shoemaker made money by showing the shoe he was making for the Countess of Coventry." Sir Joshua declared that whenever a new sitter came to him, even till the last years of his life, he always began his portrait with the determination that that one should be the best he had ever painted. Success was bound to attend that sort of man.

He painted every picture almost as an experiment; meaning to learn something new with every work, and he spent more than he made in perfecting his art. As he said: "He would be content to ruin himself" in order to own one of the best works of Titian.

His deeds of kindness are beyond counting. He rescued his friend Dr. Johnson from debt--thereby saving him from prison; and when a young lad, "a son of Dr. Mudge," who was very anxious to visit his father on the occasion of his sixteenth birthday, grew too ill to make the journey. Reynolds said gaily: "No matter my boy. *I* will send you to your father." He painted a splendid portrait of the boy and sent it to Dr. Mudge. This gift of a picture, however, was very unusual with Reynolds, who, unlike Gainsborough who gave his by the bushel to everyone, declared that his pictures were not valued unless paid for. When Sir William Lowther, a gay and rich young man of London, died, he left twenty-five thousand dollars to each of thirteen friends, and each of the thirteen commissioned the painter to make a portrait of Lowther, their benefactor. His work room was of interest: "The chair for his sitters was raised eighteen inches from the floor, and turned on casters. His palettes were those which are held by a handle, not those held on the thumb. The stocks of his pencils were long, measuring about nineteen inches. He painted in that part of the room nearest to the window, and never sat down when he painted." The chariot in which he drove about had the four seasons allegorically painted upon its panels, and his liveries were "laced with silver"; while the wheels of his coach were carved with foliage and gilded.

Sir Joshua knew that it paid to advertise, and as he had no time to go about in that gorgeous chariot he made his sister go, for he declared that people seeing that magnificent coach would ask: "Whose chariot is that?" and upon being told could not fail to be impressed with his prestige. The comical inconsequence of this anecdote concerning a man so important robs it of vulgarity.

The graceful anecdotes told of Reynolds are without number, but one and all are to his advantage and show him to have been good and gentle, a devoted and high-bred man.

PLATE--THE DUCHESS OF DEVONSHIRE AND HER DAUGHTER

This is generally considered one of the finest of Sir Joshua's pictures, if not the most beautiful of all. He was such a welcome guest at the houses of grandees that perchance he had noticed the lovely duchess playing with her still more lovely baby, and thought what a charming picture the two would make. As a representation of the artist's ability to portray grace and sweetness it can hardly be surpassed. He painted it in 1786, half a dozen years before his death, and it now hangs in Chatsworth, the home of the present Duke of Devonshire.

Other well known Reynolds paintings are "The Hon. Ann Bingham," "The Countess of Spencer," the "Nieces of Sir Horace Walpole," and the "Angels' Heads" in the National Gallery.

XXXV PETER PAUL RUBENS.

Flemish School

1577-1640
Pupil of Tobias Verhaecht

The story of Peter Paul Rubens, whose birthday falling upon the saint days of Peter and Paul gave to him his name, is hardly more interesting than that of his parents, although it is quite different. The story of Rubens's parents seems a part of the artist's story, because it must have had something to do with influencing his life, so let us begin with that.

John Rubens was Peter Paul's father, and he was a learned man, a druggist, but he had also studied law, and had been town councillor and alderman in the town where he was born. Life went easily enough with him till the reformation wrought by Martin Luther began to change John Rubens's way of thinking, and he turned from Catholic to Lutheran.

From being a good Catholic John Rubens became a rabid reformer; and when, under the new faith, the Antwerp churches were stripped of their treasures, the magistrates were called to account for it. John Rubens, as councillor, was among those summoned. The magistrates declared that they were all good Catholics, but a list of the reformers fell into the Duke of Alva's hands and Rubens's name was there. This meant death unless he should succeed in flying from the country, which he instantly did. That was in 1568, when he had four children, but Peter Paul was not one of them--since he was a seventh son.

The Rubens family went to live in Cologne, where the father found his learning of great use to him, and he was honoured by being made legal adviser to Anne of Saxony who was William the Silent's second queen. John Rubens's behaviour was not entirely honourable and before long he was thrown into prison, but his good wife, Maria Pypelincx undertook to free him. He had treated her very badly, but her devotion to his cause was as great as if he had treated her well. Despite his wife's efforts he was kept a prisoner in the dungeon at Dillenburg for two years, and afterward he was removed to Siegen, the place where Peter Paul was born.

In the sixteenth century there were no records of any sort kept in the town of Siegen, and so we cannot be absolutely sure that Peter Paul was born there, but his mother was certainly there just before and after the date of his birth, which was the 29th of June 1577. After his birth, his father was set free in Siegen and allowed to go back to the city in which he had misbehaved himself. In Cologne he became once more a Catholic, and he died in that faith. Meantime, ten years had passed since Peter Paul's birth, and both his father and mother were determined above all things their son should have a fine education, quite unlike other artists, for the boy seemed capable of learning. While he was still very small he could speak to his tutor in French, to his mother in Flemish, and to his father in Latin. Besides these languages he spoke also Italian and English. Before he was an artist, Rubens, like Dürer and Leonardo da Vinci, was a child of rare intelligence. As a little chap he went to Antwerp with his mother--this was after his father's death--and in Belgium he took for the first time the rôle of courtier, in which he was to become so successful later in life. The charming little fellow, dressed in velvet and lace, took his place in the household of the Countess of Lalaing, in Brussels.

Very soon after entering that household, Rubens was permitted by his mother to leave it for the studio of the painter who was his first master, though not the one who really taught him much. Rubens did not stay there long, but went instead to the studio of Adam van Noort, an excellent painter of the time. After that he studied under another artist, who was both a scholar and a gentleman, Van Veen, and with him Peter Paul was able to speak in Latin and in his many other languages, while learning to paint at the same time.

Thus we find Rubens's lot was always cast, not among the rich, but among the intelligent, the well bred, and the cultivated. This fact alone would prepare us to anticipate pleasant things for him and from him.

In those days of guilds, there were many rules and regulations. Van Noort, Rubens's teacher, was dean of the painters' guild and through his influence the guild recognised Rubens as "master," which meant that he was qualified to take pupils; thus he was pupil and teacher at the same time.

One is unable to think of Rubens as having low tastes, as being morose, erratic, or anything but a refined, gracious, and brilliant gentleman. He began well, lived well, and ended well.

None of his teachers really impressed their style of art upon him. He was the model for others. Rubens became nothing but Rubens, but all the art world wished to become "Rubenesque."

Rubens went to Mantua to see the art of Italy, and while there he met the Duke of Mantua who was Vincenzo Gonzaga, the richest, most powerful personage of that region and time. The duke engaged Rubens to paint the portraits of many beautiful women--just the sort of commission that Rubens's pupil, Van Dyck, would have loved; but Rubens's art was of sterner stuff, and the work by no means delighted him. He had great ideas, profound purposes, and wished to undertake them, but just then it seemed best that he perform that which the Duke of Mantua wanted him to do; hence he set about it.

Later Rubens went to the Spanish court, not as a painter, but as a cavalier upon a diplomatic mission. Bearing many beautiful presents to King Philip III., he went to Madrid, where his elegance, manly beauty, dashing manner, and ability to speak several languages made him a wonderful success. He remained for three years at the court and studied the methods of Spanish painters. He also painted the members of the Spanish court, as Velasquez had done, but they looked like people of another world. The Spanish aristocracy had always been painted with pallid faces, languid and elegant poses; but Rubens gave them a touch of the life he loved--made them robust and apparently healthy-minded. Of all great colourists, Rubens took the lead. Titian with his golden hues and warm haired women was very great, but Rubens, "the Fleming" as he was called, revelled in richness of colouring, and flamed through art like a glorious comet.

Rubens had long been wanted in his own country. His sovereigns, Albert and Isabella, wished him to return and become their painter, but they were unable to free him from his engagements in Italy and Spain. At last Rubens received word that his mother, whom he loved devotedly, was likely to die, and what kings could not do his love for her accomplished.

Although his patron, the Duke of Mantua, was absent, and his consent could not be secured, Rubens set off post-haste to his mother's home. He arrived in Antwerp too late to see Maria Pypelincx, who had died before he reached her. Once more on his native soil, Albert and Isabella determined to induce him to remain. He had intended to go back to Mantua and continue his work under the duke, but since he was now in

Belgium he decided to stay there, and thus he became the court painter in his own country, which after all he greatly preferred to any other.

He was to have a salary of five hundred livres ($96) a year, also "the rights, honours, privileges, exemptions, etc." that belonged to those of the royal household; and he was given a gold chain. In this day of large doings there is something about such details that seems childish, but a "gold chain" was by no means a small affair at a time when $96 was considered an ample money-provision for an artist.

That gorgeous gold chain, a mark of distinction rather than a reward, is to be seen in all its glory in one of Rubens's great paintings. The artist himself is mounted upon a horse, the chain about his neck, while he is surrounded by "no fewer than eight-and-twenty life-size figures, many in gorgeous attire, warriors in steel armour, horsemen, slaves, camels, etc." This picture, "The Adoration of the Magi," was twelve feet by seventeen, and was painted at the town's expense. It was later sent to Spain and placed in the Madrid Gallery.

One of the greatest honours that could come to students of that day, was to be admitted to Rubens's studio to paint under his direction, and it is said that "hundreds of young men waited their turn, painting meanwhile in the studios of inferior artists, till they should be admitted to the studio of the great master."

Rubens was a king among painters, as well as a painter patronised by kings.

He had two wives, and he married the first one in 1609. Her name was Isabella Brant. Sir Joshua Reynolds said of her: "His wife is very handsome and has an agreeable countenance, but the picture is rather hard in manner"--by which he meant a picture which Rubens had painted of her. One of his greatest privileges when he was engaged at the court of Albert and Isabella, had been that he need obey none of the exactions of the Guild of St. Luke, none of their rigid rules concerning the employment of art students. Rubens could take into his service whom he pleased, whether they had been admitted as members of the guild or not, though to be a member of the guild was a testimony to their qualifications. In the end, this did a good deal of harm, for Rubens employed students to do the preliminary work of his pictures, who had not been his pupils and who were not otherwise qualified. Thus we read criticisms like that of Sir Joshua's; and many of Rubens's pictures are marred in this manner.

A story is told of Van Dyck and other pupils of Rubens breaking into the master's studio and smudging a picture which Van Dyck afterward repaired by painting in the damaged portion most successfully. We are also told in connection with Rubens's picture, "The Descent from the Cross," that Van Dyck restored an arm and shoulder of Mary of Magdala, but certainly Van Dyck did not become a pupil of Rubens till some time after that picture was painted.

The work of a wonderful period in Rubens's art was completely destroyed. In two years time he painted forty ceilings of churches in Antwerp, all of which were burned, but there is a record of them in the copies made by De Witt, in water colours from which etchings were afterward made. This work of Rubens was the first example of foreshortening done by a Flemish painter.

Above all things Rubens liked to paint big pictures, on very large surfaces, as did Michael Angelo. "The large size of picture gives us painters more courage to present our ideas with the utmost freedom and semblance of reality. ... I confess myself to be, by a natural instinct, better fitted to execute works of the largest size." He wrote this to the English diplomat Trumbull in 1621.

In the midst of Rubens's greatest success as a painter came his diplomatic services. It was desirable that Spain and England should be friends, and Rubens always moving about because of his work, and being so very clever, the Spanish powers thought him a good one to negotiate with England. While on a professional visit to Paris, the English Duke of Buckingham and the artist met, and this seemed to open a way for business. The Infanta consented to have Rubens undertake this delicate piece of statesmanship, but Philip of Spain did not like the idea of an artist--a wandering fellow, as an artist was then thought to be--entering into such a dignified affair. The real negotiator on the English side, was Gerbier, by birth also a Fleming, and strange to tell, he too had been an artist. The English engaged him to look after their interests in the affair, and as soon as Philip learned that their diplomat was also an artist, his prejudices against Rubens as a statesman, disappeared. So it was decided that the two Flemings, artists and diplomats, should meet in Holland to discuss matters. About that time Sir Dudley Carleton wrote to Lord Conway: "Rubens is come hither to Holland, where he now is, and Gerbier in his company, walking from town to town, upon their pretence of taking pictures, which may serve him for a few days if he dispatch and be gone; but yf he entertayne tyme here long, he will infallibly be layd hold of, or sent with disgrace out of the country ... this I have made known to Rubens lest he should meet with a skorne what may in some sort reflect upon others."

The two clever men got through with their talk, nothing unfortunate happened, and Rubens got off to Spain where he laid the result of his talk with Gerbier before the Spanish powers. He was given a studio in Philip's palace, where he carried on his art and his diplomacy. The king became delighted with him as a man and an artist, and as well as attending to state business, he did some wonderful painting while in Madrid. He was there nine months or more, and then started off for England to tell Charles I. of Philip III.'s wishes. But upon his arrival he learned that a peace had just been concluded between France and England, and all was excitement.

He was received in England as a great artist; every honour was showered upon him, and when he made Philip's request to Charles, that he should not act in a manner hostile to Spain, Charles agreed, and kept that agreement though France and Venice urged him to break it.

Charles knighted Rubens while he was in England, and the University of Cambridge made him Master of Arts. The sword used by the king at the time he gave the accolade is still kept by Rubens's descendants.

While he was in London Rubens was very nearly drowned in the Thames going down to Greenwich in a boat.

When he first went from Italy to Spain on a mission of state, he carried a note or passport bearing the following lines: "With these presents" (he took magnificent gifts to Philip, among them a carriage and six Neapolitan horses) "comes Peter Paul, a Fleming. Peter Paul will say all that is proper, like the well informed man that he is. Peter Paul is very successful in painting portraits. If any ladies of quality wish their pictures, let them take advantage of his presence." When he visited England there was no longer need of such introduction; he went in all the magnificence that his genius had earned for him.

Rubens was always a happy man, so far as history shows. He married the first time, a woman who was beautiful and who loved him, as he loved her. He was able to build for himself a beautiful house in Antwerp. In the middle of it was a great *salon*, big enough to hold all his collection of pictures, vases, bronzes, and beautiful jewels. There was also a magnificent staircase, up which his largest pictures could be easily carried, for it was built especially to accommodate the requirements of his work.

Rubens's greatest picture was painted through a strange happening when this beautiful house was being built. The land next to his belonged to the Archers' Guild and when the workmen came to dig Rubens's cellar, they went too far and invaded the adjoining property. The archers made complaint, and there seemed no way to adjust the matter, till some one suggested that Rubens make them a picture which should be accepted as compensation for the harm done. This Rubens did, and the picture was to be St. Christopher--the archers' patron saint; but when the work was done "Rubens surprised them" by exhibiting a picture "of all who could ever have been called 'Christ-bearers.'" This was "The Descent from the Cross"--not a single picture but a picture within a picture, for there were shutters folding in front of it, and on these was painted the archers' patron, St. Christopher.

Rubens's daily life is described thus: "His life was very methodical. He rose at four, attended mass, breakfasted, and painted for hours; then he rested, dined, worked until late afternoon; then, after riding for an hour or two one of his spirited horses, and later supping, he would spend the evening with his friends.

"He was fond of books, and often a friend would read aloud to him while he worked." This is a pleasant picture of a reasonable and worthy life.

It is said that once he painted eighteen pictures in eighteen days, and it is known that he valued his time at fifty dollars a day.

His pupil, Van Dyck, being pushed for money, turned alchemist and tried to manufacture gold, but when Rubens was approached by a visionary who wanted him to lend him money by which he might pursue such a work, promising Rubens a fortune when he should have discovered how to make his gold, the artist laughed and said: "You are twenty years too late, friend. When I wield these," indicating his palette and brush, "I turn all to gold."

Many are the delightful anecdotes told of Rubens. It is said that while he was at the English court he was painting the ceiling of the king's banqueting hall, and a courtier who stood watching, wished to say something *pour passer le temps*, so he asked: "Does the ambassador of his Catholic Majesty sometimes amuse himself with painting?"

"No--but he sometimes amuses himself with being an ambassador," was the witty retort, which showed how he valued his two commissions.

When King Charles I. knighted Rubens he gave him, beside the jewelled sword, a golden chain to which his miniature was attached. If Rubens had gone about with all the chains and decorations given him by kings and other great ones of the earth he would have been weighted down, and would have needed two pairs of shoulders on which to display them.

Rubens's first wife died; and when he married again, he was as fond of painting pictures of the second wife as he had been of the first. The name of the second was Helena Fourment, and she is called by one author "a spicy blonde." Certainly she was very gay, big, and robust, and only sixteen years old when she married Rubens who was then a man of fifty-three. Of one picture, "The Straw Hat," for which he is supposed to have used his wife's sister as model, he was so fond that he would not sell it at any price.

Rubens had a rare mother, as shown in her letters to her husband, John, when he was in prison for his wrongdoing. It would seem that such a mother must have a strong, forceful son, and Rubens is less of a surprise than many artists who had no such influence in their childhood. The history of Rubens's mother is worthy of being told even had she not had a famous son who painted a beautiful picture of her.

Rubens's "Holy Families" are like those of no other painter. The Virgin, the Child, all the others in the picture, are quite different from the Italian figures. These are human beings, good to look upon; full of love and joy, softness and beauty.

It was his learning that first won favour for him in Italy. The Duke of Mantua hearing him read from Virgil, spoke to him in Latin, and being answered in that tongue was so charmed that the foundation of their friendship and the duke's patronage was laid. In Italy he was called "the antiquary and Apelles of our time."

His nephew-biographer writes of him: "He never gave himself the pastime of going to parties where there was drinking and card-playing, having always had a dislike for such."

As Rubens grew in fame, he found that many were jealous of him, and on one occasion a rival proposed that he and Rubens each paint a picture upon a certain subject and leave it to judges to decide which work was the best--Rubens's or his own.

"No," said Rubens. "My attempts have been subjected to the scrutiny of connoisseurs in Italy and Spain. They are to be found in public collections and private galleries in those countries; gentlemen are at liberty to place their works beside them, in order that comparison may be made." This was a dignified way of disposing of the case.

Rubens loved to paint animals, and he had a great lion brought to his home, that he might study its poses and movements.

The flesh of his figures was so lifelike that Guido declared he must mix blood with his paints. He was called "the painter of life."

Rubens, a seventh child, had also seven children, two belonging to his first wife, five to the second.

Many stories are told of his patience and his kindness. It is said that at one time his old pupil, Van Dyck, returned to Antwerp after an absence, greatly depressed and in need of money. Rubens bought all his unsold pictures, and he did this charitable act more than once, and is known to have done the same thing for a rival and enemy, out of sheer goodness of heart.

Kings and queens came to the Rubens house, people of many nations did him honour; and toward his closing days, when gout had disabled him, ambassadors visited him, since he could not go to them.

In a description of his death and burial which took place at Antwerp we read: "He was buried at night as was the custom, a great concourse of citizens ... and sixty orphan children with torches followed the body." He was placed in the vault of the Fourment family, and as he had requested, "The Holy Family" was hung above him. In that picture, we find the St. George to be Rubens himself; St. Jerome, his father; an angel, his youngest son, while Martha and Mary are Isabella and Helena, his two wives.

He left many sketches "to whichever of his sons became an artist, or to the husband of his daughter who should marry an artist." But there were none such to claim the bequest.

PLATE--THE INFANT JESUS AND ST. JOHN

The little girl behind Jesus is supposed to represent his future bride, the Christian Church. The thoughtful, far-seeing look upon the face of the Christ-child, though it does not clash with His youthful charm, is meant to suggest that He has a premonition of His work in the world. The other joyous little figures also demonstrate the artist's love for children. He brings them into his pictures, as cherubs, wherever he can, and they are frequently just as well painted and more universally appreciated than his stout women. In this picture he has a good opportunity to show his adorable flesh tints, combined with the movement and freedom naturally associated with child life.

The original painting is in the Court Museum at Vienna, but it has always been so popular that many copies of it have been made, and one of these is in the Berlin Gallery.

PLATE--THE ARTIST'S TWO SONS

(See Frontispiece)

This picture hangs in the Lichtenstein Gallery at Vienna; the two boys, eleven and seven years of age, are the sons of Rubens by his first wife, Isabella Brant; and Albert, the elder of the two, greatly resembles his mother. He is evidently a student, for he wears the dress of one and carries a book in one hand. The other is placed affectionately upon the shoulder of his little brother, Nicolas, whose face, figure, and attire are all much the more childish of the two.

Critics consider this painting to mark the Highest point which Rubens reached in portraiture. It has all the colour, character, and vitality of his best work. Some of his other pictures are: "Coronation of Marie de Medicis," "The Kirmesse," "Slaughter of the Innocents," "Susanna's Bath," "Capture of Samson," "A Lion Hunt" and "The Rape of the Daughters of Leucippus."

XXXVI JOHN SINGER SARGENT

American and Foreign Schools

1856-1926
Pupil of Carolus Durand

This artist was born in Europe, of American parents; thus we may say that he was "American," though he owed nothing but dollars to the United States, since his instruction was obtained in Italy and France, and all his associations in art and friendship were there. He was probably the most brilliant of the artists termed American. His great mural work in the Boston Public Library, is hardly to be surpassed.

Above all, Sargent's portraits are masterly. He was famous in that branch of art before he was twenty-eight years old. Among his finest portraits is that of "Carmencita," a Spanish dancer, who for a time set the world wild with pleasure. The list of his famous portraits is very long.

Sargent's father was a Philadelphia physician; who originally came from New England, but the artist himself was born in Florence. He was given a good education and grew up with the beauties of Florence all about him, in a refined and charming home. He was the delight of his master, Carolus Durand for he was modest and refined, yet full of enthusiasm and energy. In his twenty-third year he painted a fine picture of his master. Sargent was a musician as well as a painter; a man of great versatility, as if the gods and all the muses had presided at his birth.

PLATE--CARMENCITA

In this picture of the famous Spanish dancer Sargent shows all the life and character he can put into a portrait. The girl seems on the point of springing into motion. She is poised, ready for flight and the proud lift of her head makes one believe that she will accomplish the most difficult steps she attempts. The painting is in the Luxembourg, Paris.

Other noted Sargent portraits are "Mr. Marquand" in the Metropolitan Museum of Art, "Lady Elcho, Mrs. Arden, Mrs. Tennant," "Mrs. Meyer and Children," "Homer St. Gaudens," "Henschel," and "Mr. Penrose."

XXXVII TINTORETTO (JACOPO ROBUSTI)

Venetian School

1518-1594
Pupil of Titian

Tintoretto was born with an ideal. As a young boy he wrote upon his studio wall: "The drawing of Michael Angelo, the colouring of Titian," and that was the end he tried to reach. His father was a "tintore"--a dyer of silk, a tinter--and it was from the character of that work the artist took his name. He helped his father with the dyeing of silks, while he was still a child, and was called "II tintoretto," little dyer.

As the little tinter showed great genius for painting, his father placed him in Titian's studio, but for some reason he only stayed there a few days, long enough, however, to permit us to call him a pupil of Titian; especially as he wrote that master's name upon his wall and determined to imitate him. After his few days with Titian, Tintoretto studied with Schiavone and afterward set up a studio for himself.

As a determined lad in this studio of his, Tintoretto tried every means of developing his art. He studied the figures upon Medicean tombs made by Michael Angelo, taking plaster casts of them and copying them in his studio. He used to hang little clay figures up by strings attached to his ceiling, that he might get the effect of them high in air. By looking at them thus from below he gained an idea of foreshortening.

Although this artist nearly succeeded in getting into line with Michael Angelo, he did not colour after the fashion of his master, Titian. Tintoretto was about twenty-eight years old before he got any very big commission, but at that age a chance came to him. In the church of Santa Maria del Orto were two great bare spaces, unsightly and vast, about fifty feet high and twenty broad. In that day anything and everything was decorated with masterpieces, and it was almost disgraceful for a church to let such a space as that go unfrescoed. Tintoretto saw an opportunity, and finally offered to paint pictures there for nothing if the church would agree to pay for the materials he needed. The church certainly was not going to refuse such an offer, even if Tintoretto was not thought to be much of an artist at the time. If the work was poor, one day they could choose to have it repainted. Thus Tintoretto got his first great opportunity. He painted on those walls "The Last Judgment" and "The Golden Calf." They made him famous, and gained him the commission to paint the picture which is used as an illustration here.

The brothers of the Scuola di San Rocco asked him to compete with Veronese, in painting the ceilings after he had done four pictures for their walls.

Tintoretto consented, and Veronese and two others who were in the competition set about making their sketches which they were to present for the brothers' consideration. Finaly the day of decision came. All were assembled, the artists armed with sketches of their plans.

"Where are yours, Tintoretto?" the others asked. "We expect a drawing of your idea."

"Well, there it is," the artist answered, drawing a screen from the ceiling. Behold! he had already painted it to suit himself. The work was complete.

"That is the way I make my sketches," he said.

Though the work was magnificent it had not been done according to the monks' ideas of business and order. They objected and objected.

"Very well," the artist cried; "I will make the ceiling a present to you." As there was a rule of their order forbidding them to refuse a present, they had to accept Tintoretto's. This did not promise very good business at the time, but the work was so splendid and Tintoretto so reasonable that they finally agreed to give him all the work of their order--nearly enough to keep him employed during a lifetime. After that he painted sixty great pictures upon their walls.

He painted so much and so fast that he did not always do good work, and one critic declares that "while Tintoretto was the equal of Titian, he was often inferior to Tintoretto"--which after all is a very fine compliment.

His life was so tranquil and uneventful that there is little to say of it; but there is much to say of his art. He lived mostly in his studio, and when he died he was buried in the Santa Maria del Orto--the church in which he had done his first work.

Veronese had given to Venice a brilliant, glowing, rich, ravishing riot of colour and figures, but Tintoretto was said to rise up "against the joyful Veronese as the black knight of the Middle Ages, the sombre priest of a gloomy art." Tintoretto was of stormy temperament, and upon one occasion he proved it by thrusting a pistol under a critic's nose, after he had invited him to his studio; it is this half savage spirit that may be seen in his paintings. He had deep-set, staring eyes, it is said, a furrowed brow and hollow cheeks, indicative of his passionate spirit. He painted very few female figures, but mostly men. When he did paint a woman, she looked mannish and not beautiful. When he painted gorgeous subjects, like doges and senators, he gave to them gloomy backgrounds, awe-inspiring poses, and he seldom painted a figure "full-face" but three-quarter, or half, so that he did not give himself a chance to presenthuman figures in beautiful postures. He is said to have been the first who painted groups of well-known men in pictures intended for the decoration of public buildings. One great critic has written that "while the Dutch, in order to unite figures, represented them at a banquet, Tintoretto's *nobili* (aristocrats) were far too proud to show themselves to the people" in so gay and informal a situation. With the coming of Tintoretto it was said "a dark cloud had overcast the bright heaven of Venetian art. Instead of smiling women, bloody martyrs and pale ascetics" were painted by him. He dissected the dead in order to learn the structure of the human body. In his paintings "his women, especially, with their pale livid features and encircled eyes, strangely sparkling as if from black depths, have nothing in common with the soft" painted flesh which he pictured in his youth while he was following Titian as closely as he could. As he grew older and his art more fixed, he followed Michael Angelo more and more. Titian's colouring was that of "an autumn day" but Tintoretto's that of a "dismal night." Yet these very qualities in Tintoretto's work made him great.

PLATE--THE MIRACLE OF ST. MARK

This painting in the Academy at Venice tells the story of how a Christian slave who belonged to a pagan nobleman went to worship at the shrine of St. Mark. That was unlawful. The nobleman had his slave taken before the judge, who ordered him to be tortured. Just as the executioner raised the hammer with which he was finally to kill the slave, St. Mark himself came down from heaven, broke the weapon and rescued the slave.

The figure of the patron saint of Venice is swooping down, head first, above the group, his garments flying in the air. A bright light touches the slave's naked body, as he lies upon his back, the executioner having turned away and raised his hammer aloft, while others have drawn back in fright at the appearance of the patron saint. We may imagine that Tintoretto was trying to acquire this power of painting wonderful figures hovering in the air when he hung his little clay images from the ceiling of his studio years before. Other pictures of his are: "The Marriage of Bacchus and Ariadne," "Martyrdom of St. Agnes," "St. Rocco Healing the Sick," "The Annunciation," "The Crucifixion," and many others.

XXXVIII TITIAN (TIZIANO VECELLI)

(Pronounced Tit-zee-ah'no (Vay-chel'lee))

Venetian School

1477-1576
Pupil of Giovanni and Gentile Bellini

Titian was a child of the Tirol Mountains, handsome, strong, full of health and fine purposes, even as a boy. He was born in a little cottage at Pieve, in the valley of Cadore, through which flows the River Piave; and he wandered daily beside its banks, gathering flowers from which he squeezed the juices to paint with. When he grew up he became a wonderful colourist, and from his boyhood nothing so much delighted him as the brilliant colours flaunted by the flowers of wood and field.

Gathered about his good father's hearth were many children, Caterina, Francesco, Orsa, and the rest, living in peace and happiness, closely bound together by love. Titian had a gentle, loving mother named Lucia, while his father was a soldier and an honoured man. In the little town where they lived, he was councillor and also superintendent of the castle and inspector of mines, no light honours among those simple country people. Doubtless Titian inherited his splendid bearing and his determined character from his soldier father.

Even while a little child, the man who was destined to become a great artist began his work with the juices of the wild-flowers, which he daubed upon the wall of the humble home in the Tirol valley, making a Madonna with angels at her feet and a little Jesus upon her knee. But if Titian was a great painter, he was never even a fair scholar. He went to school, but would not, or could not, study. His father soon saw that he was wasting his time and being made very unhappy through being forced to do that for which he had no ability; so he was soon released from book-learning and sent to Venice, seventy-five miles from home, to learn art. In Venice, the Vecelli family had an uncle, and it was with him that Titian lived, though he studied first with Sebastian Zuccato, the head of the Venetian guild of mosaic workers, and a pretty good teacher in his way. He was not able to teach Titian very much, for the boy was an inspired artist and needed a good master; so, after a little, the family held a consultation and it was decided that Titian should become the pupil of Gentile Bellini, a very clever artist indeed. There was an interesting story told about this master which made the Vecellis feel that their boy would do well to be under the influence of a kind-hearted man, as well as a genius. It seems that Bellini's fame had become so great that the Sultan had sent for him to paint the portraits of himself and the Sultana. Bellini went gladly to Turkey to do this; but he took with him certain pictures to show his patron. Among them was one of St. John the Baptist having his head cut off. The Sultan looked at it, and cutting heads off being a large part of his business, he saw that Bellini had not scientifically painted it, and in order to show him the true way to conduct such matters, he sent for a slave and ordered his head chopped off in Bellini's presence. Bellini was so terrified and sickened by the dreadful sight that he fled from Turkey and would not paint its ruler, the Sultana nor anyone else who had to do with such cruel things as he had witnessed.

It was into this man's studio that Titian went as a young boy, but after a little he displeased Gentile Bellini, who complained that his pupil worked too fast, and therefore could not expect to do great work. He declared that picture painting was serious and careful work, and that Titian was too careless and quick. As a matter of fact, Titian was too wonderful for Bellini ever to do much for; and since he could not get on with him, he went to another master--Gentile Bellini's brother, Giovanni. One of Titian's chief troubles in the studio of Gentile had been that he was not allowed to use the gorgeous colouring he loved, but in the brother's studio he found to his joy that colour was more valued, and he was given more freedom to use it. Also there was a young peasant pupil with Giovanni, who, like Titian, loved to use beautiful colours, and he and the newcomer became fast friends.

The other artist's name was Giorgione, and he had the most delightful ways about him, winning friends wherever he went, so it was no wonder that the warm-hearted Titian sought his companionship. One day those two young comrades left their master's studio, to have a good time off by themselves. There was a stated hour for their return; but they had spent all their money, and forgot that Giovanni Bellini was expecting them home. When they did return the door was closed and locked. What were they to do? They did the only thing they could. As comrades in misfortune they joined forces, set up a studio of their own, and went to work to earn their living as best they might. At first it was hard sledding, but in time they got a good job, namely to decorate the walls of a public building in Venice which was used by foreign merchants for the transaction of their business, a sort of "exchange," as we understand it. This was the Fondaco de' Tedeschi, and it had two great halls, eighty rooms, and twenty-six warehouses. It was indeed a big undertaking for the two young men, and they divided the business between them. Their joy was great, their cartoons successfully made and the work well begun, when, alas, they fell to quarreling simply because someone had declared that Titian's work upon the building was a little better than Giorgione's.

This dispute parted the two friends, who had had good times together, and it must have been Giorgione's fault, because Ludovico Dolce, one who knew Titian well, said that "he was most modest ... he never spoke reproachfully of other painters ... in his discourse he was ever ready to give honour where honour was due ... he was, moreover, an eloquent speaker, having an excellent wit and perfect judgment in all things; of a most sweet and gentle nature, affable and most courteous in manner; so that whoever once conversed with him could not choose but love him henceforth forever." That is a most loving and splendid tribute for one man to pay another. Not long after Giorgione died, and Titian took up his unfinished work, doing it as well as his own.

There was a brilliant and mature artist called Palma Vecchio, in Venice, and Titian painted in his studio, where he saw and loved Vecchio's daughter, Violante. The young artist was not very well off financially, and therefore could not marry; hence he was not specially happy over his love affair. About that time he took to painting after the manner of Vecchio, through being so much influenced by his soft feelings for the older artist's daughter. He used the lovely Violante again and again for his model, and many of the beautiful faces which Titian painted at that time show the features of his lady-love. With his new love Titian's serious work seemed to begin, and at twenty-one he painted his first truly great picture, "Sacred and Profane Love." To day this picture hangs upon the walls of the Borghese Palace, in Rome.

Raphael painted a great many pictures, but Titian must have painted more. At least one thousand have his signature.

Now came wars and troubles for Venice. The Turks, French, and Venetians became at odds, and during the strife many fine works of art were lost, among them many of Titian's pictures. He had painted bishops, also the wicked Borgias, and many other great personages, but all of these are gone and to this day, no one knows what became of them.

At last Titian began one of his greatest paintings, "The Tribute Money," and he set about it because he had been criticised. Some German travellers in Venice visited Titian's studio, and though they found his work very fine, one of them said that after all there was only one master able to finish a painting as it should be finished, and that was the great Dürer. The German pointed out the differences between Titian's method and Dürer's, and declared that Venetian painters never quite came up to the promise of their first pictures. Dürer's wonderful pictures were quite different from Titian's, inasmuch as his work was fuller of detail and careful finishing, but Titian was as great in another way. His effects were broader, but quite as satisfying. However, the German criticism put him on his mettle, and he answered that if he had thought the greatest value of a painting lay in its fiddling little details of finishing, he too would have painted them. To show that he could paint after Dürer's fashion, as well as his own, he undertook the "Tribute Money," and the result was a wonderful picture.

Soon Rome sent for Titian. The Florentines, Raphael and Michael Angelo, were already there doing marvellous things, but the pope wished to add the genius of Titian to theirs and made him a great offer to go and live in Rome and do his future work for that city. This was an honour, but amid all his fame and the homage paid him, Titian had remembered the old home in the vale of Cadore. It was there his heart was, and he determined to return to the home of his boyhood to do his best work. So he sent his thanks and refusal to the pope, and he wrote as follows to his home folks, through the council of his town:

"I, Titian of Cadore, having studied painting from childhood upward, and desirous of fame rather than profit, wish to serve the doge and signorini, rather than his highness the pope and other signori, who in past days, and even now, have urgently asked to employ me. I am therefore anxious, if it should appear feasible to paint the hall of council, beginning, if it pleases their sublimity, with the canvas of the battle on the side toward the Piazza, which is so difficult that no one as yet has had the courage to attempt it."

Then in stating his terms he asked for a very moderate sum of money and a "brokerage" for life. The Government did not have to think over the matter long. Titian's father had been honoured among them, Titian's genius was well known, and the commission was gladly given him. As soon as he got this business affair settled he moved into the palace of the Duke of Milan "at San Samuele; on the Grand Canal, where he remained for sixteen years," so says his biographer.

Titian's affairs were not yet entirely smooth, because both of the Bellinis having painted for his patrons, they naturally considered Titian an intruder, and thought that the work should have been given to them. They did all they could to make trouble for the younger artist, but after a time Titian came into his rights, receiving his "brokerage" which gave to him a yearly sum of money 120 crowns, $126.04. His taxes were taken off for the future, provided he would agree to paint all the doges that should rule during his lifetime.

Titian undertook to do this, but he did not keep his word, for he painted only five doges, though many more followed. He had no sooner received his commission from the council of his native place than he began to neglect it, and to paint for the husband of the wicked poisoner--Lucretia Borgia--whose name was Alfonso d'Este, the Duke of Ferrara. It was for him he painted the "Venus Worship," now in the Museum of Madrid, also "The Three Ages," which belongs to Lord Ellesmere, and the "Virgin's Rest near Bethlehem," now in the National Gallery. Afterward he painted "Noli Me Tangere," which is in the same London Gallery.

There is a picture of great size in the Academy of Arts in Venice, which was first seen on a public holiday nearly four hundred years ago. It is the "Assumption of the Virgin," first shown on St. Bernardino's day, when all the public offices were closed by order of the Senate, and the whole city had a gay time. This occasion made Titian the most honoured artist of his time, but still the Venetians had cause to complain; because now their painter took so much work in hand that he nearly ceased doing the work on the council hall. The council sent him word that unless he attended to business the paintings should be finished by some one else and he would have to pay the new artist out of his own pocket; but in waywardness he paid no attention to this summons. Lucretia Borgia died, and her husband having never loved her, fell at once in love with a girl of a lower class, who was very good and worthy to be loved. The duke wanted Titian to paint them both, and so once more the great painter neglected his contract with the council. The girl's name was Laura, and Titian painted her and the duke in one picture, which now hangs in the Louvre.

At last, after seven years of his neglecting to do his promised work the council became enraged and threatened to take the artist's property away from him. That frightened Titian very much, and he began frantically to work on the battle piece on the hall wall. It was about this time that he married. He had probably forgotten Violante in the passing of so many years; at any rate it was not she whom he married, but a lady whose first name was Cecilia. Soon he had a little family of children, but one of them was destined to make Titian very unhappy. This was Pomponic who became a priest, but he was also a wicked spendthrift, and kept his father forever in trouble, trying to pay his debts and keep him out of scrapes. Another son became an artist; not great like his father, but very helpful and a comfort to him. Then his wife died, and Titian had loved her so dearly that for a long time he had not the heart to paint much. His sister, Orsa, came to live at his home and take care of his motherless children.

He left the palace on the Grand Canal and bought a home north of Venice, with beautiful gardens attached, and there he lived and worked, entertaining the most illustrious men. Titian's house and gardens became the show place of the country, so many geniuses and famous people visited there. It was there that he painted "The Martyrdom of Saint Peter," and the picture was so loved by the Venetians that the signori threatened with death any one who should take the picture from the chapel where it hung. In spite of this caution the picture was burned in the fire that destroyed the chapel in 1867.

Titian was now getting to be old, but he was yet to do great work and to have kingly patrons. Charles V. visited Bologna, and, seeing Titian's great work, wanted him to paint his portrait. So the artist went to Bologna and painted the portrait of the king, clothed in armour, but without any head-covering, making Charles V. look so fine a personage, that he was delighted. Charles said he had always been painted to look so much uglier than he really was that when people who had seen his portraits, actually saw himself they were pleasantly disappointed. While Titian was painting his picture, Lombardi, the sculptor, wished above all things to see Charles, so Titian said: "You come with me to the sittings, and act as if you were some apprentice, carrying my colours and brushes, and then you can watch the king as easily as possible." Lombardi did as Titian suggested, but he hid in his big and baggy sleeve a tablet of wax, on which to make a relief picture of Charles. One day the king surprised the sculptor and demanded to be shown what he was doing. Thereupon he was so much pleased that he commissioned Lombardi to make the model in marble. While the king was sitting for two portraits to Titian, the artist one day dropped his brush. The king looked at the courtiers who were lounging about watching the work, but none of them picked it up, so the king himself did so. Titian was distressed over this and apologised to the king. "There may be many kings," said Charles, "but there will never be more than one Titian--and he deserves to be served by Caesar himself." After that he would allow no other artist to paint his portrait, declaring that Titian alone could do it properly, and for the two pictures Titian received two thousand scudi in gold, was made a Count of the Lateran Palace, of the Aulic Council and of the Consistory; with the title of Count Palatine and all the advantages attached to those dignities. His children were thereby raised to the rank of nobles of the empire, with all the honours appertaining to families with four generations of ancestors. He was also made Knight of the Golden Spur, with the right of entrance to court. This was great return for two portraits of a king, but it shows what a king could do if he chose.

Titian had a brother who also became an artist, less famous than himself, and it was that brother, who, when their father died in the Cadore home, went back to care for the old place and to keep it in readiness so that the famous Titian might return to it for rest and peace. Foreign sovereigns had invited Titian to end his days with them, but they could not tempt him from that vale of Cadore nor his country home in Venice.

All this time he had been neglecting the work upon the hall of council, and at last, the councillors gave the work to another, took away Titian's "brokerage" and told him he must return to Venice all the moneys they had given him for twenty years back. This finally cured him of his neglect, and he went to work in earnest painting so rapidly that he finished the work in two years.

Before he died Titian went to Rome, where he painted Pope Paul's portrait, and the story is told that when the portrait was set to dry upon the terrace--which it probably was not,--the people who passed took off their hats to it, thinking it was the pope himself.

Besides his bad son and his good one, Titian had a beautiful daughter whom he painted again and again. He went to Augsburg once more to paint King Charles, who for that work added a pension of five hundred scudi to what he had already done for him. This made the artist "as rich as a prince, instead of poor as a painter." King Philip II. loved art as his father had, and he took a painting of Titian's with him to the convent of Yuste, where he went to die, wishing to have it near to console him. In those days art had become a religion for high and low. Great personages still went to Casa Grande, Titian's Venetian home, where he entertained like a prince. No one knew better than he how princes behaved, and when a cardinal came to dine with him, he threw his purse to his servant, crying: "Prepare a feast, for all the world is dining with me!" Henry III. of France visited Titian and ordered sent to him every picture of which he had asked the price.

His friends stood by him all his life, but in his old age his beautiful daughter, Lavinia, died, leaving behind her six children for him to love as his own. The brother had died before that, in the old home at Cadore, and at more than eighty years of age Titian was still painting from morning till night. About this time he sent to King Philip "The Last Supper," which was to be hung in the Escorial. The monks found it too high to fill the space, and though the artist in charge, Navarrette, begged them to let it be, they cut a piece off the top, that it might be hung where they wanted it. Titian had so far had to pay no taxes, but at that time an account of his property was demanded and this is what he owned: "Several houses, pieces of land, sawmills, and the like," and he was blamed because he did not state the full value of his possessions. At ninety-one he painted a picture which became the guide of Rubens and his brother artists, so wonderful was it. Again, at ninety-nine he began a picture, which was to be given to the monks of the Frari in return for a burial place for the artist within the convent walls, but he never finished it. He died during the time of the plague, but of old age alone, though his son, Orzio, died of the disease. The alarm of the people was so great that a law had been passed to bury all who died at that time, instantly and without ceremony, but that law was waived for the painter. Titian, in the midst of a nation's tragedy was borne to the convent of the Frari, with honours. Two centuries later the Austrian Emperor commanded the great sculptor, Canova, to make a mausoleum above the tomb.

It was said that shortly before he died Titian began to be less sure in his use of colours, and would often daub on great masses, but his students came in the night and rubbed them off, so that the master never felt his failing.

As King Charles had said, there was never but one such artist in the world.

Titian prepared his canvas by painting upon it a solid colour to serve for the bed upon which the picture itself was to be painted. To quote more exactly from a good description--some of these foundation colours were laid on with resolute strokes of his brush which was heavily laden with colour, while the half-tints were made with pure red earth, the lights with pure white, softened into the rest of the foundation painting with touches of the same brush dipped into red, black, and yellow. In this way he could give the "promise" of a figure in four strokes. After laying this foundation, he turned his picture toward the wall and left it there for months at a time, frequently turning it around that he might criticise it. If, during this time of waiting, he thought any part of the work already done was poor, he made it right, changing the shape of an arm, adding flesh where he thought it was needed, reducing flesh where it seemed to him out of proportion, and then he would again turn the canvas face to the wall. After months of self-criticism and retouching he would have the first layer of flesh painted upon his figures, and a good beginning made. "It was contrary to his habit to finish at one painting, and he used to say that a poet who improvises cannot hope to form pure verses." He would often produce a half-light with a rub of his finger, "or with a touch of the thumb he would dab a spot of dark pigment into some corner to strengthen it; or throw in a reddish stroke--a tear of blood so to speak--to break the parts ... in fact when finishing he painted more with his fingers than with his brush." He used to say, "White, red, and black, these are all the colours that a painter needs, but one must know how to use them."

PLATE--THE ARTIST'S DAUGHTER, LAVINIA.

Previous to the time of Titian, it had been the custom to paint portraits of beautiful ladies merely to their waists, just far enough to show their hands. He went further, and produced "knee portraits," which gave him an opportunity to paint their gorgeous gowns as well. He has done so in making this picture of his daughter Lavinia, probably just before her marriage to Cornelio Sarcinelli which took place in 1555. She is attired in gold-coloured brocade with pearls about her neck. Her dress, combined with the dish of fruit she holds so high, gives Titian the colour effects he always sought. A yellow lemon is specially striking, and the red curtain to the left harmonises with the whole. The uplift of the arms and the turn of the head give the desired amount of action. It is not Titian's customary style of work; he seldom did anything so intimate and personal, and the picture is the more interesting on that account. It is in the Berlin Gallery.

Some of Titian's famous pictures are: his own portrait; "Flora," "Holy Family and St. Bridget," "The Last Judgment," "The Entombment," "The Magdalene," "Bacchanal," "St. Sebastian," "Bacchus and Ariadne," and "The Sleeping Venus."

XXXIX JOSEPH MALLORD WILLIAM TURNER

English

1775-1851

Pupil of the Royal Academy

If the occupation of a shepherd produced a poet, no less did an artist of the first water come out of a barber shop. Turner's father was a jolly little fellow who dressed hair for English dandies and did all of those things which in those days fell to men of his profession. It was in this little shop that the great artist grew up. Father Turner was ambitious for his son, who was anxious to study art. The less said of the artist's mother the better, for she was a termagant and finally went crazy, so that the father and his little boy were soon left alone, to plan and work and strive to make each other happy. The pair were never apart.

Turner's art beginning was at six years of age, on the occasion of a visit his father paid to a goldsmith of whose hair curling and peruquing he had charge. Perched upon a chair too high for a little boy's comfort, and feeling that it took his father very long indeed to satisfy the customer, Joseph's eye lighted upon a silver lion which ornamented a silver tray. He studied every detail of that lion while waiting for his father, and finally when they got home, he sat down and drew it from memory. By tea time he had a lion in full action upon the paper. This delighted his father above everything, and it was settled then and there that the little fellow should have a chance to learn art.

The father could not give much time to his upbringing, but he taught him to be honest and kind-hearted and to save his money. His playground was generally the bank of the Thames, and under London Bridge where, roving with the sailors, he learned to love the ships, the setting-suns and evening waters from a daily study of them.

He did not do much at school, because the other pupils at New Brentford, learning that he could draw wonderful things upon the schoolroom walls, used to do his "sums" for him, while he sketched for them. After a while father Turner began to hang up some of his son's sketches upon the walls of the barber shop, among the wigs and curls and *toupées*, and he put little tags upon them, telling the price. The extraordinary work of his little boy began to attract the attention of the jolly barber's patrons, and by the time he was twelve years old the child had a picture upon the walls of the Royal Academy--a far-cry from barber shop to Academy!

One authority says that this first exhibition occurred in his fourteenth year, but by that time he was a pupil of the Academy, and it is not unlikely that he had shown his mettle before.

He now began to earn his own living, but he still dwelt in the barber shop with his father. While in the Academy he coloured prints, made backgrounds for other painters, drew architect's plans, and in that way made money. He had been sent to a drawing master to study "the art of perspective," but having no mathematical knowledge he had been unable to learn it, and the teacher had advised his father to put little Turner to cobbling or making clothes. However, William was to learn perspective, and even to be made master of that branch of art in the Academy itself.

In after years, when he had become a great artist, someone spoke pityingly of the drudgery he had had to do to make money as a young boy--referring to his painting of backgrounds and the like. "Well! and what could be better practice?" Turner answered cheerfully.

He used to go to the house of Dr. Munro, who lived in fine style on the Strand. This gentleman owned Rembrandts, Rubenses, Titians, and other great masterpieces, and in that house the "little barber" had a chance to see the best of art, and also to copy it. This was a great opportunity for him and he made the most of it. Besides the chance for study, he earned about half a crown an evening and his supper, for his copying.

Turner was the first painter to make "warm moonlight." All other artists had given cold, silvery effects to a moonlit atmosphere, but Turner had seen a mellow, sympathetic moon, and he first showed it to others. About this time he went travelling; for an engraver of the *Copper Plate Magazine* had engaged the young boy to go into Wales and make sketches for his work. Turner set off on a pony which a friend had lent him, with his baggage done up in a bundle--it did not make a very big one--and thus he voyaged. It was a fine experience, and he came home with many beautiful scenes on paper, which he in after years made into complete pictures. Next he made the acquaintance of Thomas Girtin, the first in his country of a fine school of water-colour painters, and this acquaintance grew into a close friendship. The two were devoted to each other and worked together at any sort of mechanical art work that would bring them a living. When Girtin died Turner said: "Had Tim Girtin lived, I should have starved," showing how highly he valued Girtin's work.

Turner is said to have been "a stout, clumsy little fellow, who never cared how he looked. He wore an ill-fitting suit, and his luggage tied up in a handkerchief was slung over his shoulder on a cane. Sometimes he carried a small valise and an old umbrella, the handle of which he converted into a fishing rod, for Turner dearly loved both hunting and fishing."

The hero travelled a great deal, because above every thing he loved the fields and streams, and to tramp alone. It is said that it was his habit to walk twenty-five miles a day, seeing everything on the way, letting no peculiarity of nature escape him. His sketchbook was a curiosity, because he not only made sketches in it, but jotted down his travelling expenses, what he thought about things that he saw, and all the gossip he heard in the towns through which he passed. Because he liked best to travel alone he was called "the Great Hermit of Nature."

One memorable day--of which he thought but little at the time--he stopped on the road to make a sketch of Norham Castle. Later he completed the picture, and it became famous, so successful that from that hour he had all the work he could do. Years afterward, when passing that way again in company with a friend, he was seen to take off his hat to the castle.

"Why are you doing that?" his friend asked, in amazement.

"Well, that castle laid the foundation of my success," he answered, "and I am pleased to salute it."

During his young manhood Turner had fallen in love with a girl, and planned to marry, but after he returned from one of his country trips he found she had married another, and from that moment the artist was a changed man. He had been generous and gay before, now he began to save his money, so that people thought him miserly-- but he was forgiven when it became known what he finally did with his fortune. After the young woman deserted him he wandered more than ever, and one of his fancies was to keep boys from robbing birds' nests. He looked after the little birds so carefully that the boys named him "old Blackbirdy." He had already begun those wonderful pictures of ships and seas, and his house was ornamented with full-rigged little ships and water plants, which he carefully raised to put into his pictures. By that time he had bought a home of his own in the country, and his father the barber went to live with him. The old man's trade had fallen off, because the fashions had changed, wigs were less worn, and hair was not so elaborately dressed. In the country home the old man took charge of all the household affairs, prepared his son's canvases for him, and after the pictures were painted it was the ex-barber who varnished them, so that Turner said, "Father begins and finishes all my pictures." There the father and son lived, in perfect peace and affection, till Turner decided to sell the place and move into town, "because," said he, "Dad is always working in the garden and catching cold."

Meanwhile he had been made master of perspective in the Academy, and it was expected that he would lecture to the students, but he was not cut out for a lecturer. He was not elegant in his manners, nor impressive in his speech. On one occasion, when he had risen to deliver a speech, he looked helplessly about him and finally blurted out: "Gentlemen! I've been and left my lecture in the hackney coach!"

During these years he had tried to establish a studio like other masters and to have pupils and apprentices about him; but the stupid ones he could not endure, having no patience with them, and he treated all the fashionable ones so bluntly they would not stay; so the idea had to be given up.

He became a visitor at Farnley Hall in Yorkshire, where a friend, Mr. Hawksworth Fawkes lived, and in the course of his lifetime Fawkes put fifty thousand dollars worth of Turner's pictures upon his walls. The Fawkes family described Turner as a most delightful man: "The fun, frolic, and shooting we enjoyed together, and which, whatever may be said by others of his temper and disposition, have proved to me that he was, in his hours of distraction from his professional labours as kindly hearted a man and as capable of enjoyment and fun of all kinds as any I ever knew."

Another friend writes: "Of all light-hearted, merry creatures I ever knew, Turner was the most so; and the laughter and fun that abounded when he was an inmate of our cottage was inconceivable, particularly with the juvenile members of our family."

The story of his disappointment in marriage is an interesting one. It is said that the young lady whom he loved was the sister of a schoolmate. They had been engaged for some time, but while he was on one of his travels his letters were stolen and kept from the young woman. She believed he had forgotten her, and her stepmother, who had taken the letters, persuaded the girl to engage herself to another. Turner returned just a week before her marriage and tried to win her back, but although she loved him, she felt herself then bound to her new suitor and therefore married him. Her marriage was very unhappy and her misery, as well as his own, distressed the artist till his death. Almost all his life, in spite of his seeming gaiety, he worked like a slave, rising at four o'clock in the morning and working while light lasted. When remonstrated with about this he would sadly say: "There are no holidays for me."

All his ways were honest and simple, and his election to the Academy was very exceptional in the way it came about. Most Academicians had graces and airs and good fellowship to commend them, as well as their works, but Turner had none of these things. He had given no dinners, nor played a social part in order to get the membership. When the news was brought him that he was elected, some one advised him to go and thank his fellow Academicians for the honour, as that was the custom; but Turner saw no reason in it. "Since I am elected, it must have been because they thought my pictures made me worthy. Why, then should I thank them? Why thank a man for performing a simple duty." In half a century Turner was absent only three times from the Academy exhibitions, and his. membership was of very great value to him.

At this time Turner had an idea for an art publication to be called *Liber Studiorum*. He meant to issue this in dark blue covers and to include in each number five plates. There was to be a series of five hundred plates altogether, and these were to be divided, according to subject, into historical, landscape, pastoral, mountainous, marine, and architectural studies. After seventy plates had been, published, the enterprise fell through, because no one bought the periodical, and there was no money to keep it going. The engraver of the plates, Charles Turner, became so disgusted with the failure that he even used the proofs of these wonderful studies to kindle the fire with. Many years later, a great print-dealer, Colnaghi, made Turner, the engraver, hunt up all the proofs that he had not used for kindling paper, and these he bought for £1,500.

"Good God!" cried Charles Turner, "I have been burning banknotes all my life."

Some years later still £3,000 was paid for a single copy of the *Liber Studiorum*.

Turner was a most conscientious man, and many stories are told of his manner of teaching. He could not talk eloquently nor give very clear instructions, talking not being his forte, but he would lean over a student's shoulder, point out the defects in his work, and then on a paper beside him make a few marks to illustrate what he had said. If the artist had genius enough then to imitate him, well and good; if not, Turner simply went away and left him. His own ways of working were remarkable. He often painted with a sponge and used his thumbnail to "tear up a sea." It mattered little to him how he produced his effects so long as he did it. His impressionistic style confused many of his critics, and it is told how a fine lord once looked at a picture be had made, and snorted: "Nothing but daubs, nothing but daubs!" Then catching the inspiration, he leaned close to the canvas, and said: "No! Painting! so it is!"

"I find, Mr. Turner," said a lady, "that in copying your pictures, touches of red, blue and yellow appear all through the work."

"Well, madam, don't you see that yourself, in nature? Because if you don't, heaven help you!" was the reply.

"Once, after painting a summer evening, he thought that the picture needed a dark spot in front by way of contrast; so he cut out a dog from black paper and stuck it on. That dog still appears in the picture."

Another time he painted "A Snow-storm at Sea," which some critics called "Soap-suds and Whitewash." Turner, who had been for hours lashed to the mast of a ship in order to catch the proper effect, was naturally much hurt by the criticism. "What would they have!" he exclaimed. "I wonder what they think a storm is like. I wish they'd been in it."

Turner was conscientiously fond of his work, and when he sold a picture he said that he had lost one of his children.

He grew rich, but he never was knighted, because his manners were not fine enough to suit the king. He wished to become President of the Royal Academy, but that was impossible because he was not polished enough to carry the honour gracefully.

After selling his place in the country Turner bought a house in Harley Street, where he lived a strange and lonely life. A gentleman has written about this incident, which shows us his manner of living:

"Two ladies called upon Turner while he lived in Harley Street. On sending in their names, after having ascertained that he was at home, they were politely requested to walk in, and were shown into a large sitting-room without a fire. This was in the depth of winter; and lying about in various places were several cats without tails. In a short time our talented friend made his appearance, asking the ladies if they felt cold. The youngest replied in the negative; her companion, more curious, wished she had stated otherwise, as she hoped they might have been shown into his sanctum or studio. After a little conversation he offered them biscuits, which they partook of for the novelty-- such an event being almost unprecedented in his house. One of the ladies bestowing some notice upon the cats, he was induced to remark that he had seven, and that they came from the Isle of Man."

Thus we learn that Turner's desolate house was full of Manx cats, and of many other pets. When he had moved elsewhere--to 47 Queen Anne Street--one of the pictures he cared most for, "Bligh Shore," was put up as a covering to the window and a cat wishing to come in, scratched it hopelessly. The housekeeper started to punish it for this but Turner said indulgently, "Oh, never mind!" and saved the cat from chastisement.

The place he lived in, where his "dad was always working in the garden and catching cold," he called Solus Lodge, because he wished his acquaintances to understand that he wanted to be alone. One picture painted by him to order, was to have brought him $2,500; but when it was finished the man was disappointed with it and would not take it. Later, Turner was offered $8,000 for it, but would not sell it.

Turner again fell in love, but his bashfulness ruined his chances. He wrote to the brother of the lady. "If she would only waive her bashfulness, or, in other words, make an offer instead of expecting one, the same (Solus Lodge) might change occupiers." Faint heart certainly did not win fair lady in this case, for she married another. Before he died Turner was offered $25,000 for two pictures which he would not sell. "No" he said. "I have willed them and cannot sell them." He disposed of several great works as legacies. One picture of which he was very fond, "Carthage," was the occasion of an amusing anecdote. "Chantry," he said to his friend the sculptor, "I want you to promise that when I am dead you will see me rolled in that canvas when I'm buried."

"All right," said Chantry, "I'll do it, but I'll promise to have you taken up and unrolled, also."

A remarkable incident of generosity is told of Turner. In 1826 he hung two exquisite pictures in the Academy. One, "Cologne," having a most beautiful, golden effect. This was hung between two portraits by Sir Thomas Lawrence. The golden colouring of Turner's picture entirely destroyed the effect of the Lawrence pictures, and without a word, Turner washed his lovely picture over with lampblack. This gave the Lawrence, pictures their full colour value. A friend who had been enthusiastic about the "Cologne" was provoked with Turner. "What in the world did you do that for?" he demanded. "Well, poor Lawrence was so unhappy. It will all wash off after the exhibition." Turner had his reward in cash, for the picture sold for 2,000 guineas.

Above all things Turner hated engravings, or any process that cheapened art, and one day he stated this to his friend Lawrence. "I don't choose to be a basket engraver," he declared.

"What do you mean by that," Sir Thomas inquired.

"Why when I got off the coach t' other day at Hastings, a woman came up with a basket of your 'Mrs. Peel,' and offered to sell me one for a sixpence."

Turner dearly loved his friends, and the story of Chantry's death, illustrates it. He was in his room when the sculptor breathed his last, and just as he died, the artist turned to another friend, George Jones, and with tears streaming down his face, wrung Jones's hand and rushed from the room, unable to speak.

Again, when William Frederick Wells, another friend, died, Turner rushed to the house of Clara Wells, his daughter, and cried: "Oh Clara, Clara! these are iron tears. I have lost the best friend I ever had in my life."

In his old age Turner suddenly disappeared from all his haunts, and his friends could not find him. They were much troubled, but one day his old housekeeper found a note in a pocket of an old coat, which made her think he had gone to Chelsea. She looked there for him, and found him very ill, in a little cottage on the Thames River. Everybody about called him Admiral Booth, believing him to be a retired admiral. He had felt his death near and had tried to meet it quite alone. He died the very day after his friends found him, as he was being wheeled by them to the window to look out upon the river for the last time. He was buried in St. Paul's Cathedral between Sir Joshua Reynolds and James Barry. He left his drawings and pictures to a "Turner Gallery," and $100,000 to the Royal Academy, to be used for a medal to be struck every two years for the best exhibitor. The rest of his fortune went to care for "poor and decayed male artists born in England and of English parents only." This was to be known as Turner's Gift, and that is why he had saved money all his life.

A few more of the numberless stories of his generosity should be told. A picture had been sent to the Academy by a painter named Bird It was very fine, and Turner was full of its praise, but when they came to hang it no place could be found.

"It can't be hung," the others of the committee said.

"It must be hung," returned Turner, but nothing could be done about it, for there was absolutely no place. Then Turner went aside with the picture and sat studying it a long time. Finally he got up, took down a picture of his own and hung Bird's in its place. "There!" he said. "It is hung!"

Again, an old drawing-master died and Turner who had known the family for a long time, was aware that they were destitute, so he gave the widow a good sum of money with which to bury her husband and to meet general expenses. After some time she came to him with the money; but Turner put his hands in his pockets. "No," he said; "keep it. Use it to send the children to school and to church."

On one occasion when he had irritably sent a beggar from his house, he ran out and called her back, thrusting a £5 note into her hand before letting her go.

There was a man who in Turner's youth, while the little fellow was making pictures in the cheerless barber shop bought all of these drawings he could find. He often raised the price and in every way tried to help Turner. In after years that old patron went bankrupt. Turner heard that his steward had been instructed to cut down some fine old trees on this man's estate, and sell them. Turner, without letting himself be known in the matter, at once stopped the cutting and put into his old patron's hands about £20,000. The rescued man, afterward, through the same channels that he had received the money, paid it all back. Years passed, and the son of that same man got into the same difficulties, and again, without being known in the matter, Turner restored his fortune. That son, in his turn, honestly paid back the full amount. This was the miser who saved all his money--to do good deeds to his friends. Ruskin wrote that in all his life he had never heard from Turner one unkind or blameful word for others.

PLATE--THE FIGHTING TÉMÉRAIRE

This was the picture which Turner loved best of all, the one he would never sell; but at his death ho gave it to the English nation.

"Many years before he painted it, he had gone down to Portsmouth one day to see Nelson's fleet come in after the glorious victory of Trafalgar. The *Téméraire* was pointed out to him--a battle ship that had very proudly borne the English flag, for during the battle it had run in between two French frigates and captured them both.

"And now between thirty and forty years later, he lingered one afternoon on the banks of the Thames. As he looked over the water he saw the grand old hulk being towed down the river by a noisy little tug to be broken up at Deptford. 'There's a fine subject!' he exclaimed as he looked at the heroic ship thathad known many glorious years; and in his thought he compared it to 'a battle-scarred warrior borne to the grave.'

"Then he painted the picture. The glow of the setting sun irradiates the scene and bids farewell to the old ship. Twilight is coming on, and the new moon has just risen in its pearly light. It is a pathetic picture," and well illustrates how truly a "master of sunsets and waves" the artist was.

Among his other paintings are several of Venice; "The Slave Ship" and many other sea pieces.

XL SIR ANTHONY VAN DYCK

Flemish School

1599-1641
Pupil of Rubens

Anthony Van Dyke's father was neither a gentleman nor an ill-born person. He was "betwixt-and-between," being a silk merchant, who met so many fine folk that he seemed to be "fine folk" himself; and by the time Anthony had grown up, he actually believed himself to be one of them. If manners stand for fineness Sir Anthony must have been superfine, because he was almost overburdened with "manners."

He became a wonderful, be-laced, perfumed, shiny gentleman who never stooped to paint anything less than royalty and its associates, nor in anything less than velvets and laces. Like Rembrandt and Gainsborough, he set a fashion--or rather the style in which he painted came to be known after his name. We are all familiar with the kind of ornamentation on clothes called Van Dyck--pointed lace, or trimmings--and pointed beards.

As a very young lad he was almost too dainty to be liked by healthy boys; and the worst of it was he did not care whether healthy, robust chaps liked him or not; certainly he did not care for them. He liked to sit in his father's shop and be smiled upon by the great ladies who came to buy, and in turn to smile shyly at them; this tendency became stronger as he grew to be a man.

Anthony's mother made the most exquisite embroideries, and this may mean that some part of his art was inherited. She handled lovely colours, and tried to fashion beautiful flower shapes for customers. She was a fragile, tender sort of woman, while the father was doubtless a dapper, over-nice little fellow.

Anthony was born in Antwerp, and the facts concerning his education, as in the case of most artists, are lost to our knowledge. He probably had a little of some sort outside of painting, but it certainly was not enough to hurt him, nor to make a fine healthy man of him. He was very beautiful, in a lady-like, faint-coloured way, not in the least resembling the handsome, gorgeous, elegant, robust Rubens, a true cavalier, of a dashing sort.

He was apprenticed to a painter when he was ten years old, and later on became the pupil of Rubens. He painted a whole series of Apostles' heads, about which a lawsuit took place. The papers relating to this were found about twenty years ago, though the lawsuit occurred as far back as 1615. Several of the Apostles' heads that brought about the suit are to-day to be seen in the gallery at Dresden.

Everything in those days--especially in Germany and Holland--was represented by a "guild." In reading about the Mastersingers of Nuremberg we are told that on the day when the trial of singers was to take place, dozens of "guilds" assembled in the meadow--guilds of bakers, of shoemakers--of which Hans Sachs was the head--guilds of goldsmiths, etc. Van Dyck was a member of the painters' guild when he was no more than nineteen. His work at that time showed so much strength that there is a picture of his, an old gentleman and lady, in the Dresden gallery, which for a long time was supposed to have been painted by his master, Rubens.

An intimate friend of Van Dyck, Kenelm Digby, says that Van Dyck's first relations with Rubens came about by Van Dyck being employed to make engravings for the reproduction of Rubens's great works. After that he studied painting with him.

One of his friends of that time wrote that at twenty Van Dyck was nearly as great as Rubens, though this is hardly substantiated by the verdict of time, and that being a man with very rich family connections, he could hardly be expected to leave home. On every hand we have signs of the artist's affected feeling about himself and other people.

However, an annual pension from the King of England seems to have made travelling possible to this fine gentleman of lace ruffles, pale face, and lady-like ways.

There is an entry about him on the royal account book of "Special service ... performed for His Majesty." Also "Antonio Van Dyck, gent., *His Majesty's servant*, is allowed to travaile 8 months, he havinge obtayneid his Majesty's leave in that behalf, as was signified to the E. of Arundel." Certainly by that time Van Dyck had become a truly great portrait painter; not the greatest, because every picture showed the same characteristics in its subject--elegance, fine clothes, languid manners, without force of great truth or any excellent moral quality to distinguish one from another. Nevertheless, the kind of painting that he did, he did better than anyone else had ever done, or probably ever will do.

While in England he painted all the royalties and many aristocrats, and wherever he went he was always painting pictures of himself.

He travelled about a good deal, always painting people of the same class--kings and queens and fine folk, and painting them pretty nearly all alike.

When he went to Italy he was everywhere received as a great painter, but while artists agreed that his work was excellent he was not much liked by them, and many tales are told about that journey which are interesting, if not entirely true. Van Dyck was the sort of man about whom tales would be made up. One, however, sounds true. It is said that he fell in love--which of course he was always doing--with a beautiful country girl, and that for love of her he painted an altar piece into which he put himself, seated on the great gray horse which Rubens had given him. That picture is in St. Martin's Church at Saventhem, near Brussels, but although one is inclined to believe this story because it was quite the sort of thing which might be expected of Van Dyck, even this is not true, because the painting was done long after the artist had made his Italian journey, and it was commissioned by a gentleman living at Saventhem, whose daughter Van Dyck undoubtedly liked pretty well; but he made the picture for money, not for love.

While he was in Italy he lived with a cardinal, and painted languid pictures of sacred subjects, which were far from being his best work. The best that he did was in portraiture. Distinguished though he was, he did not have a very good time in Italy, because he would not join the artists who worked there, nor associate with them in the least, and naturally this made him disliked.

We see a good many portraits painted by Van Dyck, of persons mounted upon or standing beside the gray horse, and these were painted about the time of that Italian journey. He used the Rubens horse in many paintings.

Of all the people with whom he painted, he most valued the knowledge he got from a blind woman painter of Sicily, called Sofonisba Anguisciola, and he often said that he had learned more from a blind woman than from all the open-eyed men he ever knew. This woman artist was over ninety years old at the time he learned from her.

While he was in Italy the plague broke out, and Van Dyck fled for his life, leaving an unfinished picture behind him, one ordered by the English king, the subject being Rinaldo and Armida, which had gained for the artist his knighthood pension.

It is said that during his first year in England he painted the king and queen twelve times. He had an extraordinary record for industry, and painted very quickly, as he had need to do, because it took a great deal of money to buy the sort of things Van Dyck liked--fine laces and velvets, perfumes and satins. His plan was to sketch his subject first on gray paper with black and white chalk, and after that he gave the sketch to an assistant who increased it to the size he wished to paint. The next step was to set his painter to work upon the clothing of his figures. This was painted in roughly, together with background and any architectural effect Van Dyck wanted. After this the artist himself sat down and in three or four sittings, of not more than an hour each, he was able to finish a picture worth to-day thousands of dollars.

He painted hands specially well, and kept certain models for them alone.

Van Dyck had eleven brothers and sisters, whom he always kept in mind. Some of his sisters had become nuns while some of his brothers were priests, and Van Dyck's influence got a monkish brother called to the Dutch court to act as chaplain to the queen.

By this time every royal personage in the world, nearly, had sent for Van Dyck to paint his portrait, for he could make one look handsomer than could any other painter in existence. If the king was very ugly, Van Dyck painted such beautiful clothes upon him that nobody noticed the plainness of the features.

When Van Dyck was about thirty-six years old he married a great lady, the Lady Mary Ruthven, granddaughter of the Earl of Gowrie, but before that he had had a lady-love, Margaret Lemon, whom he painted as the Virgin and in several other pictures. When he married Lady Mary, Margaret Lemon was so furiously jealous that she tried to injure Van Dyck's right hand so that he could paint no more.

About this time Rubens died in Flanders, leaving behind him an unfinished series of pictures which had been commissioned by the king of Spain. Van Dyck was asked to finish these, but declined until he was asked to make an independent picture, to complete the series, and this he was delighted to do. Ferdinand of Austria wrote to the king of Spain that Van Dyck had returned in great haste to London to arrange for his change of home, in order to do the work. "Possibly he may still change his mind," he added, "for he is stark mad." This shows how Van Dyck's erratic ways appeared to some people.

He had a sister, Justiniana, who was also something of an artist and she married a nobleman when she was about twelve years old.

When Van Dyck died he was buried in St. Paul's, London, and Charles I. placed an inscription on his tomb.

In the "Young People's Story of Art," is the following anecdote: "A visit was once paid by a courtly looking stranger passing through Haarlem, to Franz Hals, the distinguished Dutch painter.

"Hals was not at home but he was sent for to the tavern and hastily returned. The stranger told him that he had heard of his reputation--had just two hours to spare--and wished to have his portrait painted. Hals, seizing canvas and brushes fell vigorously to work; and before the given time had elapsed, he said, 'Have the goodness to rise, sir, and examine your portrait!' The stranger looked at it, expressed his satisfaction, and then said, 'Painting seems such a very easy thing, suppose we change places and see what I can do!'

"Hals assented, and took his position as the sitter. The unknown began, and as Hals watched him, he saw that he wielded the brush so quickly, he must be a painter. His work, too, was rapidly finished, and as Hals looked at it he exclaimed, 'You must be Van Dyck! No one else could paint such a portrait!'

"No two portraits could have been more unlike. The story adds that the famous Dutch and Flemish masters heartily embraced each other."

The stories of Van Dyck's youth are interesting, and probably true. It is said that he drew so well when he was a pupil of Rubens that the great master often allowed him to retouch his own works. Once in Rubens's studio, some of the students got the key and went in to see what the master was doing, when he was absent. Rubens had left a painting fresh upon the easel, and in looking about them one of the boys rubbed against it. This frightened them all. What should they do? Rubens would find his picture ruined and know that they had broken in.

After consultation they decided there was no one with them who could repair the damage as well as Van Dyck, who set about it, and soon he had painted in the smudged part so perfectly that when Rubens saw it, he did not for some time know that anything had happened to his picture. Later he suspected something, and when he learned of the prank and its outcome, he was so delighted with Van Dyck's work that he praised him instead of blaming him for it.

Van Dyck had a very precise method of working. When sitters came to him he would paint for just one hour. Then he would politely dismiss them, and his servant would wash his brushes, and clear the way for the next sitter. He dined with his sitters often that he might surprise in them the expression which he wanted to paint. Also, he had their clothing sent to his studio, that it might be exactly imitated by himself or by those assistants who painted in the foundation for his finished work.

While attached to King Charles I.'s court, Van Dyck was given a fine house at Blackfriars, on the Thames, and he had a private landing place made for boats, so that the royal family might visit him at their convenience. Charles I. used often to go to Van Dyck's studio to escape his many troubles, and thus the artist's home became as fashionable a gathering place, as Gainsborough's studio was in Bath. He painted Queen Henrietta not less than twenty-five times. He often furnished concerts for his sitters, for he himself was passionately fond of music, and moreover he believed that music often brought to the faces of his sitters, an expression that he loved to paint.

He painted so many pictures of a certain kind of little dog, in the pictures of King Charles I. that ever since that breed has been known as the King Charles spaniel.

After a while Van Dyck got heavily into debt. King Charles himself was in great trouble, and he had no money with which to pay his painter's pension. The artist had lived so extravagantly that he did not know at last which way to turn, so in desperation he thought to try alchemy and maybe to learn the secret of making gold. He wasted much time at this, as cleverer men have done, but at last he became too ill for that or for his own proper work, and badly off though Charles was himself, he offered his court physician a large sum if he could cure his court painter. But Van Dyck had enjoyed life too well, and nothing could be done for him.

He was the seventh child of his parents--which some have thought had something to do with his genius and success; he lived gaily all the years of his life, going restlessly from place to place, and having many acquaintances but probably few friends, outside of his old master, Rubens, who loved him for his genius.

PLATE--CHILDREN OF CHARLES THE FIRST

Van Dyck painted the family of the unfortunate king of England four times. There are five children in the Windsor Castle picture, and this one, which hangs in the Turin Gallery, was probably painted before the birth of the fourth child in 1636. It is celebrated for its colouring as well as for its great artistic merit. The children are surely childlike enough, despite their stately attire, and they little dream of the sad fate awaiting the whole of the Stuart family to which they belong.

Other Van Dycks are: "The Blessed Herman Joseph," "Lords Digby and Russell," "Lord Wharton," "Countess Folkestone," and "William Prince of Orange."

XLI VELASQUEZ (DIEGO RODRIGUEZ DE SILVA)

(Pronounced Vay-lahs'keth)

Castilian School

1599-1669
Pupil of Herrera

It is pretty difficult to find out why a man was named so-and-so in the days of the early Italian and Spanish painters. More likely than not they would be called after the master to whom they had been first apprenticed; or after their trade; after the town from which they came, and rarely because their father had had the name before them. In Velasquez's case, he was named after his mother.

No one seemed to be certain what to call him, but he generally wrote his name "Diego de Silva Velasquez." His father was Rodriguez de Silva, a lawyer, but in calling the boy Velasquez the family followed a universal Spanish custom of naming children after their mothers.

Little Velasquez was well taught in his childhood; he studied many languages and philosophy, for he was intended to be a lawyer or something learned, anything but a painter. The disappointment of parents in those days, when they found a child was likely to become an artist is touching.

Despite his equipment for a useful life, according to the ideas of his parents, this little chap was bound to become nothing but a maker of pictures.

Herrera was a bad-tempered master and little Velasquez could not get on with him, so after a year of harsh treatment, he went to another master, Pacheco, but by that time he had learned a secret that was to help make his work great. Herrera had taught him to use a brush with very long bristles, which had the effect of spreading the paint, making it look as if his "colours had floated upon the canvas," in a way that was the "despair of those who came after him."

Velasquez was born in Seville at a time when about all the art of the world was Italian or German; thus he became the creator of a new school of painting.

He stayed five years in Pacheco's studio and pupil and master became very fond of each other. Pacheco was not a great master--not so good as Herrera--but he was easy to get on with, and knew a good deal about painting, so that as Velasquez had the genius, he was as well placed as he needed to be.

In Pacheco's studio there was a peasant boy whose face was very mobile, showed every passing feeling; and Velasquez used to make him laugh and weep, till, surprising some good expression, he would quickly sketch him. With this excellent model, Velasquez did a surprising amount of good work.

Spain had just then conquered the far-off provinces of Mexico and Peru, and was continually receiving from its newly got lands much valuable merchandise. Rapidly growing rich, this Latin country loved art and all things beautiful, so its money was bound to be spent freely in such ways. Madrid had been made its capital, and at that time there were few fine pictures to be found there. The Moors who had conquered Spain had forbidden picture making, because it was contrary to their religion to represent the human figure, or even the figures of birds and beasts. Then the Inquisition had hindered art by its rules, one of which was that the Virgin Mary should always be painted with her feet covered; another, that all saints should be beardless. There were many more exactions.

While cathedrals were being built elsewhere, the Moors had been in control of Spanish lands, so that no cathedral had been built there, and when Velasquez came upon the scene the time of great cathedral building was past. It had ceased to be the fashion. Although there had been such painters as Beneguette, Morales, Navarrette, and Ribera, all Spanish and of considerable genius, they had been too badly handicapped to make painting a great art in Spain. When Madrid became the capital of Spain, it had no unusual buildings, unless it was an old fortress of the Moors, the Alcazar, Caesar's house, but the nation was buying paintings from Italy, and it began to beautify Madrid, which had the advantage of the former Moorish luxury and art, very beautiful, though not pictorial.

In Madrid, then, there seemed to be great opportunity for a fine artist like Velasquez, and his master urged him to go there and try his fortune. So he set out on mule-back, attended by his slave, but unless he could get the ear of the king, it was useless for him to seek advancement in Madrid. Without the king as patron at that time, an artist could not accomplish much. After trying again and again, Velasquez had to return to his old master, without having seen the king; but after a time a picture of his was seen by Philip IV., and he was so much pleased with it that he summoned the artist. Through his minister, Olivares, he offered him $113.40 in gold (fifty ducats) to pay his return expenses. The next year he gave him $680.40 to move his family to Madrid.

At last the artist had found a place in the rich city, and he went to live at the court where the warmest friendship grew between him and the king. The latter was an author and something of a painter, so that they loved the same things. This friendship lasted all their lives, and they were together most of the time, the king always being found, in Velasquez's studio in the palace when his duties did not call him elsewhere. During the many many years--nearly thirty-seven--that Velasquez lived with Philip IV. he employed himself in painting the scenes at court. Thus he became the pictorial historian of the Spanish capital. He was a man of good disposition, kindly and generous in conduct and in feeling, so that he was always in the midst of friends and well-wishers.

Philip IV. was indeed a noble companion, but he was not a gay one, being known as the king who never laughed--or at least whose laughter was so rare, the few times he did laugh became historic. One would expect this serious and depressing atmosphere to have had an effect upon a painter's art; but it chanced that Rubens visited Spain, and there, Velasquez being the one famous artist, it was natural they should become interested in each other. Rubens told Velasquez of the wonders of Italian painting, till the Spaniard could think of nothing else, and finally he begged Philip to let him journey to Italy that he might see some of those wonders for himself. The request made the king unhappy at first, but at last he gave his consent and Velasquez set out for Italy. The king gave him money and letters of introduction, and he went in company with the Marquis of Spinola.

After Velasquez had stayed eighteen months in Italy, Philip began to long for his friend and sent for him to return. He came back full of the stories of brilliant Italy, and charmed the king completely.

There is as absurd a story of Velasquez's perfection in painting as that of Raphael's, whose portrait of the pope, left upon the terrace to dry, imposed upon passers by. It is said of Velasquez's work that when he had painted an admiral whom the king had ordered to sea, and left it exposed in his studio, the king, entering, thought it was the admiral himself, and angrily inquired why he had not put to sea according to orders. On the face of them these stories are false, but they serve to suggest the perfection of these artists' paintings.

Philip, being a melancholy man, had his court full of jesters, poor misshapen creatures--dwarfs and hunchbacks--who were supposed to appear "funny," and Velasquez, as court painter, painted those whom he continually saw about him, who formed the court family. Thus we have pictures of strange groups--dwarfs, little princesses, dressed precisely as the elders were dressed, favourite dogs, and Velasquez himself at his easel.

In 1618, while still with his master, Pacheco, he had married the master's daughter, a big, portly woman. Before he left Seville he bad two daughters.

These were all the children he had, although he painted a picture of "Velasquez's Family" which includes a great number of people. The figures in that painting are the children of his daughter, not his own; and this may account for one biographer's statement that the artist had "seven children." He was devoted to and happy in his family of children and grandchildren.

He did not grow rich, but received regularly during his life in Madrid, twenty gold ducats ($45.36) a month to live upon, and besides this his medical attendance, lodging, and additional payment for every picture. The one which brought him this good fortune was an equestrian portrait of Philip; first uncovered on the steps of San Felipe. Everywhere the people were delighted with it, poets sung of it, and the king declared no other should ever paint his portrait. This picture has long since disappeared.

In 1627 Velasquez won the prize for a picture representing the expulsion of the Moors from Spain and was rewarded by "being appointed gentleman usher. To this was shortly afterward added a daily allowance of twelve reals--the same amount which was allowed to court barbers--and ninety gold ducats ($204.12) a year for dress, which was also paid to the dwarfs, buffoons, and players about the king's person--truly a curious estimate of talent at the court of Spain."

The record of Philip IV. with unpleasing, even degenerate characters, about him, is brightened by the thought of his loyalty to his court painter and life-long friend. When the king's favourites fell, those who had been the friends of Velasquez, the artist loyally remained their friend in adversity as he had been while they were powerful. This constancy, even to the royal enemies, was never resented by Philip. He honoured the faithfulness of his artist, even as he himself was faithful in this friendship. Philip's court was such that there was little to paint that was ennobling, and so Velasquez lacked the inspiration of such surroundings as the Italian painters had.

Philip IV. was hail-fellow-well-met with his stablemen, his huntsmen, his cooks, and yet he seems to have had no sense of humour, was long faced and forbidding to look at, and despite his strange habits considered himself the most mighty and haughty man in the world. He felt himself free to behave as he chose, because he was Philip of Spain; and he chose to do a great many absurd and outrageous things. In all Philip's portraits, painted by Velasquez, he wears a stiff white linen collar of his own invention, and he was so proud of this that he celebrated it by a festival. He went in procession to church to thank God for the wonderful blessing of the *Golilla*--the name of his collar. This unsightly thing became the fashion, and all portraits of men of that time were painted with it. "In regard to the wonderful structure of Philip's moustaches it is said, that, to preserve their form they were encased during the night in perfumed leather covers called *bigoteras*." Such absurdities in a king, who had the responsibilities of a nation upon him, seem incredible.

Velasquez made in all three journeys to Italy, and the last one was on a mission for the king, which was much to the latter's credit. Philip had determined to have a fine art gallery in Madrid, for Spain had by this time many pictures, but no statuary; so he commissioned his painter to buy whatever he thought well of and *could* buy, in Italy. Hence the artist set off again with his slave--the same one with whom he had journeyed to Madrid so long before. His name was Pareja, and his master had already made an excellent artist of him.

They went to Genoa, thence to the great art-centres of Italy, were received everywhere with honour, and the artist bought wisely. Velasquez did not care for Raphael's paintings as much as for Titian's, and he said so to Salvator Rosa, an honoured painter in Italy.

While in Rome Velasquez painted the pope, also his own slave, Pareja.

When he returned to Spain he took with him three hundred statues, but a large number of them were nude, and the Spanish court, not over particular about most things, was very particular about naked statues, so that after Philip's death, they nearly all disappeared. After his return, and after the queen had died and Philip had married again, Velasquez was made quartermaster-general, no easy post but not without honour, though it interfered with his picture painting a good deal. He had to look after the comfort of all the court, and to see that the apartments it occupied, at home or when it visited, were suitable.

"Even the powerful king of Spain could not make his favourite a belted knight without a commission to inquire into the purity of his lineage on both sides of the house. Fortunately, the pedigree could bear scrutiny, as for generations the family was found free from all taint of heresy, from all trace of Jewish or Moorish blood, and from contamination from trade or commerce. The difficulty connected with the fact that he was a painter was got over by his being painter to the king and by the declaration that he did not sell his pictures."

The red Cross of Santiago conferred upon him by Philip, made Velasquez a knight and freed him also from the rulings of the Inquisition, which directed so largely what artists could and could not do. Thus it is that we come to have certain great pictures from Velasquez's brush which could not otherwise have been painted.

This action of the king, setting free the artist, made two schools of art, of which the court painter represented one; and Murillo the other, under the command of the Church. Although not so rich perhaps as Raphael, Velasquez lived and died in plenty, while Murillo, the artist of the Church of Rome, was a poverty-stricken man.

Finally, while in the midst of honours, and fulfilling his official duty to the court of Spain, Velasquez contracted the disease which killed him. The Infanta, Maria Theresa, was to wed Louis XIV., and the ceremony was to take place on a swampy little island called the Island of Pheasants. There he went to decorate a pavilion and other places of display. He became ill with a fever and died soon after he returned to Madrid.

He made his wife, his old master Pacheco's daughter, his executor, and was buried in the church of San Juan, in the vault of Fuensalida; but within a week his devoted wife was dead, and in eight days' time she was buried beside him.

He left his affairs--accounts between him and the court--badly entangled, and it was many years before they were straightened out. His many deeds of kindness lived after him. He made of his slave a good artist and a devoted friend, and by his efforts the slave became a freedman. The story of his kindly help to Murillo when that exquisite painter came, unknown and friendless to Madrid, has already been told.

The Church where Velasquez was buried was destroyed by the French in 1811, and all trace of the resting place of the great Spanish artist is forever lost to us.

He is called not only "painter to the king," but "king of painters."

PLATE--EQUESTRIAN PORTRAIT OF DON BALTHASAR CARLOS.

Philip of Spain had long prayed for a son and when at last one was granted him his pride in his young heir was unbounded. The little Don Carlos was not unworthy, for he was a cheerful, hearty boy, trained to horsemanship, from his fourth year, for his father was a noted rider and had the best instructors for his son. The prince was a brave hunter too and we are told that he shot a wild boar when he was but nine years of age. In this portrait which is in the Museo del Prado he is six years old, and it was neither the first nor the last that Velasquez made of him. It was one of the court painter's chief duties to see that the heir to the throne was placed upon canvas at every stage of his career, and he painted him from two years of age till his lamented death at sixteen.

The young prince wears in this picture a green velvet jacket with white sleeves and his scarf is crimson embroidered with gold. The lively pony is a light chestnut and the foreshortening of its body must be noticed. The steady grave eyes of the lad are gazing far ahead as they would naturally be if he were riding rapidly, but his princely dignity is shown in his firm seat in the saddle and his manner of holding his marshal's batôn.

The great art of the painter is also shown in the way he subordinates the landscape to the figure. He will not allow even a tree to come near the young horseman, but brings his young activity into vivid contrast with the calm peacefulness of the distant view.

With the death of Don Carlos the downfall of his father's dynasty was assured, though for a time his little sister, the Infanta Maria Theresa, was upheld as the heiress. She married Louis XIV. and had a weary time of it in France. Velasquez painted her picture too, in the grown up dress of the children of that day. It is in the Vienna Gallery. Among his best known pictures are "The Surrender of Breda," "Alessandro del Borro," and "Philip IV."

XLII PAUL VERONESE (PAOLO CAGLIARI)

(Pronounced Vay-ro-nay'zay and pah'o-lah cal-ee-ah'ree)

Venetian School

1528-1588
Pupil of Titian

"One has never done well enough, when one can do better; one never knows enough when he can learn more!"

This was the motto of Paul Veronese. This artist was born in Verona--whence he took his name--and spent much of his life with the monks in the monastery of St. Sebastian.

His father was a sculptor, and taught his son. Veronese himself was a lovable fellow, had a kind feeling for all, and in return received the good will of most people. When he first went to Venice to study he took letters of introduction to the monks of St. Sebastian, and finally went to live with them, for his uncle was prior of the monastery, and it was upon its walls that he did his first work in Venice. His subject was the story of Esther, which he illustrated completely.

He became known in time as "the most magnificent of magnificent painters." He loved the gaieties of Venice; the lords and ladies; the exquisite colouring; the feasting and laughter, and everything he painted, showed this taste. When he chose great religious subjects he dressed all his figures in elegant Venetian costumes, in the midst of elegant Venetian scenes. His Virgins, or other Biblical people, were not Jews of Palestine, but Venetians of Venice, but so beautiful were they and so inspiring, that nobody cared to criticise them on that score. He loved to paint festival scenes such as, "The Marriage at Cana," "Banquet in Levi's House," or "Feast in the House of Simon." He painted nothing as it could possibly have been, but everything as he would have liked it to be.

Into the "Wedding Feast at Cana," where Jesus was said to have turned the water into wine, he introduced a great host of his friends, people then living. Titian is there, and several reigning kings and queens, including Francis I. of France and his bride, for whom the picture was made. This treatment of the Bible story startles the mind, but delights the eye.

It was said that his "red recurred like a joyful trumpet blast among the silver gray harmonies of his paintings."

Muther, one who has written brilliantly about him, tells us that "Veronese seems to have come into the world to prove that the painter need have neither head nor heart, but only a hand, a brush, and a pot of paint in order to clothe all the walls of the world with oil paintings" and that "if he paints Mary, she is not the handmaid of the Lord or even the Queen of Heaven, but a woman of the world, listening with approving smile to the homage of a cavalier. In light red silk morning dress, she receives the Angel of the Annunciation and hears without surprise--for she has already heard it--what he has to say; and at the Entombment she only weeps in order to keep up appearances."

Such criticism raises a smile, but it is quite just, and what is more, the Veronese pictures are so beautiful that one is not likely to quarrel with the painter for having more good feeling than understanding. His joyous temperament came near to doing him harm, for he was summoned before the Inquisition for the manner in which he had painted "The Last Supper."

After the Esther pictures in St. Sebastian, the artist painted there the "Martyrdom of St. Sebastian," and there is a tradition that he did his work while hiding in the monastery because of some mischief of which he had been guilty.

At that time he was not much more than twenty-six or eight, while the great painter Tintoretto was forty-five, yet his work in St. Sebastian made him as famous as the older artist.

There is very little known of the private affairs of Veronese. He signed a contract for painting the "Marriage at Cana," for the refectory of the monastery of St. Giorgio Maggiore, in June 1562, and that picture, stupendous as it is, was finished eighteen months later. He received $777.60 for it, as well as his living while he was at work upon it, and a tun of wine. One picture he is supposed to have left behind him at a house where he had been entertained, as an acknowledgment of the courtesy shown him.

Paul had a brother, Benedetto, ten years younger than himself, and it is said that he greatly helped Paul in his work, by designing the architectural backgrounds of his pictures. If that is so, Benedetto must have been an artist of much genius, for those backgrounds in the paintings are very fine.

Veronese married, and had two sons; the younger being named Carletto. He was also the favourite, and an excellent artist, who did some fine painting, but he died while he was still young. Gabriele the elder son, also painted, but he was mainly a man of affairs, and attended to business rather than to art.

Veronese was a loving father and brother, and beyond doubt a happy man. After his death both his sons and his brother worked upon his unfinished paintings, completing them for him. He was buried in the Church of St. Sebastian.

PLATE--THE MARRIAGE AT CANA

This painting is most characteristic of Veronese's methods. He has no regard for the truth in presenting the picture story. At the marriage at Cana everybody must have been very simply dressed, and there could have been no beautiful architecture, such as we see in the picture. In the painting we find courtier-like men and women dressed in beautiful silks. Some of the costumes appear to be a little Russian in character, the others Venetian; and Jesus Himself wears the loose every-day robe of the pastoral people to whom he belonged. We think of luxury and rich food and a splendid house when we look at this painting, when as a matter of fact nothing of this sort could have belonged to the scene which Veronese chose to represent. Perhaps no painter was more lacking in imagination than was Veronese in painting this particular picture. He chose to place historical or legendary characters, in the midst of a scene which could not have existed co-incidently with the event.

Among his other pictures are "Europa and the Bull," "Venice Enthroned," and the "Presentation of the Family of Darius to Alexander."

XLIII LEONARDO DA VINCI

(Pronounced Lay-o-nar'do dah Veen'chee)

Florentine School

1451-1519
Pupil of Verrocchio

Leonardo da Vinci was the natural son of a notary, Ser Pier, and he was born at the Castello of Vinci, near Empoli. From the very hour that he was apprenticed to his master, Verrocchio, he proved that he was the superior of his master in art. Da Vinci was one of the most remarkable men who ever lived, because he not only did an extraordinary number of things, but he did all of them well.

He was an engineer, made bridges, fortifications, and plans which to this day are brilliant achievements.

He was a sculptor, and as such did beautiful work.

He was a naturalist, and as such was of use to the world.

He was an author and left behind him books written backward, of which he said that only he who was willing to devote enough study to them to read them in that form, was able to profit by what he had written.

Finally, and most wonderfully, he was a painter.

He had absolute faith in himself. Before he constructed his bridge he said that he could build the best one in the world, and a king took him at his word and was not disappointed by the result.

He stated that he could paint the finest picture in the world--but let us read what he himself said of it, in so sure and superbly confident a way that it robbed his statement of anything like foolish vanity. Such as he could afford to speak frankly of his greatness, without appearing absurd. He wrote:

"In time of peace, I believe I can equal anyone in architecture, in constructing public and private buildings, and in conducting water from one place to another. I can execute sculpture, whether in marble, bronze, or terra cotta, and in painting I can do as much as any other man, be he who he may. Further, I could engage to execute the bronze horse in eternal memory of your father and the illustrious house of Sforza." He was writing to Ludovico Sforza whose house then ruled at Milan. "If any of the above-mentioned things should appear to you impossible or impracticable, I am ready to make trial of them in your park, or in any other place that may please your excellency, to whom I commend myself in proud humility."

Leonardo's experiments with oils and the mixing of his pigments has nearly lost to us his most remarkable pictures. His first fourteen years of work as an artist were spent in Milan, where he was employed to paint by the Duke of Milan, and never again was his life so peaceful; it was ever afterward full of change. He went from Milan to Venice, to Rome, to Florence, and back to Milan where his greatest work was done.

While Leonardo was a baby he lived in the Castle of Vinci. He was beautiful as a child and very handsome as a man. When a child he wore long curls reaching below his waist. He was richly clothed, and greatly beloved. His body seemed no less wonderful than his mind. He wished to learn everything, and his memory was so wonderful that he remembered all that he undertook to learn. His muscles were so powerful that he could bend iron, and all animals seemed to love him. It is said he could tame the wildest horses. Indeed his life and accomplishments read as if he were one enchanted. One writer tells us that "he never could bear to see any creature cruelly treated, and sometimes he would buy little caged birds that he might just have the pleasure of opening the doors of their cages, and setting them at liberty."

The story told of his first known work is that his master, being hurried in finishing a picture, permitted Leonardo to paint in an angel's head, and that it was so much better than the rest of the picture, that Verrocchio burned his brushes and broke his palette, determined never to paint again, but probably this is a good deal of a fairy tale and one that is not needed to impress us with the artist's greatness, since there is so much to prove it without adding fable to fact.

Leonardo was also a very far seeing inventor and most ingenious. He made mechanical toys that "worked" when they were wound up. He even devised a miniature flying machine; however, history does not tell us whether it flew or not. He thought out the uses of steam as a motive power long before Fulton's time.

Leonardo haunted the public streets, sketchbook in hand, and when attracted by a face, would follow till he was able to transfer it to paper. Ida Prentice Whitcomb, who has compiled many anecdotes of da Vinci, says that it was also his habit to invite peasants to his house, and there amuse them with funny stories till he caught some fleeting expression of mirth which he was pleased to reproduce.

As a courtier Leonardo was elegant and full of amusing devices. He sang, accompanying himself on a silver lute, which he had had fashioned in imitation of a horse's skull. After he attached himself to the court of the Duke of Milan, his gift of invention was constantly called into use, and one of the surprises he had in store for the Duke's guests was a great mechanical lion, which being wound up, would walk into the presence of the court, open its mouth and disclose a bunch of flowers inside.

Leonardo worked very slowly upon his paintings, because he was never satisfied with a work, and would retouch it day after day. Then, too, he was a man of moods, like most geniuses, and could not work with regularity. The picture of the "Last Supper" was painted in Milan, by order of his patron, the Duke, and there are many picturesque stories written of its production. It was painted upon the refectory wall of a Dominican convent, the Santa Maria delle Grazie; and at first the work went off well, and the artist would remain upon his scaffolding from morning till night, absorbed in his painting. It is said that at such times he neither ate nor drank, forgetting all but his great work. He kept postponing the painting of two heads--Christ and Judas.

He had worked painstakingly and with enthusiasm till that point, but deferred what he was hardly willing to trust himself to perform. He had certain conceptions of these features which he almost feared to execute, so tremendous was his purpose. He let that part of the work go, month after month, and having already spent two years upon the picture, the monks began to urge him to a finish. He was not the man to endure much pressure, and the more they urged the more resentful he became. Finally, he began to feel a bitter dislike for the prior, the man who annoyed him most. One day, when the prior was nagging him about the picture, wanting to know why he didn't get to work upon it again, and when would it be finished, Leonardo said suavely: "If you will sit for the head of Judas, I'll be able to finish the picture at once." The prior was enraged, as Leonardo meant he should be; but Leonardo is said actually to have painted him in as Judas. Afterward he painted in the face of Christ with haste and little care, simply because he despaired of ever doing the wonderful face that his art soul demanded Christ should wear.

The one bitter moment in Leonardo's life, in all probability, was when he came in dire competition with Michael Angelo. When he removed to Florence he was required to submit sketches for the Town Hall--the Palazzo Vecchio--and Michael Angelo was his rival. The choice fell to Angelo, and after a life of supremacy Leonardo could not endure the humiliation with grace. Added to disappointment, someone declared that Leonardo's powers were waning because he was growing old. This was more than he could bear, and he left Italy for France, where the king had invited him to come and spend the remainder of his life. Francis I. had wished to have the picture in the Milan monastery taken to France, but that was not to be done.

Doubtless the king expected Leonardo to do some equally great work after he became the nation's guest.

Before leaving Italy, Leonardo had painted his one other "greatest" picture--"La Gioconda" (Mona Lisa)-and he took that wonderful work with him to France, where the King purchased it for $9,000, and to this day it hangs in the Louvre.

But Leonardo was to do no great work in France, for in truth he was growing old. His health had failed, and although he was still a dandy and court favourite, setting the fashion in clothing and in the cut of hair and beard, he was no longer the brilliant, active Leonardo.

Bernard Berensen, has written of him: "Painting ... was to Leonardo so little of a preoccupation that we must regard it as merely a mode of expression used at moments by a man of universal genius." By which Berensen means us to understand that Leonardo was so brilliant a student and inventor, so versatile, that art was a mere pastime. "No, let us not join in the reproaches made to Leonardo for having painted so little; because he had so much more to do than to paint, he has left all of us heirs to one or two of the supremest works of art ever created."

Another author writes that "in Leonardo da Vinci every talent was combined in one man."

Leonardo was the third person of the wonderful trinity of Florentine painters, Raphael and Michael Angelo being the other two.

He knew so much that he never doubted his own powers, but when he died, after three years in France, he left little behind him, and that little he had ever declared to be unfinished--the "Mona Lisa" and the "Last Supper." He died in the Château de Cloux, at Amboise, and it is said that "sore wept the king when he heard that Leonardo was dead."

In Milan, near the Cathedral, there stands a monument to his memory, and about it are placed the statues of his pupils. To this day he is wonderful among the great men of the world.

PLATE--THE LAST SUPPER

This, as we have said, is in the former convent of Santa Maria delle Grazie, in Milan. It was the first painted story of this legendary event in which natural and spontaneous action on the part of all the company was presented.

To-day the picture is nearly ruined by smoke, time, and alterations in the place, for a great door lintel has been cut into the picture. Leonardo used the words of the Christ: "Verily, I say unto you that one of you shall betray me," as the starting point for this painting. It is after the utterance of these words that we see each of the disciples questioning horrified, frightened, anxious, listening, angered--all these emotions being expressed by the face or gestures of the hands or pose of the figures. It is a most wonderful picture and it seems as if the limit of genius was to be found in it.

The company is gathered in a half-dark hall, the heads outlined against the evening light that comes through the windows at the back. We look into a room and seem to behold the greatest tragedy of legendary history: treachery and sorrow and consternation brought to Jesus of Nazareth and his comrades.

This great picture was painted in oil instead of in "distemper," the proper kind of mixture for fresco, and therefore it was bound to be lost in the course of time. Besides, it has known more than ordinary disaster. The troops of Napoleon used this room, the convent refectory, for a stable, and that did not do the painting any good. The reason we have so complete a knowledge of it, however, is that Leonardo's pupils made an endless number of copies of it, and thus it has found its way into thousands of homes. The following is the order in which Leonardo placed the disciples at the table: Jesus of Nazareth in the centre, Bartholomew the last on the left, after him is James, Andrew, Peter, Judas--who holds the money bag--and John. On the right, next to Jesus, comes Thomas, the doubting one; James the Greater, Philip, Matthew, Thaddeus, and Simon. Jesus has just declared that one of them shall betray him, and each in his own way seems to be asking "Lord, is it I?" In the South Kensington Museum in London will be found carefully preserved a description, written out fairly in Leonardo's own hand, to guide him in painting the Last Supper. It is most interesting and we shall quote it: "One, in the act of drinking puts down his glass and turns his head to the speaker. Another twisting his fingers together, turns to his companion, knitting his eyebrows. Another, opening his hands and turning the palm toward the spectator, shrugs his shoulders, his mouth expressing the liveliest surprise. Another whispers in the ear of a companion, who turns to listen, holding in one hand a knife, and in the other a loaf, which he has cut in two. Another, turning around with a knife in his hand, upsets a glass upon the table and looks; another gasps in amazement; another leans forward to look at the speaker, shading his eyes with his hand; another, drawing back behind the one who leans forward, looks into the space between the wall and the stooping disciple."

Other paintings of Leonardo's are: "Mona Lisa," "Head of Medusa," "Adoration of the Magi," and the "Madonna della Caraffa."

XLIV JEAN ANTOINE WATTEAU

(Pronounced in French, Vaht-toh; English, Wot-toh)

French (Genre) School

1684-1721
Pupil of Gillot and Audran

Watteau's father was a tiler in a Flemish town--Valenciennes. He meant that his son should be a carpenter, but that son tramped from Valenciennes to Paris with the purpose of becoming a great painter. He did more, he became a "school" of painting, all by himself.

There is no sadder story among artists than that of this lowly born genius. He was not good to look upon, being the very opposite of all that he loved, having no grace or charm in appearance. He had a drooping mouth, red and bony hands, and a narrow chest with stooping shoulders. Because of a strange sensitiveness he lived all his life apart from those he would have been happy with, for he mistrusted his own ugliness, and thought he might be a burden to others.

Such a man has painted the gayest, gladdest, most delicate and exquisite pictures imaginable.

He entered Paris as a young man, without friends, without money or connections of any kind, and after wandering forlornly, about the great city, he found employment with a dealer who made hundreds of saints for out-of-town churches.

It is said that for this first employer Watteau made dozens and dozens of pictures of St. Nicholas; and when we think of the beautiful figures he was going to make, pictures that should delight all the world, there seems something tragic in the monotony and common-placeness of that first work he was forced by poverty to do. Certainly St. Nicholas brought one man bread and butter, even if he forgot him at Christmas time.

After that hard apprenticeship, Watteau's condition became slightly better. He had been employed near the Pont Notre Dame, at three francs a week, but now in the studio of a scene painter, Gillot, he did work of coarse effect, very different from that exquisite school of art which he was to bring into being. After Gillot's came the studio of Claude Audran, the conservator of the Luxembourg, and with him Watteau did decorative work. In reality he had no master, learned from nobody, grovelled in poverty, and at first, forced a living from the meanest sources. With this in mind, it remains a wonder that he should paint as no other ever could, scenes of exquisite beauty and grace; scenes of high life, courtiers and great ladies assembled in lovely landscapes, doing elegant and charming things, dressed in unrivalled gowns and costumes. Until Watteau went to the Luxembourg he had seen absolutely nothing of refined or gracious living. He had come from country scenes, and in Paris had lived among workmen and bird-fanciers, flower sellers, hucksters and the like. This is very likely the secret of his peculiar art.

Watteau would have been a wonderful artist under any circumstances, no matter what sort of pictures he had painted; but circumstances gave his imagination a turn toward the exquisite in colourand composition. Doubtless when he first looked down from the palace windows of the Luxembourg and saw gorgeous women and handsome men languishing and coquetting and revelling in a life of ease and beauty, he was transported. He must have thought himself in fairyland, and the impulse to paint, to idealise the loveliness that he saw, must have been greater in him than it would have been in one who had lived so long among such scenes that they had become familiar with them.

After Watteau there were artists who tried to do the kind of work he had done, but no one ever succeeded. Watteau clothed all his shepherdesses in fine silken gowns, with a plait in the back, falling from the shoulders, and to-day we have a fashion known as the "Watteau back"--gowns made with thisshoulder-plait. He put filmy laces or softest silks upon his dairy maids, as upon his court ladies, dressing his figures exquisitely, and in the loveliest colours. He had suffered from poverty and from miserable sights, so when he came to paint pictures, he determined to reproduce only the loveliest objects.

At that time French fashions were very unusual, and it was quite the thing for ladies to hold a sort of reception while at their toilet. A description of one of these affairs was written by Madame de Grignon to her daughter: "Nothing can be more delightful than to assist at the toilet of Madame la Duchesse (de Bourgoyne), and to watch her arrange her hair. I was present the other day. She rose at half past twelve, put on her dressing gown, and set to work to eat a*méringue*. She ate the powder and greased her hair. The whole formed an excellent breakfast and charming *coiffure*." Watteau has caught the spirit of this strange airy, artificial, incongruous existence. His ladies seem to be eating *meringues* and powdering their hair and living on a diet of the combination. One hardly knows which is toilet and which is real life in looking at his paintings.

He quarreled with Audran at the Luxembourg, and having sold his first picture, he went back to his Valenciennes home, to see his former acquaintances, no doubt being a little vain of his performance.

After that he painted another picture which sold well enough to keep him from poverty for a time, and on his return to Paris he was warmly greeted by a celebrated and influential artist, Crozat. Watteau tried for a prize, and though his picture came second it had been seen by the Academy committee.

His greatness was acknowledged, and he was immediately admitted to the Academy and granted a pension by the crown, with which he was able to go to Italy, the Mecca of all artists the world over.

From Italy he went to London, but there the fogs and unsuitable climate made his disease much worse and he hurried back to France, where he went to live with a friend who was a picture dealer. It was then that he painted a sign for this friend, Gersaint, a sign so wonderful that it is reckoned in the history of Watteau's paintings.

Soon he grew so sensitive over his illness, that he did not wish to remain near his dearest friends, but one of them, the Abbé Haranger, insisted upon looking after his welfare, and got lodgings for him at Nogent, where he could have country air and peace.

Watteau died very soon after going to Nogent in July, 1721, and he left nine thousand livres to his parents, and his paintings to his best friends, the Abbé, Gersaint, Monsieur Henin, and Monsieur Julienne. He is called the "first French painter" and so he was--though he was Flemish, by birth.

PLATE--FÊTE CHAMPÊTRE

This exquisite picture displays nearly all the characteristics of Watteau's painting. He was said to paint with "honey and gold," and his method was certainly remarkable. His clear, delicate colours were put upon a canvas first daubed with oil, and he never cleaned his palette. His "oil-pot was full of dust and dirt and mixed with the washings of his brush." One would think that only the most slovenly results could come from such habits of work, but the artist made a colour which no one could copy, and that was a sort of creamy, opalescent white. This was original with Watteau, and most beautiful.

In this "Fête Champêtre," which is now in the National Gallery at Edinburgh, he paints an elegant group of ladies and gentlemen indulging in an open air dance of some sort. One couple are doing steps facing one another, to the music of a set of pipes, while the rest flirt and talk, decorously, round about. There is no boisterous rusticity here; all is dainty and refined.

The same characteristics are to be found in Watteau's other pictures such as, "Embarkation for the Island of Cythera," "The Judgment of Paris," and "Gay Company in a Park."

XLV SIR BENJAMIN WEST

American

1738-1820

Pupil of the Italian School

The beautiful smile of his little niece helped to make this man an artist. This is the story:

Benjamin West was born down in Pennsylvania, at Westdale, a small village in the township of Springfield, of Quaker parentage. The family was poor perhaps, but in America at a time when everybody was struggling with a new civilisation it did not seem to be such binding poverty as the same condition in Europe would have been. Benjamin had a married sister whose baby he greatly loved, and he gave it devoted attention. One day while it was sleeping and the undiscovered artist was sitting beside it he saw it smile, and the beauty of the smile inspired him to keep it forever if he could. He got paper and pencil and forthwith transferred that "angel's whisper."

No child of to-day can imagine the difficulties a boy must have had in those days in America, to get an art education, and having learned his art, how impossible it was to live by it. Men were busy making a new country and pictures do not take part in such pioneer work; they come later. Still, there were bound to be born artistic geniuses then, just as there were men for the plough and men for politics and for war. He who happened to be the artist was the Quaker boy, West.

He took his first inspiration from the Cherokees, for it was the Indian in all the splendour of his strength and straightness that formed West's ideal of beautiful physique.

When he first saw the Apollo Belvedere, he exclaimed: "A young Mohawk warrior!" to the disgust of every one who heard him, but he meant to compliment the noblest of forms. Europeans did not know how magnificent a figure the "young Mohawk warrior" could be; but West knew.

After his Indian impetus toward art he went to Philadelphia, and settled himself in a studio, where he painted portraits. His sitters went to him out of curiosity as much as anything else, but at last a Philadelphia gentleman, who knew what art meant, recognised Benjamin West's talent, and made some arrangement by which the young man went to Italy.

Life began to look beautiful and promising to the Pennsylvanian. He was in Italy for three years, and in that home of art the young man who had made the smile of his sister's sleeping baby immortal was given highest honours. He was elected a member of all the great art societies in Italy, and studied with the best artists of the time. He began to earn his living, we may be sure, and then he went to England, where, in spite of the prejudice there must have been against the colonists, he became at once a favourite of George III., a friend of Reynolds and of all the English artists of repute-- unless perhaps of Gainsborough, who made friends with none.

West was appointed "historical painter" to his Majesty, George III., and he was chosen to be one of four who should draw plans for a Royal Academy. He was one of the first members of that great organisation, and when Sir Joshua Reynolds, the first president, died, West became president, remaining in office for twenty-eight years.

About that time came the Peace of Amiens, and West was able to go to Paris, where he could see the greatest art treasures of Europe, which had been brought to France from every quarter as a consequence of the war. At that time, before Paris began to return these, and when she had just pillaged every great capital of Europe, artists need take but a single trip to see all the art worth seeing in the whole world.

After a long service in the Academy, West quarreled with some of the Academicians and sent in his resignation; but his fellow artists had too much sense and good feeling to accept it, and begged him to reconsider his action. He did so, and returned to his place as president. When West was sixty-five years old he made a picture, "Christ Healing the Sick," which he meant to give to the Quakers in Philadelphia, who were trying to get funds with which to build a hospital. This picture was to be sold for the fund; but it was no sooner finished and exhibited in London before being sent to America, than it was bought for 3,000 guineas for Great Britain. West did not contribute this money to the hospital fund, but he made a replica for the Quakers, and sent that instead of the original.

West was eighty-two years old when he died and he was buried in St. Paul's Cathedral after a distinguished and honoured life. Since Europe gave him his education and also supported him most of his life, we must consider him more English than American, his birth on American soil being a mere accident.

PLATE--THE DEATH OF WOLFE

This death scene upon the Plains of Abraham, without the walls of Quebec in 1759, must not be taken as a realistic picture of an historic event. West drew upon his imagination and upon portraits of the prominent men supposed to have been grouped around the dying general, and he has produced a dramatic effect. One can imagine it is the two with fingers pointing backward who have just brought the memorable tidings, "They run! They run!"

"Who run?" asks Wolfe, for when he had fallen the issues of the fight were still undecided. "The French, sir. They give way everywhere." "Thank God! I die in peace," replied the English hero. At a time when the momentous results of this battle had set the whole of Great Britain afire with enthusiasm it is easy to understand the popularity of a picture such as this. It was sold in 1791 for £28, and now belongs to the Duke of Westminster. There is a replica of it in the Queen's drawing-room at Hampton Court.

Another famous historical picture by West is "The Battle of La Hogue."

INDEX

"Rape of the Daughters of Leucippus, The"

Raphael (Sanzio)

Reade, Charles

"Reading at Diderot's, A"

"Reaper, The"

"Regions of Joy"

Rembrandt (van Rijn)

"Retreat from Russia"

Reynolds, Samuel

Reynolds, Sir Joshua

Ribera

Rinaldo and Armida

"Road over the Downs, The"

"Robert Cheseman with his Falcon"

Robusto, Jacopo. *See* Tintoretto

Romano, Guilio

Rood, Professor

"Rosary, Story of the"

Rossetti, Dante Gabriel

Rossetti, W. M.

Rothschild, Lord

Rousseau

Royal Princess

Rubens, Albert

Rubens, John

Rubens, Nicholas

Rubens, Peter Paul

Ruisdael, Jacob van

Ruskin, John

Ruthven, Lady Mary

Sachs, Hans

"Sacred and Profane Love"

"St. Anthony of Padua"

"St. Augustine"

"St. Barbara"

St. Bernard dog

"Wedding Feast at Cana, The"

Wells, Frederick

West, Sir Benjamin

"Weymouth Bay"

Whitcomb, Ida Prentice

"William, Prince of Orange"

William the Silent

"Will-o'-the-Wisp"

"Willows near Arras"

Wilson

"Winnower, The"

"Winter"

Wolgemuth

"Woodcutters, The"

"Wooded Landscape"

"Wood Gatherers, The"

Yarmouth

"Young People's Story of Art"

"Youth Surprised by Death"

"Zingarella"

Zuccato, Sebastian

* END OF PICTURES EVERY CHILD SHOULD KNOW *

24010592R00162

Printed in Great Britain
by Amazon